Jewish Russians

Jewish Russians

Upheavals in a Moscow Synagogue

Sascha L. Goluboff

PENN

University of Pennsylvania Press

Philadelphia

10 9 8 7 6 5 4 3 2 1

Published by
University of Pennsylvania Press
Philadelphia, Pennsylvania 19104-4011

Library of Congress Cataloging-in-Publication Data

Goluboff, Sascha L.
   Jewish Russians : upheavals in a Moscow synagogue / Sascha L. Goluboff.
      p. cm.
   Includes bibliographical references and index.
   ISBN 0-8122-3705-6 (cloth : alk. paper)—ISBN 0-8122-1838-8 (pbk. : alk. paper)
   1. Synagogues—Russia (Federation)—Moscow—History—20th century. 2. Jews—
Russia (Federation)—Moscow—History—20th century. 3. Jews, Georgian
(Transcaucasian)—Russia (Federation)—Moscow—Social conditions—20th century. 4.
Jews, Bukharan—Russia (Federation)—Moscow—Social conditions—20th century. 5.
Mountain Jews—Russia (Federation)—Moscow—Social conditions—20th century. 6.
Goluboff, Sascha L. 7. Moscow (Russia)—Ethnic relations. I. Title.

BM333.M672 M674 2002
296'.0947'3109049—dc21

                                                                    2002031966

To my parents,
Diane Kandle Goluboff
and Barry Stephen Goluboff

Contents

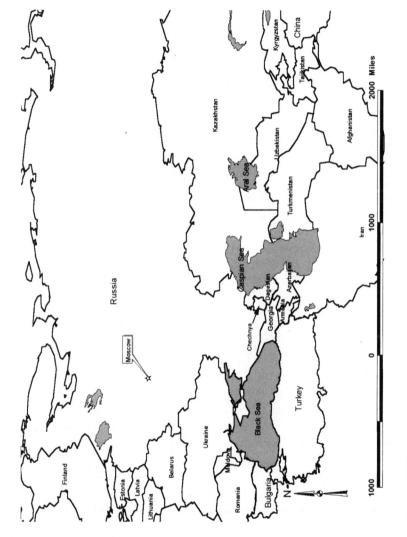

Figure 1. The former Soviet Union and surrounding countries.

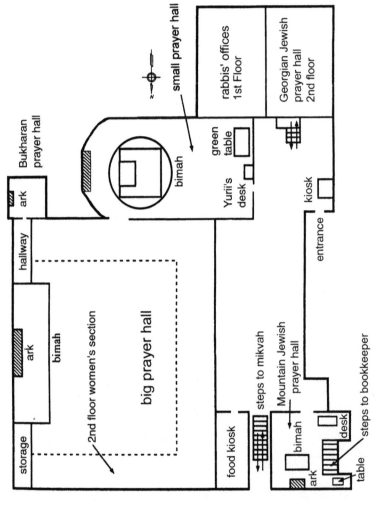

Figure 2. Key features of the synagogue floor plan.

Introduction

This is a book about the end of an era. Combining ethnographic methodology with archival research, it documents the decline of the historically dominant Russian Jewish community at the Central Synagogue in Moscow from 1995 to 1996. It also traces the rapid rise of a transnational congregation headed by a Western rabbi and primarily made up of Georgian Jews from Georgia, Bukharan Jews from Central Asia, and Mountain Jews from Azerbaijan, Dagestan, and Chechnya. This ethnography focuses on events in the synagogue that led to this transformation. It outlines how emigration, cultural shifts, capitalist investment, and unstable borders have affected the composition and trajectory of post-Soviet Jewry. I believe this kind of in-depth anthropological study provides new insights into both the meaning of Jewish identity in Russia and the future of the Russian nation.

Since the collapse of the Soviet Union in 1991, Russia has been in a state of flux on state and local levels. The socialist economy was organized around the notion of paternalistic redistribution whereby the state, through local distribution centers, obtained and handed out products according to a system of bureaucratic privileges (Verdery 1996). Because of its inefficiency, this official economy relied on a second economy, an illegal black market, to acquire all the materials needed by the state and its citizens. With the change in the post-Soviet economy, from a state-led system to an entrepreneurial one, young men in prominent positions within the bureaucratic elite and the black market personally profited from international aid earmarked for the development of a capitalist system in Russia (Wedel 1998). Claiming to defend the "free market" in Russia from the communists, this group of oligarchs achieved political authority, influencing the outcome of regional and presidential elections (Klebnikov 2000). The sharp devaluation of the rouble, the influx of foreign goods and services into Moscow, and the wars and economic crises in the former republics of the Soviet Union created a widening gap between the newly rich and the increasing numbers of poor, destitute, and displaced persons (Arkhangelsky 1998; Pilkington 1998).

To escape the wars and economic crises in their homelands after the dissolution of the Soviet Union, large numbers of Georgian Jews from Georgia, Bukharan Jews from Central Asia, and Mountain Jews from the Dagestan Republic of Russia and Azerbaijan have come to Moscow. Post-Soviet Jewish Moscow is thus undergoing a transnational transformation: Bukharan Jews are Sephardim (having ties to Jews from Spain), Georgian and Mountain Jews are *Mizrahim* (Oriental Jews from lands either once ruled by Persia or located "in the East"), and local Russian Jews are Ashkenazim (whose ancestors came from Germany). Historical and cultural distinctions such as these were very important in the context of the Central Synagogue. While some were elderly, the majority of these Bukharan, Georgian, and Mountain Jewish migrants who became involved in the Central Synagogue were young to middle-aged businessmen wanting to take advantage of new business opportunities in Moscow. They opened up retail stores offering imports from Western Europe and China, took over ownership of classy Moscow restaurants, and bought, rented, or worked at kiosks selling books, food, and alcohol. Unlike Russian Jews from Moscow whose religious practices had been extremely curtailed by the Soviet government, Georgian, Mountain, and Bukharan Jews had experienced fewer state restrictions regarding their religion, and they lived openly among observant Christians and Muslims (Zand 1991). Although Russian Jews have always represented the largest number of Jews in Moscow, unofficial estimates claim that Jews from the republics averaged from 30,000 to 44,000, or 22 percent, of the 200,000 Jews living in Moscow in 1995.

An influx of Ashkenazic Jews from Europe, America, and Israel also affected the negotiation of Jewish religious life in post-Soviet Moscow. Western Jews arrived in Russia in large numbers beginning in the late 1980s, under the rubric of *perestroika* (reconstruction) and *glasnost'* (openness), two policies that promised Soviet citizens a restructuring of the state and freedom of expression. The government at that time attempted to normalize religious life by calling it a "healthy force" in society and by allowing Russia's different nationalities to organize themselves as they wished (Ramet 1993:33). As a result, increasing numbers of Western Jews received visas to visit Russia to help reestablish Jewish religious institutions. Most Western Jews came to Russia in the 1990s for religious, philanthropic, and/or business reasons, believing that the new economy would bring them profits, as well as provide solid financial help to local Jewish communities.

Many Georgian, Mountain, and Bukharan Jews who attended the

Central Synagogue were able to adjust to the new atmosphere of commercial openness in Russia because of their involvement with the black
market during the Soviet period. However, Russian Jews at the synagogue bemoaned their poverty, blaming it on the new economy and
its investors. Middle-aged and elderly, they had belonged to two different social strata in Soviet Russia—petty laborers and university-
educated intelligentsia. Unlike Jews from the republics, who kept up
family connections, the majority of Russian Jews lived alone and were
visibly destitute. Unwilling to emigrate for personal or financial reasons, they attempted to hold on to their Soviet Jewish traditions in the
face of a rapidly changing world. To preserve a place for themselves in
the synagogue, the Russian state, and the diasporic Jewish nation,
Russian Jews made claims to specific self-perceptions that placed them
in opposition to Jews from the republics and the West. These endeavors created ethnic and racial identities based on varying images of the
new market economy.

In this ethnography, I expand on two theories of ethnicity and race.
First, I detail how ethnicity in the post-Soviet Jewish context is the
construction and articulation of group identities based on difference
(Appadurai 1996:15). For example, during my research, Russian Jews
talked about themselves as "Russians," and Georgian Jews called themselves "Georgians" when explaining distinctions between one another.
And yet, they both referred to themselves and one another as "Jews"
when they wanted to highlight their common heritage and ritual practices. This type of categorization challenges earlier survey research on
post-Soviet Russian Jews that claims that "in the Soviet Union and its
successor states, 'Russian' and 'Jewish' are mutually exclusive, since they
are both ethnic categories (*natsional'nost'*)" (Chervyakov et al. 1997:289).
In contrast, I show that post-Soviet Jews' constant use of ethnic labels
reveals a larger power struggle over who rightfully belonged in the
Central Synagogue and, ultimately, who was a "true" Jew and Russian
citizen. Being an authentic Jew meant being a foundational part of
Jewish culture and history; being a real Russian citizen meant exhibit-
ing characteristics that positively contributed to building the new Russian society. Jews at the synagogue argued over what comprised these
significant Jewish and Russian traits.

Second, following Brackette Williams (1989:436), I propose that
ethnic groups are defined as racially inside the nation but inferior to
the dominant group, while racialized populations are defined as essentially outside the nation. In the case of the Central Synagogue,
because they contested the large number—and loud presence—of
Georgian Jews who participated in morning ritual, Russian Jews labeled themselves as "Jewish" and "Russian" and called Georgian Jews

ethnic "Georgians." This placed Russian Jews in charge of ritual as the "true" Jews, but it still acknowledged Georgian Jews as contributing men and financial assistance to the prayer community. However, in certain situations Russian Jews also recognized the Georgian Jews' long history of religious observance and, at those times, Russian Jews saw themselves as "Russian" in relationship to the "Jewish" Georgian Jews. In this context, being Russian was negative; it signified being assimilated into the dominant culture.

Race complicated this labeling when Russian Jews described Mountain Jews as *chernye* ("blacks") from the Caucasus, who worked in the "immoral," profit-mongering marketplace. In relation to Mountain Jews, Russian Jews saw themselves as "moral," "Russian," and "Jewish" intellectuals who had been taught under the Soviet system to abhor commerce. This book will show how post-Soviet Jewish identity corresponds to perceived ethnic and racial lines that relate to each group's (Georgian Jews', Mountain Jews', and Russian Jews') supposed success or failure in the new market economy.

This focus on race, in addition to ethnicity, attempts to fill a gap in recent discussions about class change in Russia. Perhaps the lack of attention to race stems from how Soviet and post-Soviet literature and discourse have conflated race *(rasa)* with nationality *(natsional'nost')* and ethnicity *(etnos)* (Slezkine 1991). In Soviet and post-Soviet common discourse, each nationality, like each *etnos* (a term used in Soviet anthropological literature), has its own "natural" mentality *(mentalitet)* and traditions (Verdery 1988). Post-Soviets continue to use the terms *natsional'nost'* and *etnos* to refer to the notion of a people *(narod)* that have their own customs and geographical origins. However, although the word *rasa* does not appear often in everyday talk, Russians frequently define non-Russians by their skin color. For example, Muscovites accused the *chernye*—dark-skinned Gypsies and migrants from the southern republics who sold goods in open-air bazaars—of sabotaging Russia by causing crime, terrorism, and social unrest in the capital (Humphrey 1995; Lemon 1998).

These claims portray the physical marketplace as dangerous and the new economy, and those who engage in it, as morally corrupt. While there has been much debate on whether current anti-immigrant sentiments in Europe are a new form of racism or should be called something else, the rapid marketization of the Russian economy points to the former conclusion. Robert Miles' study of capitalism and migration on a global scale shows how racialization—"the process of signification in which human beings are categorized into 'races' by reference to real or imagined phenotypic difference"—is concomitant with the complex interplay of international labor mobilization and migration, especially as migrants become new class agents (Miles 1987:7). Statements about unwelcome *chernye* in Moscow point to how race, at times more than ethnicity or nationality, is a salient marker of who belongs in the Russian and Jewish nations. Therefore, an investigation into the production of race, ethnicity, and class can get to the heart of what makes Russia Russian and the Jewish people Jewish.

The conflicts that arose among the Mountain, Bukharan, Georgian, Western, and Russian Jews at the Central Synagogue in 1995 and 1996 provided me with a unique opportunity to observe on a microcosmic level how Russia is experiencing and responding to the collapse of the Soviet empire and the permeability of its borders with Asia and the Caucasus. My work speaks to recent anthropological studies of the former Soviet Union that seek to understand the rapid changes occurring there by focusing on how the creation and re-creation of the Russian nation-state—its economy, politics, and ideology—affect life on institutional and everyday levels (Hann 1993; Kideckel 1995; Burawoy and Verdery 1999; Verdery 1999; Berdahl, Bunzl, and Lampland 2000). These investigations highlight what Michael Burawoy and Katherine Verdery call "local improvisations," activities that move Russia in novel directions and/or "return" it to socialism (Burawoy and Verdery 1999:2). While some studies focus on the reconfiguration of class and identity in Russia (Burawoy 1995; Ledeneva 1998), others look at how minority ethnic groups fight for autonomy in the Russian nation, basing their claim on citizenship rights they enjoyed within the Russian state (Balzer 1999; Golovnev and Osherenko 1999; Rethmann 2000). In this book, I explain how being a *Russian* Jew, *Mountain* Jew, *Georgian* Jew, or *Bukharan* Jew is intimately linked to the Jewish struggle to be valuable members of Russian society. Jewish assertions of Russian identity and belonging shake up ideological notions of Russian and Jewish national purity, and they lead Russian culture in new directions.

Researching Jews as a way to study race and ethnicity in Russia entails a new approach to Jewish studies. Until recently, research on Jews in the Soviet Union has concentrated mainly on Russian Jews, discussing the policy of forced assimilation and its failure due to anti-Semitism supported by the Soviet policy of indicating nationality on passports (Baron 1976; Gitelman 1988; Levin 1990). Russian Jews were Jewish by nationality but Soviet by citizenship. Like other Soviet citizens, they had to present their passports when interacting with the Soviet bureaucracy at job interviews and when registering for scarce goods and housing. They were constantly discriminated against due to their nationality. Recent scholarship on post-Soviet Jewry continues to stress the paradoxical nature of Jewish self-identification by defining Jewish ethnicity either as "self-evident," "an immutable biological and social fact, ascribed at birth like sex and eye color" (Markowitz 1988:81), or as symbolic, "largely emptied of its cultural content" (Chervyakov et al. 1997:289). According to these studies, Jews are once again caught in the quandary of being Jewish yet not quite knowing what that means beyond sentiment and a sense of responsibility for others like themselves.

I conceptualize this quandary differently: Jews at the synagogue were constantly engaged in contradictory, but always culturally meaningful and contextual, processes of identity formation. Because the Jewish people are diasporic, there is a constant tension between universal Jewish doctrine and the rich diversity of Jewish experience in Russia. In writing a story that argues for localism within the context of Judaism's transnational ideology, I take my cue from Lila Abu-Lughod (1993) as well as from other anthropologists who study the performative and contextual nature of Jewish identity within community and synagogue life (Myerhoff 1979 and 1992; Kugelmass 1986; Dominguez 1989; Prell 1989; Shokeid 1995). What I found at the Central Synagogue signals the disappearance of a dominant Russian Jewish influence and the development of a post-Soviet Jewry based on perceived cultural, racial, and ethnic differences as they emerge within the discourse of belonging to the new Russian nation. Russian Jewry can no longer dictate the rules of engagement for post-Soviet Jewry at large due to the increasing multinational face of Moscow Jewry.

To focus readers on the important ethnographic and theoretical issues at hand rather than on the details of my specific place of research, I changed the name of the synagogue and slightly altered its floor plan. For the purpose of anonymity, I provided pseudonyms for all the congregants and synagogue staff whom I met with and interviewed. I slightly altered the position of each speaker to mask some of his or her personal characteristics, while not disrupting the meaning and poignancy of his or her comments, since each person's worldview is distinctly tied to class, status, and racial or ethnic affiliation. I chose not to change the names of those who were deceased when I did my fieldwork in 1995 and 1996, because they appear in both archival files and other published manuscripts. All translations from Russian are my own unless otherwise noted.

My Arrival in the Field

It was difficult for me to sleep the first night I arrived in Moscow. I had been to Moscow two times before, once as part of a four-month study group in college in 1990 and again on a preliminary research visit in the summer of 1994. Now, as I was lying in bed in the dark of my rented apartment, images of the city flashed through my mind. Flying into Moscow, I had felt a sense of familiarity. The green grasses and trees at the airport gave way to the concrete of the city as I rode in a taxi into downtown. The crispness of mid-October accentuated the grayness of the city. The taxi zoomed along the wide main street, past steel and cement metro stations; sprawling two-floored *magazini* (department stores); bulky, high-rise Soviet apartment buildings with decaying balconies and crumbling facades; and billboard ads in Russian for cigarettes and detergent. Traffic was heavy, and the acrid smells of the city—nonfiltered cigarettes, leaded gas, and dirt—came into the car. These sensations were oddly comforting, reminding me of my college days and the thrill I had experienced being a young American woman abroad for the first time.

My apartment was small. Although conveniently located in the center of the city, the rooms were far from clean, so I spent my first hours in the city cleaning up the dust and dog hair. In the darkness of the bedroom that night, with the orange curtains shut, the street was quiet, except for the intermittent noises coming from the small zoo across the street. One animal started to bray and others joined in, making a weird cacophony of sounds. Wild dogs on the street barked.

Dawn's weak light seeped in through the curtains and gave the whole room an orange glow. Anxious to start my research, I threw off the covers and walked onto the small balcony off the living room. Moscow seemed like a range of dreary buildings, jutting out of the flat earth. Some were wide and others tall, clustered together like coral reefs; a scattering of prerevolutionary architecture, survivors hidden in a cement jungle, provided respite from sensual boredom. Across from my apartment building, there was a red brick building with a silver cupola and large windows made out of little glass squares. The point of the cupola stood above the surrounding buildings, touching the sailing gray clouds. Sounds were no longer dismembered; mournful moaning at night was by day the usual noises of the zoo. It was Monday morning. I was ready to begin.

The Central Synagogue is located in the center of the city, close to Red Square and the Kremlin. With nervous anticipation, I exited the metro station closest to the synagogue and walked through the underground passageway, past small kiosks selling music tapes and CDs, videos, clothes, makeup, and accessories. I emerged into the sunlight of the street. Along the road were yellow and white painted three-story buildings, housing private residences and small grocery and clothing stores. The architecture in this area has not changed much since the end of the seventeenth century. At that time, this area was then the suburbs outside the royal residence.

It was about one hundred years later, in the early 1800s, when the tsarist government allowed Jews who belonged to the first and second merchant guilds to live here near the Kremlin for up to six months at a time.[1] The rest of the Jewish population was required to stay in the Pale of Settlement, an area that included modern-day Ukraine and Poland. These Ashkenazic Jews spoke Yiddish, a combination of Hebrew and German. In 1859, the Jewish population of Moscow increased rapidly when Tsar Aleksandr II opened the Russian interior to Jewish guild merchants, university graduates, and artisans. By 1889, the Jewish population had grown so large (26,000 persons) that it established its own prayer house. In 1883, Lazar Poliakov, a banker and the chairman of the Jewish religious community, donated money to build the present-day Central Synagogue on what was then called *Spasoglinishchevskii pereulok* (Spasoglinishchevskii Lane), a name honoring the nearby Church of the Transfiguration of the Savior. Although the synagogue was completed in 1891, it closed later that year when Tsar Aleksandr III, reacting against the liberal policies of his father, expelled the Jews from Moscow. It reopened in 1905 under the rubric of Tsar Nicholas II's manifesto of October 17, which promised civil liberties to the Russian people. On June 1, 1906, the Central Synagogue was officially consecrated, and it has stayed open ever since.[2]

When the new Bolshevik government eliminated restrictions on Jewish settlement in 1917, Jews streamed into Russia proper, many of them settling in Moscow. The synagogue grew, and the new Jewish residents established other places of worship around the city, the most notable of which were synagogues with a strong Hasidic influence in the heavily Jewish populated suburbs of Mar'ina Roshche and Cherkizovo. Although the synagogue in Cherkizovo closed in the early 1970s, the one in Mar'ina Roshche continued to function through the Soviet period as the underground center of Lubavitcher Hasidism, and in 1992, the Lubavitchers acquired a synagogue on Bolshaia Bronnaia Street. Immediately after the collapse of the Soviet state, this synagogue became the second most popular place of Jewish worship after the Central Synagogue.[3]

In 1958, Spasoglinishchevskii Lane became *ulitsa Arkhipova* (Arkhipova Street) in honor of Abram Efimovich Arkhipov, a Jewish intel-

lectual who became a People's Artist of the Russian Republic of the Soviet Union. Although the Russian government recently changed the
name back to Spasoglinishchevskii Lane, to reaffirm the Russian Orthodox heritage of the country, local Jews still referred to it as Arkhipova Street. Throughout my time in Moscow, I heard both religious
and nonobservant Jews frequently talk about the synagogue with
phrases like, *Ty idyosh na Arkhipova?* ("Are you going to Arkhipova?")
and *Kak eto bylo na Arkhipova?* ("How was it at Arkhipova?"), which re-
veales how the synagogue continues to function as a main place of
Jewish identity within the capital. Its congregation is formally known
as MERO, which stands for *Moskovskaia evreiskaia religioznaia obshchina*
(Moscow Jewish Religious Community).

Arkhipova is a narrow street that turns slightly and rises sharply. It
is difficult to see the synagogue in full detail, because it is not possible
to stand far enough away from it, but it nonetheless makes a formidable impression. Throughout my fieldwork, the facade, which has two
rows of fat, large columns in a classical Greco-Roman style, was under
restoration. The cement bricks were a creamy yellow, and the bottoms
of the columns were painted white, while the top was stripped of color.

I walked up the stairs to open the large wooden door. It was locked.
The synagogue was closed because of the break between morning and
afternoon services for Simchat Torah, the holiday celebrating the end
of the yearly cycle of Torah readings.

Just then, I heard someone greet me in Russian from across the
street. It was Yaakov, the beggar whom I met during my summer research trip. He was a seventy-eight-year-old Russian Jew, and today he
was wearing a brown overcoat and a nappy fur hat. He was smoking a
cigarette, holding it in his right hand, between his third finger and the
stumps of what was left of his ring finger and pinkie. He had lost them
in an industrial accident in the 1940s. He smiled at me: "How are
you? We got your two letters. How long are you here? To study?
What? How much do they pay you? Yurii Isaakovich is not here. He'll
be here tomorrow. How much can you give me?" He stood close to
me. His face was small and shrunken, making his nose and ears seem
extra large. "I don't have dollars with me right now," I said. He did
not want roubles, and I did not want to fish around in my purse for
one-dollar bills in front of him. I remembered last summer when I
gave him five dollars. Yurii Isaakovich, the administrator of the small
prayer hall at the synagogue with whom I had corresponded since
then, admonished me for handing out so much money. I decided that
paying him a little would not hurt.

As we were talking, an old woman came by, asking for money, telling
us that her children were sick. He shooed her away so he could talk to

me. He told her to come tomorrow morning to the synagogue for charity. "How much?" she said. "Come at ten o'clock," he said, pushing her behind him.

"Come tonight and tomorrow, it will be a big celebration," he said to me as he walked away.

It was still light out when I returned to the synagogue at 5:30 P.M. Twenty or so Russian Jews of all ages stood outside. As I later came to find out, the majority of them did not follow the Jewish law of no work on Shabbat (the Jewish Sabbath, observed on Saturdays) and holidays, a law that prohibits driving cars and using electrical equipment so that one fully observes the day of rest and contemplation. Yaakov was at the top of the stairs. He waved me inside through a side door that led into a small corridor. The walls were dark wood, and the floor was covered in maroon tile. To the right was a kiosk selling colorful books about the Jewish holidays and pocket-sized blue booklets containing the Jewish calendar. Straight ahead was a set of stairs leading to the women's section of the large main prayer hall (separation of the sexes during prayer is an official Orthodox Jewish practice). The landing between the first and second floors connected to an addition to the building that housed the rabbis' offices and, on the floor above, a large room that until recently functioned as a religious kindergarten and elementary school. I walked past the door to the small prayer hall (which was locked tonight) and into the main hallway that leads to the main prayer hall.

A wall of glass-framed wooden doors separated the main prayer hall from the hallway. The two center doors stood open, and yellow light from the lamps on the bimah (the raised portion of a prayer hall at the front of the room) flooded the dark hallway. Standing at the open doors, I could see about thirty men inside. Two aisles led to two sets of stairs on either side of the bimah, separating the room into three long rows of pews. Centered on the wall behind the bimah was the ark that housed the Torah scrolls. The ark, the wall behind the bimah, and the prayer table in front of the ark were made out of white marble with gold trim. The cantor and an all-male choir were already leading the service from the bimah. On either side of the ark were two large wooden chairs; one was for Rabbi Mark Samuelovich Dubinovich, chief rabbi of Russia, and the other was for Rabbi Simcha Silverstein, chief rabbi of the Central Synagogue and head of the Rabbinical Court of Russia. Both men were out among the congregation. Rabbi Dubinovich served as the rabbi of this synagogue's congregation from 1983 until 1990, when Rabbi Silverstein, a French Jew in his thirties, replaced him. Holiday and Shabbat speeches by the rabbis were given at the podium at the foot of the bimah. The white austerity of the bimah contrasted with the bright fresco on the wall above the ark. In gold and green, it depicted two Trees of Life, symbolizing the Torah. They stretched high above the women's section, an area that curved around the room, providing box seats and a balcony view of the men congregated below.

I made my way to the women's section to join several middle-aged Russian Jewish women who had already found their seats. From that vantage point, I watched Rabbi Silverstein walk up an aisle, talking to people while the cantor continued to pray. The rabbi wore a celebratory black hat and long black coat with a black velvet collar. When he reached the row closest to the bimah, he and about fifteen men began to dance in a circle, holding hands and singing in Hebrew in the customary Ashkenazic way of celebrating the Torah. The room was composed entirely of Muscovite Russian Jews of all ages. They had come in from the street and were now crowded at the back of the room, and they clapped with enthusiasm.

This scene reminded me of the countless stories I had read about the Central Synagogue during Soviet times. After World War II, Soviet officials brought Western journalists and interested visitors to the synagogue to see "evidence" of Jewish religious freedom in order to repudiate Western reports that anti-Semitism existed in the Soviet Union. After they watched a service from a place where it was difficult for them to interact with the congregants, the journalists interviewed the rabbi, who always confirmed the Soviets' claim that there was no anti-Semitism. Between World War II and 1983, when Rabbi Dubinovich began his tenure, there had been three rabbis at the synagogue: Rabbi Solomon Shliefer (1943–57), Rabbi Yegudah-Leib Levin (1957–71), and Rabbi Yaakov Fishman (1971–83).

Beginning in the late 1960s, journalists reported on what they called the "refusnik" movement. Refusniks (*otkazniki* in Russian) were those Jews whom the government refused permission to emigrate due to Soviet anti-Zionist policies. Thousands of these Russian Jews protested for their right to live in Israel. Russian Jewish *samizdat* (self-published illegal literature) described how Russian Jews gathered in front of the synagogue to exchange information and to meet one another while other Russian Jews, more interested in renewing their religious faith, congregated inside to pray. For Western and Soviet Jews, the Central Synagogue became a symbol of the survival and strength of the Russian Jewish people in the face of Soviet power. It became synonymous with the image of Russian Jewry.

But there was something about this Simchat Torah scene that did not echo the numerous stories I had read. When Rabbi Silverstein stepped onto the bimah, four Mountain Jews came up the right aisle, walked onto the bimah, and opened the ark. As Mountain Jews usually have darker complexions than Russian Jews, these four men were easily recognizable. Taking out two Torah scrolls, they paraded them down the aisle, past the crowd, and out of the main prayer hall. Interested in the cultural significance of this event, I left the women's section and went down to the main hallway on the first floor. Shalom, the fifty-five-year-old head of the Mountain Jewish community, and about ten other Mountain Jewish men were gathered in a small room tucked in the far left-hand corner of the main hallway. They were having their own Simchat Torah service.

In fact, when I returned to observe the holiday celebrations the next day, I found even more of these separate services. Fifteen elderly Russian Jews, including Yurii Isaakovich, were reading the Torah in the small prayer hall on the first floor. On the addition's second floor, Georgian Jews came together for a service of their own, and Bukharan Jews gathered in the synagogue library. Thus, what looked like a Russian Jewish synagogue from the outside was really a multinational synagogue on the inside. The synagogue's tiny corridors and half-hidden rooms revealed complex negotiations of identity and space. It was clear that this synagogue was experiencing many changes, and I wanted to find out what they were and why they were happening. This book is a result of that quest.

Finding a Seat at Morning Services

The various Jewish groups divided the synagogue space. In addition to being welcome to participate in the official service in the main prayer hall, each Jewish community had its own smaller prayer space that it used on Shabbat and holidays. Georgian Jews congregated on the second floor of the synagogue addition, Mountain Jews had a little room on the first floor, and Russian Jews used the small prayer hall. Bukharan Jews met either in the library or in a small room to the left of the bimah in the main prayer hall, a room that had functioned as the rabbi's office after the Soviet state had confiscated the synagogue addition for use as a hospital and then a school. Each of these communities had its own cantor and/or rabbi who led its religious service. Khakham David was the Georgian Jews' main rabbi,[4] and another Georgian rabbi named Khakham Eliahu arrived in Moscow from Georgia in the middle of my fieldwork. Isaak Khaimov, in his late seventies, was the religious authority among the Bukharan Jews, and they called him their "mullah."[5] Unlike the Georgian and Bukharan Jews, the Mountain Jews did not have their own rabbi, as there was not one living in Moscow at the time. They occasionally borrowed Khakham

David or Khakham Eliahu. The Russian Jews relied on Shloimie to lead the services and Moshe to read the Torah. Both men were congregants in their eighties and from Ukraine. Despite having their own religious authorities, all of these groups relied on Rabbi Silverstein to answer higher religious questions, since he was the head of the Central Synagogue and the Rabbinical Court of Russia. He also controlled much of the synagogue funding and had the ear of international Jewish organizations.

Although the holidays and weekly Shabbat services drew large numbers of worshipers and spectators, the heart of synagogue life was the community of about thirty men who attended the daily *Shacharit* (morning prayer) service in the small prayer hall. Unlike many Eastern European synagogues,[6] the Central Synagogue continued to function daily. Orthodox Jewish law requires adult men to pray three times a day—morning, afternoon, and evening—in a *minyan* (a prayer quorum of ten that, according to Orthodox Jewish law, cannot include women). To an anthropologist searching for social interaction and cultural meaning, this seemed to be the most likely place to start. Worshipers packed into the small hall on Monday and Thursday mornings to hear the reading of the Torah; this space, rather than the main hall, was more suited for a gathering of thirty men. Georgian, Mountain, and Bukharan Jews prayed together with the Russian Jews in the small hall from Sunday to Friday because they usually did not have enough men to form their own *minyans*. Georgian and Russian Jews made up the majority of the morning *minyan* members, averaging about twelve persons each. Unlike the main hall (or as people called it, the *bol'shoi zal*—big hall), the small hall *(malen'kii zal)* did not have a women's section. Because Jewish law does not allow men and women to pray together side by side, it was a challenge for me to find a way to observe morning prayer.

Morning services began at 8:30. As the administrator of the small hall since 1989, Yurii Isaakovich, age fifty-nine, arrived first to prepare the room for morning prayer. Every morning at 6:00, he left his wife and twenty-year-old son sleeping in their two-bedroom apartment on the outskirts of the city to take the metro one hour to the synagogue. We had agreed that I would accompany him as he worked on October 25, 1995, and when I came in at 7:15, he was already taking plastic shopping bags out of the closet and placing them on his desk. Each *minyan* member had his own bag that included his *tallis* (prayer shawl), *tefillin* (phylacteries),[7] and *siddur* (prayer book).

I sat down toward the back of the room, near the entrance. The furniture in the small hall faced the ark standing against the curved east wall. The bimah was in the center of the room; a prayer table was set

half way between the bimah and the ark. All of these items were ve-
neered with an extremely weathered dark wood. On either side of the
bimah, seven rows of pews extended to the back of the room, leaving
an aisle between Yurii's desk and a green-topped wooden table on the
right. Magazines and newspapers were stacked high on the window-
sills, and old religious texts stood haphazardly in a glass-doored bookcase behind the green table. The white walls had yellowed with age. A
gray sleepiness absorbed the sanctuary. Even with the large windows
closed and locked, a cold draft made its way inside, bringing with it a
sour smell from the synagogue's cafeteria in the courtyard. The chill
continued throughout the day, but the silence soon gave way to conversation and prayer.

An elderly Russian Jew arrived at 7:45. Yurii shook his hand as he
passed by the desk. The old man took one of the plastic bags and
sat down at the green table. They both mumbled small prayers to
themselves, and the old man continually wiped his teary eyes with a
handkerchief.

After several minutes, they went up to the ark at the front of the
room to remove a Torah scroll. Rolling it out on the prayer table on
the bimah, they searched for the day's passage, to make it more acces-
sible when Moshe was ready to read during the service. Passage found,
the old man took a small bottle of black paint from his bag and placed
his white and blue phylacteries on the table, fingering the ragged tas-
sels hanging off the ends. He said to Yurii, "Tell me, how do you paint
phylacteries?" I asked Yurii what the man was doing. He said, "This is
a poor synagogue. We have what we need, but it is of poor quality."
"Why?" I asked. "They make a business, so we must pay to get good
stuff. He [the old man] does not have the money. I cannot say what I
want to say because he is here."

A second elderly man arrived. He picked up a plastic bag from Yurii's
desk and then gave Yurii some money—roubles clipped together with
a piece of paper on top. Yurii put the money in a tin box where he
kept the *tzedoka* (charity money) collected from the congregation.

More elderly Russian Jewish men arrived, and, after picking up
their prayer equipment, they walked about, whispering to one another in Russian and Yiddish. As the time approached 8:30, several
young Georgian and Mountain Jews entered the room. With them
was Shalom, the head of the Mountain Jewish community, who made
it his business to council me. "You will insult the worshipers if you stay
here," he said. He set up a place for me in the main hall, behind the
doors that led into the small hall. He propped open one of the doors
so I could hear the service. As I put my long winter coat down, Shalom
said, "The wind will blow, so you should wrap your coat around you."

He picked up my coat and tried to place it around my shoulders, but he was holding it sideways, and he looked confused. I told him that I would do it myself. He went into the small hall, and I sat down.

From my vantage point, I could see Yurii get ready for prayer. He had on a black robe with the left sleeve hanging loose, so as to have access to his left arm. He picked up his prayer shawl, held it out in front of him to say the blessing for putting it on, kissed the top, swung it behind him, and then placed it on his head. Yurii took out his pair of phylacteries, two small black lacquered boxes with black leather straps on each side. He rolled up his left sleeve, revealing the fleshy part of his upper arm, and placed the box of the phylactery there. He then wrapped the leather straps down to his hand and secured them. He centered the other phylactery box on his forehead and tied the straps behind his head. He then put his black square silk hat on, but farther back than usual, making a small lock of hair curl down over the box.

As the service got underway, I could hear Shloimie, the eighty-three-year-old cantor, lead prayer. I also heard Yose, a thirty-year-old Israeli, who did charity work in Moscow and owned his own retail business. His voice was easy to pick out—melodiously loud and authoritative. I later found out that he usually came late and that he said his beginning morning prayers with gusto, regardless of when he entered the room.

A short, Georgian Jewish young man came to the door to ask me if he could shut it because of the draft. An older Georgian Jew followed behind him, saying, *"Ne razreshaetsia"* to both of us, meaning that my watching the service and talking to him was "not allowed." He closed the door.

Needless to say, I was distressed at the thought of not being able to observe services, but I did not get up the nerve to try to observe morning services again until two months later. By then, I was familiar with more of the congregants, having met and talked with them after services. On Thursday, January 4, I watched the service from the same doorway. Returning the next Monday, I expected to do the same thing. As I walked through the small hall to take my research spot, Zviad, a largely built Georgian Jew in his early thirties, called out to me: *"Devushka* [girl], it is too cold in there. Sit here." He pointed to the pew in the corner where I had first sat before Shalom said I should sit in the doorway. "Can I?" I said, walking back into the room. I took off my coat and sat down. No one complained. I came back the following Thursday. Not sure if Zviad's invitation was a permanent one, I sat in the main hall. This situation continued for two weeks until Zviad's older brother Aleksei called out to me as I headed for the door: *"Devushka,* it is too cold there. Sit in here. There is nothing strange about that." Yurii, standing at his desk, looked over and winked at me as I sat down.

At the time, I was not certain why Zviad and his brother Aleksei had insisted that I sit in the small hall with them. I was surprised at this since it broke the unspoken rules of Orthodox prayer, and yet no one visibly objected. The location of my seat placed me inside the room, but, because I sat by the door, I symbolically was not a member of the *minyan*. The real motivation for Aleksei's repeated insistence that I sit in the small hall and the consequences of his invitation only became apparent to me later when several serious situations emerged that threatened both my research and my safety. But for now, I was right where I wanted to be—in the center of the action and ready to take notes.

Images of the Other: A Brief History of the Russian Jews

I had managed to get myself inside morning prayer, but taking notes was harder than I had expected due to the opinions that many of the congregants had about me. Similar to the experiences of other Western anthropologists studying the former Soviet Union, people judged me based on media images of America (Kuehnast 2000). This was especially true with the Georgian and Mountain Jews, who, for the most part, envisioned me to be a "typical" independent and promiscuous "American woman" as portrayed on American televisions shows, like *Dynasty* and *Santa Barbara*. They had difficulty understanding that I was at the synagogue to conduct research and not to pick up men; and their assumptions directly shaped the kinds of interactions I was able to have with—and the type of information I was able to obtain from—them (Rosaldo 1989).

Russian Jews were more prone to categorize me in terms of a Cold War ideology that divided the world into "us versus them" (De Soto and Dudwick 2000). At times, Russian Jews at the synagogue expressed their concern that I was spying. Even though I had explained my project to them, and Yurii and Rabbi Silverstein had endorsed my efforts, people made comments like "Why are you writing this down?" and "What are you, a KGB agent?" when they saw my pen and notepad. Such comments made it clear that Soviet policies, specifically regarding the situation of Jews in the Soviet Union, continued to influence post-Soviet synagogue life. Having a fear of surveillance, Russian Jews were wary of questions about their decision to stay in Russia even though they had opportunities to emigrate. They also were embarrassed at times about their level of assimilation into Soviet Russian society compared to Jews in the West, who were free to practice Judaism, as well as to Jews from the republics who had fewer restrictions on their religious activities. These feelings and reactions stemmed from the history of Russian Jews in the Soviet Union.

The Soviet state did not see the Jews as a "nation," but rather as having a Jewish "religion" and "nationality." According to Stalin, a nation is "a historically evolved stable community of language, territory, economic life, and psychological make up manifested in a community of culture" (d'Encausse 1992:36), and because Jews did not have a common territory within the Soviet Union, they did not qualify to be a nation. In addition, the Bolsheviks declared that a Jewish nation could not exist because the Jewish people's only characteristic was its attachment to a religion, a social phenomenon that would supposedly disappear under communism. However, Lenin did acknowledge that Jews had been oppressed under the tsarist regime, and, in 1918, he gave Jews representation as a nationality via their own organization, called Evkom, within the Commissariat of Nationalities. He also set up Evsektsiia, a Jewish section of the Communist Party, which would express and defend Jewish interests. The purpose of Evsektsiia was to modernize and integrate Russia's Jewish population into Soviet society by eliminating the traditional structures of Jewish life, including Hebrew (Redlich 1982:xii). By concentrating on Jews from the Pale of Settlement, Evsektsiia established Yiddish as the official Jewish language, with the intent of making Jewish culture national in form and socialist in content.

Evsektsiia's policy to develop national Jewish culture corresponded with the revised version of the Soviet policy on nations that limited the right of national self-determination. According to the Constitution of the USSR, ratified on January 31, 1924, the final phase of national evolution would be the economic, political, and ethnic fusion of all nations (d'Encausse 1992:69). Because this would be a slow and complex process, the Soviet state's recognition of the rights of ethnic groups to develop their own culture and autonomy would help them transcend their national consciousness. In general, this fusion policy permitted temporary cultural, political, and economic autonomy of all ethnic groups, Jews included. For example, Evsektsiia passed a decree in 1918 that prohibited the teaching of religious dogma in schools, denied property rights to religious groups, closed synagogues and Hebrew schools, and outlawed Hebrew as the language of the Jewish religion (Levin 1990:70). In tandem with tearing down the remnants of the traditional Jewish culture, Evsektsiia promoted Yiddish literature and theater as legitimate art forms, increased the publication of

Yiddish books and periodicals, and established Soviet Yiddish schools in order to "popularize the principles of proletarian education and communist doctrines" (Levin 1990:177).

Under the state rhetoric of providing for all citizens of the Soviet Union, Evsektsiia and Evkom attempted to establish a Jewish territory inside the USSR in order to redirect Russian Jewish Zionists away from Palestine and to improve the economic status of Jews who remained in the Pale of Settlement by providing them work as farmers. In January 1925, the Soviet government set up a new body called the Society to Settle Working Jews on the Land in the USSR, known by its acronym GESERD (in Yiddish; OZET in Russian). Soon after, the leaders of GESERD took over Evsektsiia. After much negotiation about where to place the new territory, GESERD finally established a settlement called Birobidzhan, a piece of land between the Biro and Bidzhan Rivers on the southeastern border of the Soviet Union. The Soviet government liked the idea, since it would safeguard its far eastern frontier against the Japanese (Abramsky 1970:68).

Despite this plan to create a territorial Jewish nation in the Soviet Union, the liquidation of Evsektsiia in 1930 marked the disappearance of an official Jewish center and the emergence of a less cohesive Jewish agenda. At the same time as the Jews were losing their collective voice in the government, Stalin was gaining power and starting to eliminate his rivals. His ascension marked the end of the plan to make Jews into a territorial nation. On November 25, 1936, Stalin stated in his "On the Draft Constitution of the USSR" that autonomous regions could become Soviet national republics only if they were located on a border of the Soviet Union and if the nationality was a majority in that republic. Birobidzhan did not fit these criteria. With this decree, Jews obtained the legal-political status of an "extraterritorial minority," a minority that had "lost" its national attributes.

By the end of the 1930s, Stalin had increased his attack on the sovereignty of all nationalities and nations by abolishing their autonomous administrative institutions and drastically diminishing both their educational systems and their national cultural frameworks (Pinkus 1991:292). Accordingly, the Soviet government closed almost all Yiddish institutions and theaters, and by 1941 it had totally eliminated Jewish education.

At the same time, roughly from 1929 to 1939, the Soviet government embarked on its most savage persecution of religion in the Soviet Union. During these ten years it was almost impossible for religious groups to meet and distribute materials (Walters 1993:13); however, the abolition of Jewish education and Yiddish institutions and the persecution of religious Jews did not affect all Jews from Eastern Europe living in Soviet Russia. Many Jews who had abandoned the Pale realized that, in order to become well established in the Soviet proletariat and managerial and professional classes, they had to abandon Yiddish for Russian, Ukrainian, or Byelorussian (Gitelman 1988:165). By the end of the 1930s, they had become "educationally the most mobile, geographically the most urban, and linguistically one of the most Russified of the non-Russian nationalities" (Gorlizki 1990:339). These Jews became a part of the larger Soviet society through their contacts at work as well as through their friendships and marriages with non-Jews (Tsigelman 1991:45).

While the Soviet government banned the culture and politics of nationalities and nations, it instituted a number of policies that counteracted this assimilationist stance and stabilized ethnic group membership. When it issued a policy of passportization in December 1932 that obligated all urban dwellers to hold an internal passport indicating their nationality (Pinkus 1991:293), it also introduced a population census that required Soviet citizens to identify themselves as members of a certain nationality and measured their proficiency in the national language. Over time, the majority of Jews put down Russian as their native language.

From 1936 to 1938, the Soviet government brought the Jewish nationality into public view by using Jews as scapegoats for the economic, social, and political problems in the Soviet Union. This trend created an official and contradictory narrative of Jews as both an internal enemy and a weak nationality unable to defend itself. There were two causes for this abuse. First, because the creation of the totalitarian Soviet state required mass energy, the Soviet government did not tolerate any "genuinely autonomous or corporate units independent of the central manipulation of power" (Korey 1973:70). The government targeted Jews, since they had "cultural, emotional, and family ties that transcended national borders" (Tsigelman 1991:46). This fear of internationalism was a common characteristic of the Stalinist regime. For example, in 1941, the government charged the Volga Germans with cooperating with the Nazis and subsequently dissolved the Autonomous German Republic of the Volga.

The second reason for scapegoating Jews had to do with the repression of minorities with international ties, which was a response to a deepening Russian nationalism. This "nationalism, bordering on xenophobia, was a dominant character of the struggle against the 'internationalism of the Old Guard' " (Korey 1973:69). The purge of Old Bolsheviks and Jews coincided, culminating in a government-led assault against Jews in the Communist Party, state, and intelligentsia (Schapiro 1979:45).

By the time Stalin denied Birobidzhan republic status, most Jewish leaders, as well as supporters of the autonomous region, were imprisoned or expelled from the party. Many Jews reacted to the negative stereotypes of Jewishness and violent acts against Jewish leaders by "distancing themselves from their Jewishness, sometimes even going to the extreme of Jewish self-hate and total rejection of their nationality" (Tsigelman 1991:46). They subordinated any Jewish identification to a focus on building socialism.

The non-aggression pact with Germany in 1939 and the onset of World War II reinvigorated dormant Soviet Jewish institutions. The annexed territories of Eastern Poland, the Baltic States, Bessarabia, and Bucovia brought religious Jews into the Soviet Union. In "assimilating" these new territories, the Soviet government shut down their Jewish communal organizations and set up more proletarian ones similar to the Yiddish institutions formerly established in the Russian Republic (Szmeruk 1960:110). Taking advantage of this new Jewish activity as a way to defend the country against the German invasion, the Soviet government encouraged expressions of national and religious sentiments at home to increase patriotism. Accompanying this change in policy were a shrinking of party influence in the ideological sphere and the setting up of national and special interest groups under the Sovinform Bureau, a branch of the Commissariat for Soviet Wartime Propaganda (Redlich 1982:5).

In 1941, the Sovinform Bureau established the Jewish Antifascist Committee (JAC). Members included Jewish intelligentsia such as the famous actor Solomon Michoels, the Yiddish writers David Bergelson and Itzik Feffer, and Rabbi Solomon Shliefer, the head of the Moscow Jewish Religious Community at the Central Synagogue. The JAC was to be a completely loyal tool of the Soviet war propaganda. Its job was to gather positive materials about Soviet Jews for distribution to the Western press, especially America, where there was a large and influential number of Jews (Redlich 1982:39, 40). The Soviet government hoped these Western Jews would be so moved by the propaganda that they would send aid to the Red Army and Soviet citizens. The authorities did not realize that the Jewish Antifacist Committee's meetings, radio broadcasts, and contact with Western Jews created a new form of Soviet Jewish identification that opposed the official nationality policy of assimilation. In a time when Nazis were destroying the historical centers of Jewish life and murdering millions of Jews (Gitelman 1988:222), the JAC created a positive Jewish identity based on a feeling of kinship and ancestry with world Jewry through a common religion and history of suffering. B. Z. Goldberg, the son-in-law of Sholom Aleichem (a famous Yiddish writer) who was invited to visit the Soviet

Union by the JAC in 1946, wrote that "Soviet Jews had begun to regard the committee as their representative body, big brother, advisor, defender" (Goldberg 1961:59). All kinds of Jews sent letters to the committee and came to it "with personal problems involving real or imaginary discrimination, lack of pull, or any matters relating to Jewish cultural or religious life" (Goldberg 1961:59).

These liberal policies and attitudes regarding religious and national freedom were a front. For propaganda purposes, the government was prepared to take the risk of going quite a long way to stimulate national feeling among Soviet Jews, no doubt fully confident that this sentiment could be kept under control (Schapiro 1974:291). The JAC's narrative of an international Jewish people challenged the official Soviet policy of Jews as an extraterritorial minority. According to Soviet dogma, the Jewish nation could not exist, because Jews did not have their own territory. In addition, the international nature of this new Jewish feeling challenged the Soviet state's borders, causing, by 1948, the state to launch an assault against the JAC by condemning Western influences, refusing to defend and rebuild the lives of Jews returning from the concentration camps, and purposely omitting references to the wartime Jewish tragedy in the press. The Soviet Union also ended its support of Israel, since this new country did not prove to be a loyal pro-Soviet and anti-British satellite (Schapiro 1974:294). Meanwhile the Cold War had begun, leading to a renewed sense of Soviet isolationism. The Soviet state prepared itself for battle with the West, especially with the "fifth column" of Jews located within its borders.

The attack on internal enemies culminated in a "quiet liquidation" of "dangerous Jewish nationalism" under the rubric of an anti-cosmopolitan campaign (Schapiro 1974:294). All leaders of the JAC, except Rabbi Shliefer, were either executed or sent to prison camps in Siberia. The Soviet authorities also punished Russian Jews for their growing interest in the state of Israel and their applications to emigrate, as well as their revival of Jewish cultural institutions outside the boundary of socialism. The press called the Jews "rootless cosmopolitans," "bourgeois nationalists," and "Zionists" (Frankel 1991:318). In this context, Zionism became a code word for imperialism and bourgeois (anti-Soviet) activity. The term "Zionist" also allowed the authorities to persecute Jews without mentioning their Jewish origin. In this way, the Soviet government claimed that these practices were not anti-Semitic. Zionism soon became a primary concern of the Soviet government since it employed anti-Semitism as a major weapon in the politics and information policies of the USSR and the Soviet bloc (Frankel 1991:314). In the end, the Soviet government aimed to separate the Soviet Jews from one another, the United States, and Israel.

This kind of Soviet discourse placed Jews in a precarious situation. On the one hand, it perpetuated the image of the existence of a powerful Jewish nation, and, on the other hand, it declared the Jewish nation as a thing of the past. The label of "extraterritorial minority" made Jews an officially recognized nationality: Jews had "Jew" written in their passports. And yet, according to the Soviet nationality policy, Jews, like many other ethnic groups in the Soviet Union, had "lost" their "national characteristics," meaning that Jews had no need for their own educational and religious institutions. However, the real ties that Soviet Jews established with Western Jews during World War II revived the spirit of Jews as a people. This concept threatened the new isolationist policy of the Soviet government. The very diasporic nature of the Jewish nation—that Jewish networks transcend state boundaries—endangered the solidarity of the Soviet Union. According to official policy, the Jewish nation was dangerous. It had to be contained and monitored. As such, the Soviet government focused its attacks on Jewish religious institutions.

The groundwork for these assaults was laid out at the end of the 1940s, when the synagogue became the unofficial center for Soviet Jewry after the liquidation of the JAC. As one Soviet official commented, "they [synagogues] serve as the last assembly for our Jews, often even for those who are no longer religious. They help to maintain cohesion, to nurture the feeling of belonging to a distinct Jewish entity. And this is what we are trying to prevent. The fewer the synagogues, the fewer the opportunities to congregate and to keep Jewish separateness" (Rothenberg 1970:177).

It is important to note that Jews came under state supervision because the state had a keen interest in regulating all religions in order to decrease their influence on Soviet people at large. In the 1930s, synagogues were under the supervision of the NKVD (the forerunner of the KGB), but by 1944 the Council for the Affairs of Religious Cults (hereinafter "the Council") had become responsible for surveying the activity of synagogues (Anderson 1994:25). Established as a state commission to regulate religious groups other than the Russian Orthodox Church, the Council implemented decisions made by the Central Committee regarding religious policy (Anderson 1994:27). Through its Committees (later Sections) for Religious Matters in each city, the Council oversaw registration of religious groups and exercised control over congregations, their elected officials, and their clergymen (Rothenberg 1971:22; Anderson 1994). Through this organization, the state attempted to make Jewish culture, like all other ethnic cultures, national in form and socialist in content, and a major part of this transformation was the state's crackdown on Jewish religious practice. Specifically, the state portrayed the Jewish religion as inherently nationalistic because it supposedly fostered the creation of a separate Jewish state and declared that Jews wanted to live apart from other ethnic and religious groups.

In short, the state saw Judaism as a threat to Soviet order, and it aimed to eliminate the influence of Judaism on Jewish people. Accordingly, by 1947, all synagogues in the Soviet Union were the property of the state, and their finances were under direct state supervision.[8] The Soviet state was specifically interested in the Central Synagogue because the Soviet authorities understood it to be a vehicle for regulating Jewish religious practice. The Central Synagogue officially represented the Soviet Jewish population to the West; Soviet authorities always told foreign delegates and visitors who were interested in finding out about the situation of Soviet Jews to talk with the rabbi at the Central Synagogue. The rabbi then reported these conversations back to the authorities.[9] This synagogue also supplied prayer books and various religious materials to synagogues throughout the Soviet Union.[10] With these potentially dangerous activities in mind, state policies focused on regulating the production of ritual goods and supervising the performance of "nationalistic" religious ritual at the Central Synagogue.

Council officer Tagaev's report written in 1948 provides a clear example of the state's impressions of the supposedly separatist practices at the Central Synagogue:

Under the rubric of the Jewish religion, laid out in its dogmas and drenched with its rights and customs, the [Jewish] communities [here] develop charity under national signs and try to set up memorials to those who fell pray to fascism and to the Jewish heroes of the Fatherland War [World War II]. They [also] create ties with religious communities in the USSR and abroad; revive the customs and rights that were already obsolete and forgotten even by the most believing [Jews] ([customs such as] the *mikvah*, kosher meat, the selling of seats and *aliyot* [privileges to be called up to the Torah when portions are read during prayer] in the synagogue, etc.); the return of the national-religious holidays, which exist with festivity; and take all measures in order to attract bigger numbers of believers and non-believers to the synagogue.

These national tendencies are apparent in recent times in connection with the creation of the government of Israel. On May 20, 1948, the Central Synagogue held a "festive" celebration. The prayer service was put on with special pomposity. More than ten thousand people gathered at the service, and they filled up the space of the synagogue and almost all of Spaso-Glinishchevskii [*sic*] Lane. Inside, the synagogue was decorated with a large quantity of stars of David, [a sign] which is the true emblem of Zionism [Jewish nationalism]. Inside the synagogue, the walls and the pulpit were decorated with a green color, and a wide ribbon of light blue color (one of the component colors of the white-blue flag [of Israel]) was spread out along the walls under the chorus. On the portals opposite the pulpit, there were two framed posters. One of the posters was set on a light blue background and said in silver writing: "On May 14, 1948, the government of Israel was proclaimed." The second poster said in biblical Hebrew "Am Isroel Chai," which means "The Jewish people live."[11]

Throughout the Soviet period, state officials worried about how "nationalist propaganda" at the Central Synagogue continued to attract many "non-believers" and state workers on Jewish holidays.[12] In addition, the state's negative attitude toward Jewish religious activity created an image of religious Jews as using their "rites" such as circumcision, making matzah (unleavened bread), collecting *tzedoka*, and providing the invitation to read the Torah to make personal profits.[13] The Soviet state defined criminals as those people who make "a profit by buying and re-selling goods without adding any value by means of their own labor" (Humphrey 1995:61). This ideology of the market as immoral, coupled with the anti-Semitic image of the Jew as a "greedy" tradesman, continued to shape synagogue life in the post-Soviet period. In order to defeat Jewish nationalism and crush the influence of other religious groups on the Soviet population, Khrushchev launched a severe anti-religious campaign in the 1960s.

Although he began his tenure with the "secret speech" in 1956 that accused Stalin of being a criminal, fostering a "Cult of Personality," violating "Party Democracy," and unjustly imprisoning a great number of communists (Alexeyeva and Goldberg 1990:76), Khrushchev did not reveal the anti-Semitic practices of the Stalin regime. While he exposed the Doctor's Plot as a fraud, Khrushchev was silent about how political anti-Semitism was at its root.[14] In fact, Khrushchev soon replaced anti-Semitism as a state ideology with anti-Semitism as a state policy. The government used Jews to divert resentment that might have been directed against the regime itself for poorer living standards and high rates of crime (Korey 1973:78). In order to limit Jews' influence on Soviet society, authorities denied Jews jobs in the political-security section, administration, and otherwise sensitive appointments (Korey 1973:78).

By embarking on an extreme anti-religious campaign, Khrushchev strengthened the official narrative of Jews as the enemies of the Soviet people. Anti-religious propaganda directed against Jews, in addition to having the crudity and shallowness of other anti-religious propaganda during this time, depicted the Jewish religion as reinforcing Jewish nationalism. For example, the government endorsed Trofim Kichko's book *Judaism Without Embellishment*, which built on the old

"Protocols of the Elders of Zion" fabrication involving Judaism, Zionism, Israel, Jewish bankers, and Western capitalists with a crudely concocted worldwide conspiracy (Levin 1990:618). Kichko called Judaism a stronghold of imperialism and a belief that "promotes hypocrisy, bribery, greed, and usury" (Korey 1973:80). In state discourse, "Judaism" and "Jews" became the official code words for planned revolution against the fundamentals of communism and the Soviet state—a revolution that had to be stopped.

The anti-religious campaigns subsided in 1964 due to resource exchanges between the West and the Soviet Union (Baron 1976:324). This development reestablished contact between Soviet and Western Jews, and the improved treatment of religious Jewish institutions became the definitive outcome of this relationship. For example, the government recognized the synagogue as the main institution of Jewish life in the Soviet Union. While this official sanction reinforced Khrushchev's belief in the seminal link between Judaism and Jews as a people, it also lifted some of the restrictions it had placed earlier on the production of Jewish religious items. Now, Jews could bake matzah for Passover and produce a limited amount of religious articles, such as Hebrew prayer books, prayer shawls, and phylacteries (Baron 1976:324–30).

However, the victory of Israel over its Arab neighbors in the Six Day War in 1967, and the subsequent increase of Israeli territory, rekindled the Soviet government's anti-Zionist policies. Interested in gaining influence in the Middle East, Soviet authorities sought allies with "anti-imperialist" Arab states and launched a new wave of propaganda against Israel. This anti-Zionist campaign attempted to dissuade Soviet Jews from having a positive interest in Israel and to convince Arab states that the USSR would continue to support their cause.

This anti-Zionist campaign placed Jews in difficult circumstances. On the one hand, quasi-Leninists in the Soviet government emphasized that Jews were equal and important citizens of the USSR (Frankel 1991:334). On the other hand, neo-Stalinists blamed Jews for Soviet setbacks in Czechoslovakia and the Middle East, depicting Israel, Western Jews, and Zionists as controlling almost all the world's wealth and power. Furthermore, they linked Zionism to Nazism, claiming that both shared the dogma of the existence of a "worldwide Jewish people" and a "Jewish race" (Frankel 1991:335). As a result of these accusations, no Jew could escape being charged with Zionist and anti-Soviet activity. For, "the Kremlin sees in every flickering of a true and independent Jewish consciousness among its citizens, in every attempt at contact with Israel and world Jewry—a kind of heresy" (Katz 1970:334). Aleksandr Voronel, a future Jewish activist and one of the first editors of the Jewish *samizdat* entitled *Evrei v SSSR*, explained why Soviet Jews felt alienated from Soviet society and the intelligentsia during this period: "[The] feeling of impending catastrophe is very widespread. . . . It is felt that there is a deadlock in Soviet society and . . . for the Jews emigration is the only way out. The intensity of the anti-Semitic propaganda unleashed by the Soviet authorities is so great that it is difficult to believe in the occurrence of a positive change in their way of thinking or of a reversal of this trend" (Voronel 1975:72).

By 1969, this revised anti-Zionist campaign had helped transform emergent pro-Zionist feelings existing among a minority of religious Soviet Jews into a massive movement for immigration to Israel. This took the form of appeals to the Soviet government refuting its anti-Zionist propaganda and demands to immigrate to Israel on the grounds that, as members of the Jewish nation, Jews could secede from the Soviet Union according to the Soviet constitution. These appeals were published in the West. Although many Jews had participated in the human rights movement begun by Soviet intellectuals in the late 1960s and early 1970s, more and more Jewish intellectuals began to look to Israel to replace the pride they had lost in their own country. They believed Israel could be what the Soviet Union failed to be, a nation founded on peace that worked to ensure the full social and political equality of all its citizens.

Massive emigration began in the late 1970s when the government allowed more Jews to leave due to the publicity Zionists received in the West, the increase of collective and individual letters to Soviet and international institutions, and the appearance of Jewish *samizdat* on this issue.[15] Through the years, the government changed its position many times, frequently resorting to the arrest and trial of many leaders of the Jewish emigration and *samizdat* movements. Much to the chagrin of the Soviet authorities, these trials made the Jewish situation into an international human rights issue. In 1972, despite world support of Zionists in the Soviet Union, Leonid Brezhnev made it harder for Jews to emigrate by imposing a diploma tax requiring Jews to pay back the government for their education before they could emigrate. As a result of these restrictions, the phenomenon of refusniks developed.[16]

This change in emigration patterns and policy forced many Russian Jews to rethink their positions in Soviet society and world Jewry. Many Russian Jews realized that it was not possible for all of them to leave the Soviet Union immediately, and they aimed to reach out to the greater part of Soviet Jewry who still professed conventional Soviet ideas and were not yet ready to emigrate. Some intellectuals, like Aleksandr Voronel and Victor Yakhot, wanted to help these Jews express a positive awareness of their Jewish heritage by integrating it with their "European oriented, aesthetically Russian, but ethnically undetermined Soviet culture" (Voronel 1991:258). Others, led by professors B. Fain and V. Prestin, started a movement to get Soviet Jews involved with Jewish traditions and religion. Aiming to make Jewish culture and religion legal and open in the Soviet Union, they gave practical advice and information on the Jewish holidays, strove to bring Jewish religious practice into family life, and attempted to attract Jews to the synagogue. They wanted Soviet Jewry to become an integral and viable part of world Jewry.

By the late 1970s, the emigration application process had become as strict as ever, causing an increase in the number of applicants who were refused permission to leave. Despite the appointment of Mikhail Gorbachev in March 1985, there was not much change in Soviet policy toward Jewish emigration. However, during the period of *perestroika* a few years later, the Soviet government attempted to give more power to Soviet nationalities as well as to normalize religious life by rehabilitating it as a "healthy force" in Soviet society (Ramet 1993:33). As a result, the state sponsored the publication of books on Jewish topics, endorsed Jewish cultural activities, and even released some Jewish activists from prison. It was only in 1990, right before the Soviet Union collapsed, that Jews were once again allowed to emigrate in large numbers. In 1990, 184,602 persons left, and in 1991, 147,292 emigrated, and the figures remained around 60,000 in subsequent years (Institute of the World Jewish Congress 1996). In 1995, the Jewish population of the former Soviet Union was around 1,290,000 (Institute of the World Jewish Congress 1996).

Inside the Jewish Community

Through all the emigration, post-Soviet upheaval, and influx of Jews from the former republics and the West, the Soviet state's narrative about the synagogue as the place to find "greedy," "cunning," and "corrupt" Jews continued to strongly influence post-Soviet Jewish life. Although I had read about these images in publications and archival materials, I did not understand the tenacity of the narrative and its impact on my research until I found it in a very unlikely place. In a side project about the survival tactics of blind and elderly Russian Jews (Goluboff 2000), I interviewed Anastasia Davidovna, a Russian Jew who was a retired medical doctor and professor in her late seventies. She mentioned how her father had told her to avoid the Central Synagogue:

He said, "To each clean and great deed, there is always much dirt attached." Every synagogue is full of hucksters, corruption, and profiteers. Write that down. . . . When papa first came to Arkhipova Street, which is Spasoglin-ishchevskii Lane today, he socialized with those beggars and profiteers, those primitively cunning and stupid people, those greedy and filthy people. He said, "Ninety percent of everything there is filth." That was after the war. Much filth is [still] attached. Filth is filth. Spiritual, corporal, cunning, base, greedy, unfair—that is filth. Spiritual filth. Understand?

Several weeks later, the immorality of speculation at the synagogue resurfaced in my interview with Shloimie, the eighty-three-year-old Russian Jewish cantor who led morning services in the small hall. After he told me about how he came to Moscow in 1933 from Ukraine to look for work and that he had been too sick to serve in World War II, the following unexpected (from my point of view) dialogue took place:

Shloimie: Do you need this [interview] for yourself, or are you going to give this to someone?
Sascha: It is for when I go home.
Shloimie: I thought that you would fish out everything from me and then give it to someone.
Sascha: No, I need it for . . .
Shloimie: That would be *l'shon hara*; that is "bad speech" ["gossip" in Hebrew]. If I tell you something, you should not tell anyone else.
Sascha: If you don't want to answer a question, don't answer, of course.
Shloimie: No, I will answer. I am not afraid. Why should I be afraid? If they give me something, I will take it. That's because I have a sick son. Because of that, things are bad for me.

By claiming that he was not afraid, Shloimie implied that there was something to fear in talking about himself to others, especially when it came to taking charity, but he did not explicitly discuss what that fear was. The implications of such an attitude and the larger discourses of corruption at the synagogue will become clear as I discuss more of my work, but for now, it is important to note that this unnamed fear influenced how Russian Jews interacted with me and each other. While they chatted with one another before and after services, many Russian Jews did not know each other very well. Yurii said he was not aware of Shloimie's home life even though they had been praying together for many years. Some Russian Jews, especially the elderly, limited their time with me; they talked to me formally for only ten to twenty minutes, and their informal comments were brief. There were even some who refused to converse with me, no matter how much others or I tried to encourage them. For example, Semyon was in his eighties and seemed to know a lot about Jewish traditions, judging by his avid participation in morning ritual. After six months of coming to services, I tried to introduce myself to him. His response was, "Why should I tell you what my name is?" When I tried to explain to him who I was, he responded, "I don't know who you are, and I don't want to know. I am just a *prikhozhanin* [a parishioner, a person who comes to the synagogue]. I have been coming here for seventy-five years. How long have you been coming here?"[17] A middle-aged Russian Jewish man standing next to Semyon attempted to get him to open up to me, saying, "Why don't you tell her your name? The youth need to learn." "I am not interested in that," he answered.

Looking beyond my feelings of frustration, anger, and embarrassment, I came to see that Shloimie's and Semyon's decisions to be silent about their personal lives were both a product of their experiences of repression and a tactic to refuse to become subjects of the state, the synagogue bureaucracy, and even the ethnographer. This is why some of the elderly Russian Jews in the ethnography do not appear very often—they are mainly in the background, unwilling to speak. In keeping silent about themselves, perhaps they maintained a small space of privacy, that "secret corner" that was so illegitimate in Soviet times (Boym 1994:5). In fact, the Central Synagogue never had a membership policy. While people bought seats for themselves in the main hall, so as to contribute money to the synagogue for its annual expenses of baking matzah, they were not members. They were *prikhozhanini*. I saw part of my task as an ethnographer to "measure" the silences (Visweswaran 1994:51).

Storytelling in the Field: Is There a Truth to Be Told?

Besides these awkward times, congregants and staff at the synagogue did talk with one another and me about a variety of issues and they gave me oral permission to cite them as quoted for attribution. There were many moments when these discussions turned into long monologues about the "mentalities" and activities of individuals due to their group affiliations. These stories most often focused on corruption, ranging from short comments about how so-and-so sneaked an apple into his pocket during a Shabbat meal at the synagogue to how so-and-so was making a profit off the congregation by selling ritual items for a high price. At first I thought these stories showed how some people were not "afraid" to speak their minds, but I later understood through my work in the Russian archives that these tales resembled *donosy* (denunciations) and were thus another tactic to avoid repression and representation. The state practice of surveillance informed both of these tactics.[18]

During Soviet times, members of factories and other institutions frequently wrote "abuse-of-power" letters to higher authorities to complain about how local bureaucrats took funds for personal use (Fitzpatrick 1996:845). These denunciation letters served a dual purpose: they made people feel they had a voice in local affairs, thus giving the illusion that the state was truly communist, and they informed the government of workers' attitudes, which helped the government devise policies to make workers better conform to state ideology (Holquist 1997:419). Writing denunciation letters slid easily into the practice of spying, since it was difficult to draw a sharp line between letters written by request from higher authorities and letters written in the best interest of the collective. In fact, some people might have written these letters out of jealousy or in an attempt to gain status (Fitzpatrick 1996). Complaints against persons at the synagogue reflected these kinds of narratives, especially ones I found regarding synagogue officials in files of the Council. These similarities of narration show that Soviet ways of life easily adapted to new business culture and religious freedoms in Moscow.

These stories provided me with a particular challenge, for they complicate the usual function and nature of discourse among elderly Jews facing daily challenges of change and death (Myerhoff 1979; Kugelmass 1986) and the loss of children to different cultural worlds (Boyarin 1991:11). Many seminal studies of such communities have stressed storytelling as the key to building a secure personal identity and continuing the history of Jewish people across time (Boyarin 1992:xvii). In her work on elderly Ashkenazic Jews in California, Barbara Myerhoff shows how immigrants needed to tell their life stories to others in order to gain a sense of personal continuity despite the disruptions that occurred in their lives, and yet this need was never fully realized due to their situation. She comments that elders at the community center "required witness to their past and present life and turned to each other for this, though it is a role properly filled by the succeeding generation. Lacking suitable heirs to their traditions and stories, they were forced to use peers who, they realized, would perish along with them, and thus could not assure the preservation of what they had witnessed. Center people were tightly bound to each other, but in a web of relations that never fully coalesced into the firm, clear shapes typical of many social organizations" (Myerhoff 1979:33).

By listening to and documenting their stories, Myerhoff was able to provide these elderly men and women with that sense of continuity for which they were searching. In this way, she became their surrogate child. When people at the synagogue told me tales of corruption so that I would write them down, they alienated one another, perpetuated the Soviet practice of surveillance, and put me in a very difficult position. Because I was a Westerner conducting research at the synagogue, Russian Jews were certain that I had important connections, and they expected me to do something about the "immoral activities." They wanted me to expose the "truth" to the West, since they themselves did not have any recourse to authorities beyond Rabbi Silverstein.

In fact, it was the story about how Rabbi Silverstein used synagogue funds for his own personal gain that was extremely prevalent at the synagogue during my thirteen-month research stay, and it directly impacted my research and the kinds of relationships I was able (and not able) to establish in the field. These stories were very seductive, especially during my first months in the field. As an anthropologist, I strove to understand the position of the underdog, and it was tempting to grasp onto easy explanations of complex realities. This was even more so, when the person telling the story was my most influential and important source of access in the field.

It was a week after my arrival in October when Yurii Isaakovich took it upon himself to give me some advice about whom to trust—or, more precisely, whom not to trust. Sitting next to me in the small hall, he leaned in close to me, as if to tell me a big secret. Putting his warm hand on mine, he said:

Every Jew has his own opinion about the Jewish organizations here. But I want to tell you certain things about these institutions. There are not many Jews left in Moscow, and Jews from all over the world come here to do business. Foreign organizations donate a lot of money to Moscow Jewish organizations, but the money is put into the pockets of the directors. What will you find when you ask these people about their organizations [here]? You will not find the truth. I can never find the truth, even here in the synagogue.

Simcha sees himself as the most important rabbi in Moscow. So, he does not feel bad if he takes money for himself. I can perhaps understand this because he has five children to feed. But, he gets paid a salary of thousands of dollars. Dubinovich does the same thing. For example, they got a donation of several thousands of dollars to repaint the exterior of the synagogue. A guy came and just painted the bottom of the outside columns and then disappeared. I asked around to find out what had happened, but no one knew. I asked Simcha, but he shrugged me off. I asked Dubinovich, and he did the same. I know that they took the money! They did it here, right in front of God [He looked up to the ark, raised his arms toward it, and then lowered them]. They think that they have an individual understanding with God.

There are three kinds of people in the world: rich, middle, and poor. Only the middle ones and the poor ones tell the truth. You cannot trust the rich. The poor steal too, though. They need to in order to survive. I have worked here for six years. When we bought our apartment, we paid ten roubles. That was five percent of our salary. Now, an apartment is thousands of roubles, something we cannot afford. Bread is two thousand [roubles] in the summer, but it is five thousand [roubles] in the winter. I get paid only five hundred thousand roubles a month. I survived this far by not buying any new shirts, new suits, new ties. . . . I only spend my money on food. . . . These beggars who stand out on the street [in front of the synagogue] have more money than I do. They are so bold that they ask for dollars straight off. Those Georgians [Georgian Jews] who come around, they give out dollars. The beggars should say thank you for even a *kopek*. They should be grateful. When you ask about these organizations, where will you find the truth? [19]

Even though Yurii told me that I would not be able to find the truth about synagogue affairs, it seemed that he believed his take on the situation was the most genuine. I had a strong inclination to agree with his point of view. I relied on him heavily in my first months of fieldwork for contacts and cultural understanding, and as we spent more time together, I came to love and respect him like a father. I sympathized with his suffering. His run-down apartment was sparsely furnished. He haggled over the price of bananas at the makeshift market by his metro stop, and he rotated a series of three pants and shirts to wear to work. Poor elderly Russian Jews just like Yurii who came to the synagogue for charity, and the old men looked haggard in their worn pants and sweaters at morning prayer. It was easy to see how the majority of Russian Jewish *minyan* members felt poor in relation to the comparatively well-off Rabbi Silverstein and the Mountain and Georgian Jewish businessmen, with their healthy bodies and new, dark suits.

And yet, I also got to know Rabbi Silverstein and his family. I admired how they tirelessly worked to build new schools, charity programs, and religious activities. I was grateful for their hospitality, since they frequently invited me home for Shabbat and holiday dinners. As time went on, I began to realize that Yurii's words were not so much the "truth" as they were an interpretation of the synagogue's power structure. This insight placed me in a bind, for I understood that it would be impossible for me to stay completely open to both sides— those who complained of a lack of power and those who strove to solidify their influence. This situation finally came to a head when I was forced to choose allegiances. In fact, that happened many times between different groups at the synagogue. It was not possible for me to keep a completely neutral stance, since the situations called for decisive action or the end of my fieldwork and my friendships in the field. However, I tried to never take the word of one group as the ultimate truth, and I attempted not to privilege one individual standpoint over another. I conceptualized their stories, as well as my own, as a central aspect of our subjectivity. As William Sewell writes (1992:483), "All people develop a sense of themselves as subjects in part by thinking about themselves as protagonists in stories." I have thus placed myself in this ethnography as a "heuristic devise" (Dumont 1978:12). Like Jean-Paul Dumont, I used my presence at the synagogue as a "discovery procedure" to understand "the chain reaction" that my encounter with people produced, allowing me to better "perceive the studied culture and society in action" (Dumont 1978:12). By telling stories about themselves, others, and the anthropologist, individuals constructed some sort of agency and order in their lives. I looked for how they talked about one another, how they represented their actions, and how those stories related to older, Soviet forms of protest and new market-style practices of profit making, thus providing a glimpse of the trajectory of Russian society at large.

Organization of Chapters

This book tells the story of a changing post-Soviet Jewry. Each chapter focuses on events that were "diagnostic," actions that caused conflicts and thus revealed the ways Jews at the synagogue re-created and re-shaped the Jewish nation and Russian society on the local and national levels (Moore 1987). Chapters 1 and 2 detail how Russian Jews employed stereotyping language and targeted ritual practices to place themselves at an advantage over Jews from the republics and the West. Chapter 3 provides an account of several synagogue board meetings aimed to strip the local Russian Jews of their power in the institution. Chapters 4 and 5 focus on the Mountain Jews and their attempts to empower the self-proclaimed "Sephardic" (non-Ashkenazic) Jews at the synagogue to assert their Russian citizenship. This process solidified the disappearance of a dominant Russian Jewish influence in Moscow, while it signaled the saliency of racial and ethnic differences in post-Soviet life.

This book is also a tale of an ethnographer in the field. As the chapters progress, so will the readers' understanding of the situations I experienced. As such, the people in the book reveal themselves through each chapter, mirroring the time it took me to get to know them. Readers will become acquainted with "crazy" Shalom and his plan to unite the Sephardim; follow Yehuda Levi, a local Russian Jew, on his quest to expel Rabbi Silverstein from the synagogue; and explore Aleksei's deep adherence to Georgian Jewish family honor. I tried to portray the congregants' complex lives as accurately and compassionately as I could. This work is a testament to their struggle to live with dignity in the ever-changing post-Soviet Russia.

Chapter 1
Fistfights at Morning Services

The Central Synagogue—that's a drama group!
—A Moscow-born Lubavitcher Hasid

After gaining access to morning ritual at the Central Synagogue, I spent January to May attending Monday and Thursday services. On average, the congregation consisted of thirty men: eleven local Russian Jews (Yurii, Yehuda Levi, Shloimie, Berl, Semyon, Rabbi Dubinovich, and others); twelve Georgian Jews (including the brothers Zviad and Aleksei, who invited me to sit in the small hall); two Mountain Jews (Shalom, the head of the Mountain Jewish community, and Kostia, the treasurer of the Mountain Jewish community); Isaak Khaimov (the Bukharan rabbi); and three Ashkenazic Jews from Israel and Europe (Rabbi Silverstein, Yose, the young Israeli businessman who liked to pray extremely loudly, and at least one visiting Western Jewish businessman).

At first, I spent several weeks familiarizing myself with the Orthodox Jewish service, figuring out what prayers were said and when, using my own prayer book from America as a guide. The small hall service on Mondays and Thursdays had six parts: (1) *Birkhot Hashachar* (a series of morning blessings), (2) *Pesukei de-Zimrah* (the Psalms), (3) the *Shema* and its blessings,[1] (4) the *Amidah* (the main prayer, which consists of nineteen blessings and is said standing up),[2] (5) the Torah reading, and (6) the conclusion. I then charted the seating arrangements of the various members, noticing that the Georgian Jews tended to gather together in the back of the room by the green table next to Yurii's desk, while the Ashkenazic Jews (Russian and foreign) sat closer to the front. However, the Georgian Jews left the room to have their own Torah reading in the main hall when they had ten men for a *minyan*, including the Mountain Jews. They then returned to the small hall to end services with the Ashkenazim. This arrangement ran smoothly until May 6, 1996, when a fistfight broke out between Zviad and Yose during prayer. This conflict demonstrates the tensions and history underlying morning services in the small hall. Specifically, the fight elucidates how the creation of Jewish ethnic identity was tied to the negotiation of space at the synagogue, transforming the morning *minyan* into the site of much drama and excitement.

The Fight

Morning services began as usual on May 6. After finishing the *Amidah*, the Russian Jews, three Western Ashkenazic Jews, two elderly Georgian Jews, and Isaak Khaimov gathered around the bimah to hear Moshe, the eighty-year-old Russian Jew, read the Torah. The other Georgian Jews, accompanied by Shalom and Kostia, left to read the Torah separately in the big prayer hall.

Unlike the other Ashkenazim who were listening to the day's reading, Yose watched Zviad linger by the table in the back of the small hall. Zviad was slow to join the other Georgian Jews in the main hall that morning. Visibly distressed over Zviad's tardiness, Yose walked up to him and commanded him in Russian to "go to the other room," because the Torah reading had "already started" in the main hall. Moshe thumped the bimah table with his fist to get Yose to be quiet. Zviad stared at Yose. They both looked menacing—thickly built bodies and scowling faces, muscles tense. Moshe continued to read, but soon Yose yelled, "Go! Go!!!" to Zviad. Berl, a Russian Jew in his late seventies, tried to say something to make Yose calm down. Semyon yelled out "Sha!!!" while Moshe shouted "Quiet!" and Rabbi Silverstein let out an admonishing "Yose!"

Undeterred, Yose said to Zviad, "Go there, where you usually go." Zviad went to the main hall, only to return several minutes later to stand face-to-face with Yose. "What do you want from me?" he asked Yose angrily. Yose repeated the request, pointing to the main hall. Suddenly, Zviad wrapped his hand around Yose's extended arm. Yose made a fist out of his free hand and swung it around to hit Zviad in the face, but Berl stepped in between them. Zviad stormed out of the room, but quickly returned again. In front of everyone, he started to unwrap his phylacteries to get ready to fight. Yose did the same. The Torah reading stopped, and several members of the congregation gathered around the two young men. One elderly Georgian Jew, who usually remained in the small hall for the whole prayer service, admonished Yose for assuming that all the Georgian Jews leave the room to read the Torah together. Yose responded flippantly, "Well, why not?

It is *obychno* [usual]." Clearly offended, the old man repeated, "Why assume that we go there?" Wanting to stress his point, Yose angrily approached the old man, but Aleksei, who had come into the room to support his younger brother Zviad, stepped in between them. Aleksei touched Yose on the arm to stop him from hurting the old man. In response, Yose swung a punch, but Aleksei pushed him away. The force of the push sent Yose flying back into the pew behind him and crashing with it to the ground.

I stood up near my seat, trying to stay out of everyone's way while at the same time attempting to observe everything. I had arranged for Yurii Isaakovich to audiotape the service that day from his place near the bimah, but toward the end of the fight, he turned off the tape recorder because he said the events did not properly represent Jewish ritual. And yet, when I talked to people about why they thought the fight occurred, I understood that the fight was central to the dynamics of morning prayer at the synagogue specifically and to post-Soviet society in general. Explaining the event, *minyan* members hardly mentioned the individual issues that Yose and Zviad might have had with one another. Instead, Russian and Georgian Jews interpreted the fight to be a result of their disparate ethnicities, Russian (*russkie*) and Georgian (*gruzinskie*), respectively, and they talked about them in terms of space.

Realizing that post-Soviet ritual can be the context for the production of ethnicity, I began to see that morning services comprised a symbolic system of interactions that provided the impetus for conflict and the terms in which that conflict was fought (Kertzer 1988:175). During prayer, congregants struggled over who had the right to occupy the synagogue and dictate the terms of ritual enactment. Unlike Myerhoff's elderly Jews who had the need to "fight to keep warm" in order to discover a sameness "in the midst of furor and threats of splitting apart" (Myerhoff 1979:186), Jews at the Central Synagogue used the fight to express their perceived ethnic differences and to engage in contradictory, but culturally meaningful and contextual, processes of identity formation.

Claims to a "Russian" or "Georgian" ethnicity revealed the structural inequalities that existed between the two groups in terms of access to monetary resources and synagogue space (Wilmsen 1996:4). Russian and Georgian Jews thereby interpreted their ethnic identities in terms of the nationwide market reform and its effects on Russian society. Many Russian Jews said that the new economy was responsible for their poverty and loss of status; their proximity to Georgian Jewish businessmen like Zviad and Aleksei during services exacerbated this

opinion. To regain a sense of pride in themselves, Russian Jews deliberately constructed a Soviet spacial and moral order in the synagogue
that encouraged both dissident practices and Soviet anti-commerce
discourse. This tactic gave Russian Jews agency by allowing them to
assert what they considered to be their legitimate non-business "Russian" identity and proper Jewish religious rituals. This endeavor also
slid easily into the realm of Russian national narrative, since their labeling of Georgian Jews as "Georgians" and themselves as "Russians"
is similar to incidents of nationalism in which the dominant group
uses ideological means to label subordinates as "ethnics" (people who
are part of the nation-state but are considered to be culturally and bio-
logically inferior to the dominant group) (Handler 1985; Williams
1991; Hayden 1996). Russian Jews at the Central Synagogue desired
to maintain a more central place for themselves in the new Russia,
which, by their standards, had forgotten them. The basis for their
claim to synagogue space and dominance during prayer was that the
small prayer hall was their place that historically stood in opposition to
Soviet power.

Soviet Policies That Shaped Prayer

The Soviet state had a profound influence on ritual and interpersonal
relations at the Central Synagogue. Envisioning the synagogue as a
source of Jewish nationalist propaganda, state authorities tried to curb
and eventually eliminate the influence of Judaism; they monitored
Jewish prayer services and severely limited the production and consumption of ritual objects.

The state kept track of prayer services at the Central Synagogue in
several ways, including supervising and editing the first Jewish prayer
book published in the Soviet Union. In 1954, Rabbi Solomon Shliefer
submitted to the Council a translation of the prayer book for use in
the Central Synagogue. Although one Council reviewer reported that
he "did not detect any attacks on the Soviet Union," another reader
found "the clear spirit of nationalism" in the text.[3] The latter pointed
out passages in the Jewish prayer service that request the gathering of
all Israelis "in the country of settlement."[4] He went on to quote other
passages "saturated with the spirit of nationalism from ancient times."[5]
In 1955, despite these problems, the Council authorized the publication of three thousand copies of the Soviet Jewish prayer book, entitled both *Mir* ("Peace" in Russian) and *Siddur Hashalom* ("Prayer Book
of Peace" in Hebrew), to be published in 1956 and distributed among
the worshipers at the Central Synagogue and other large religious

communities in the Soviet Union.[6] A report written in 1979, before the republication of the prayer book, details the reason why the authorities decided to print it. Despite their desire to cut out some of the "nationalistic" prayers, the Council concluded that "The text of the prayers, many of which were added two to two-and-a-half thousand years ago, and those made after, have been strengthened by centuries-old traditions. Therefore it [the prayer book] cannot be issued with such cuts. In this condition, we find it much more advisable to publish the prayer book 'Mir' *only* in the ancient Hebrew language. This would severely (at least ten times) decrease the number of people who would be able to learn, and more importantly, understand the content of these prayers."[7]

The state authorities not only monitored the words of prayer, but they also supervised the performance of prayer. As one religious Jew told me, "The spirit and atmosphere of the synagogue was official and loyal." Indeed, Rabbi Shliefer had to clear his talks to the congregation through the Council,[8] and it wrote reports about the number of worshipers attending holidays services.[9] One elderly Russian Jew told me that the main hall had a prayer for peace and a prayer for the Soviet Union flanking each side of the bimah.[10] I heard stories from other members of the congregation, and even from Jews who rarely came to the synagogue, about KGB agents camping out in the building across the street to take pictures of people going to the synagogue. These pictures supposedly wound up in the hands of employers who would sometimes fire the *vragi naroda* (enemies of the people). Yurii Isaakovich summarized this situation for me when he said, "There is a Marxist saying that religion is the opiate of the masses. Religious people were the enemies of the country. To the end of your life, you are an enemy."

Valeri, a fifty-year-old Russian Jewish intellectual, had a specific story to tell me about how he decided to attend the synagogue in the 1970s, and how he was persecuted because of it. For him, as for many other *minyan* members, the synagogue was a focal point in his life story. From Valeri's early post-socialist perspective, the synagogue symbolized his identity; he rejected communist ideology early on and chose instead to honor his Jewish heritage.

Valeri met me at the metro station near his office, in the northern part of the city on the ring road that circles around central Moscow. Trained as an engineer, he had recently begun a new job in journalism, covering stories about Jews. As we walked along the small grassy island, he commented that this part of town had the worst smog in the city. Indeed, the September air was thick with the smell of gasoline and the last of the August heat. As we walked up the hill to his office, he commented with a wry smile, "As I get older, I find that I do not always enjoy talking to Jews. As an acquaintance of mine told me once, and as I always love to quote, 'The Jews are a difficult people, but I love them anyway.' "

When we got inside, he pulled out a desk from the corner of the crowded tiny office and positioned a chair on either side. While boiling some water in an electric teakettle, he placed instant coffee, a small box of chocolate-covered raisins, and two hard small bagels *(bubliki)* on the desk. He told me that his Jewish parents always took him to the synagogue, but he did not go there regularly on his own until he was twenty-one, after his father died. He went because Jewish law dictates a person must say the mourner's Kaddish every morning in a *minyan* for eleven months following the death of a parent or loved one.[11] His decision to say Kaddish was a demanding commitment in a time when Soviet officials carefully watched synagogue attendance.

Valeri: I studied in a closed [military] institute. I had gone [to the synagogue] on holidays, although they [my parents] were scared. They said that they [the KGB] take Jewish students. They inform the *komsomol* [state youth organization], and they throw you out of school. But I went to synagogue anyway on the holidays. Even fifteen years ago, Arkhipova Street was jam-packed on the holidays. Women and men met each other. There was nowhere else to socialize. And then, I started to go regularly to the synagogue to say Kaddish.

Sascha: Was it a difficult decision to say Kaddish?

Valeri: No. I decided that I needed to do it. In general, I was not afraid, although I did have that feeling of fear, honestly speaking, when I was doing Jewish activities. By then, it was the early 1970s, and I had finished the institute and began to go to Jewish seminars in Moscow with friends. Later, when I was thirty, they tried to recruit me into the KGB. They were interested in where I had obtained some illegal Jewish literature published in Israel. They called me into the military registration and enlistment office. The young man there asked me, "Do you go to the synagogue?" "Yes, I go. I am a religious man. Is that against the law?" "No, it is not." Then he started to talk about how I had "religious" . . . no, "Zionist" material, and that they were interested in the source, and that nothing bad would happen if I informed them. He repeatedly tried to get me to use his telephone [to give the information to another agent]. I refused. They already knew about me, where I went, what I did. Maybe the police were at a seminar, maybe someone told on me. There have always been informants in Russia. There was nothing to be afraid of during that time, although many were afraid and decided to make that phone call [to inform on others].

Sascha: Why weren't you afraid?

Valeri: What could they do? They could kick me out of work or threaten me with Marxism. I worked in an open organization. We had no government secrets. I was not afraid.

In stating that he did not fear what others did, Valeri acknowledged that Jews had a constant anxiety about engaging in religious activity. Fear was thus a defining aspect of synagogue relationships and the Soviet experience at large. Because they never knew when the government was watching them or what the repercussions would be for their actions, Soviet citizens wound up scrutinizing their own and each other's behavior. This strategy was one of the main ways in which the Soviet state regulated its citizens' activities and loyalties (Berdahl 1999).

The Main Hall

State interference in the synagogue created an atmosphere of apprehension and mistrust that greatly affected prayer services in the main hall. Holiday and Shabbat celebrations took place there, while weekday services were held in the small hall. Big hall rituals were the most public, and, as such, they were subject to direct state intervention. Yurii told me, "The KGB came in here, and they told Rabbi Dubinovich [who was the chief rabbi at that time] that religion must not be against the government. We did not disagree. We had a prayer for the USSR. They told him to report *kto torgovalsia* [who was doing business] in the synagogue [because it was against the law to make a personal profit], but he did not do that. Others did. Jews told on Jews."

In an interview I conducted with Rabbi Dubinovich, he gave me another version of Yurii's story:

Rabbi: There was this committee called the Council for the Affairs of Religious Cults. Whenever we had a question, we would go to them. To tell you the truth, the people who came here often gave me more trouble than the government.

Sascha: Really? How?

Rabbi: They would write letters complaining to the Council. After each Shabbat service, they wrote that I was spreading Zionist propaganda [the result of which would have been the closing of the synagogue].[12]

Sascha: Why did they do that?

Rabbi: They were communists.

Sascha: If they were communists, why did they come to the synagogue?

Rabbi: They came to meet with others. It was like a [social] club for them.

State interference in prayer perpetuated the image of the Jew as a traitor to both other Jews and the Soviet people. And yet, many Jews came to services in the main hall on Shabbat and holidays *because of the crowds.* Russian Jews told me, "It was dangerous [to come] on other times," and "On the holidays and Shabbat, you could hide yourself in the crowd. No one could see you." This desire to pray and socialize combined with an apprehension of reprisal created vivid synagogue memories. When he applied to work at a factory in Moscow in 1933, Shloimie told his employers that he would not work on Shabbat: "I said to them that [I am] a Jew and that on Saturdays I would not work. But on Sundays I would work to make up for Saturdays. And they took me, because they needed a worker. How much and wherever I worked, I was always here on Saturdays in the synagogue, and I always prayed to the Almighty because the Almighty is always in my heart. I never hid that I was a Jew. When I came to the factory to work, I said that I was a Jew and that my name was Shloimie. I never hid it, and I was never afraid."

Berl, another regular at morning services, arrived in Moscow in 1946 when he was freed from a concentration camp in Poland and sent to work on a *kolkhoz* (collective farm). When I inquired if he were afraid to come to the synagogue in the 1940s, he responded, "Be afraid of what? I was not afraid. . . . I was saved. . . . I only came on Saturdays and on holidays." "Why only on Saturdays and holidays?" I asked. "I was a little bit afraid." "You were afraid, really? Why was it better to come on Saturdays and not every day?" "Saturday was a holiday, a joyful day, an easy day. We went around with our *tovarishchi* [comrades], and our Saturday meetings strengthened that friendship." I realized how important socializing at the synagogue was for him when, at the end of the interview, he told me, "Everyone was killed [in the camp], and I alone remained." I commented that he must still think about them a lot. "Every day," he sighed.

Russian Jews were fond of pointing out their families' seats in the

Figure 3. Prayer service in the main hall, 1972. (Photo by N. Akimov)

main hall. Valeri recalled: "When I came to the synagogue after my father's death and everyone found out that I was his son, not one person didn't express his sympathy. He prayed in the main hall on the right side. I even know exactly where." Froim, who came to Moscow in 1927 from Berdichev (Ukraine) and took part in morning prayer, showed me the two places where he had prayed in the big hall. He told me how he bought his seats, paying as much as his means allowed at the time.[13] "It was hard to get a place," he said. "There were a lot of people. So many people! There were many Jews here—rich and others—all the places were taken." David, a ninety-eight-year-old from Berdichev who regularly attended morning services, recalled how he prayed in both halls: "During the week, I prayed there [in the small hall], and on Saturdays, I prayed here [in the main hall]."

While highlighting the apprehension involved in attending services in this prayer hall, these stories also emphasized friendships forged through common religious beliefs and traditions, elucidating how fear could sometimes create bonds among people in the same situation. Warmth of spirit could minimize feelings of mistrust. This was especially true in the setting of the small hall.

Heroes of the Small Hall

In general, *minyan* members categorized the synagogue as divided into two parts during the Soviet period: the main hall, where most "communist" Jews *(kommunisty)* gathered, and the small hall, where the "believing" Jews *(veruiushchie)* prayed together. Although those who frequented the synagogue might have respected the head rabbi and enjoyed socializing in the main hall on holidays and Shabbat, they knew that it was a dangerous place. In contrast, *minyan* members recalled the Jews who gathered in the small hall as practicing a Judaism that was outside of state surveillance, and thus more "true." "On the major holidays and Shabbat, the Hasids gathered there [in the small hall],"[14] Valeri explained to me. "The people there were respected and interesting. In my time, they were excellent people. Rabbis Shliefer and Levin were strong rabbis. But an *obshchina* [community] existed only in the small hall—men like Avram Miller, Getl Vilinskii, and Motel. People went to them, not to Dubinovich, for advice. [The main hall] always had more people and concerts on the holidays. But, in general, I was in the small hall. The atmosphere was warmer there."

Unlike "communist Jews" in the main hall, who supposedly betrayed their co-religionists, the Hasidim who prayed in the small hall informally taught many young secular Jews how to lead religious lives. However, it is not clear who these Hasidim really were. Valeri could have called them Hasidim out of deference to their "holy" qualities and lifestyle. Another story was that Lazar Poliakov, the rich railroad magnate who paid for the erection of the synagogue in 1891, built the small hall so that local Hasidim would have a place to worship. It was rumored that they prayed there throughout the Soviet period. In fact, under the direction of Rebbe (Rabbi) Menachem Mendel Schneerson in New York, the Lubavitcher Hasidim worked clandestinely in the Soviet Union to pass on Jewish knowledge through their synagogue in the Mar'ina Roshche section of Moscow.

During 1995, a core group of Russian Jews who attended the weekday *minyan*, including Shloimie, Berl, David, Froim, Semyon, Moshe, and Yurii Isaakovich, preferred to celebrate Saturday morning services in the small hall, while the main service was held in the main hall. As a result, narratives about the Central Synagogue in the past created a connection between ritual space and prayer performance. These Russian Jews continued to see the main hall as an "official" (that is, Soviet) space, while associating the small hall with a Hasidic prayer style that "believing" Russian Jews practiced and secretly passed on to the next generation. They saw themselves as the bearers of the legacy of Avram, Getl, and Motel. Valeri once commented to me that the old men like Shloimie and Berl "have the strength to come [to services]. Many of them have studied. Maybe at first it seems that they do not know a lot, but then you start to talk to them and it turns out that they do. Many of them, around age seventy to eighty or so, studied in western Ukraine at Jewish schools. In principle, they know everything. But if they follow all the religious laws, well, that is their business. They come, and let them come."

And they did, but not without serious consequences. These Russian Jews used the images of the small and main halls as a tool to deal with a new reality—the demise of the socialist state and the infiltration of Jews from the West and the republics into synagogue life.

Holding on to Heroism

Russian Jews felt the presence of Western Jews most acutely during the post-Soviet administrative changes that took place in the 1990s. Many international and local Jewish organizations hoped that Rabbi Silverstein, with his highly competent rabbinical training and knowledge of English, French, Yiddish, Hebrew, and Russian, could revitalize the Jewish community after it had weathered many years under the antagonistic communist regime. I had my first extensive conversation with Rabbi Silverstein in his office a week after I arrived in Moscow. Sitting across from him at his desk, I told him in English about my project. He looked straight at me without a comment and leaned back in his chair. The silence made me nervous. After I had posed several general questions to get a sense of his stance and objectives, he said, "I can see from your questions that you are scratching the surface. You need to dig deeper. You must find out if it is possible to create a Jewish community here. This is the question I ask myself every day."

It became easier to talk with the rabbi over the following months, as he came to expect my daily presence at the synagogue and I became more relaxed around him. After observing his interaction with others and having many dinners at his house, I saw how he, in addition to setting up new Jewish schools and youth programs with his wife, worked extremely hard to get local and international sponsors to help renovate the synagogue. Many local Jews had become rich in the new economy. They, not the government, were now the main source of synagogue finances. Rabbi Silverstein was not open with many congregants about what he saw as a proper Jewish community, or about how he proposed to create it at the synagogue. Many Jews at the synagogue were skeptical of his intentions, wondering if he had the good of the local congregation in mind, since he obtained his salary from undisclosed sources outside the synagogue. In most synagogues the congregation pays the rabbi, but the Central Synagogue historically had no membership policy and therefore could not afford to pay the rabbi's salary in full.

In the winter, I heard a rumor that the rabbi planned to "modernize" the decor of the small hall to create a Russian Jewish youth *minyan* on Shabbat. The younger generation hardly came to the synagogue on weekdays, preferring to gather outside on the street during the holidays and socialize at their own schools or Jewish clubs, like Hillel, on weekends. News about the renovation caused many elderly Russian Jewish congregants to worry that they would be kicked out of the small hall, and they began to reflect on why they had prayed there. Lyonia, a forty-three-year-old Russian Jew who took over Yurii's job in the afternoons, tried to explain to me why the old men did not want to pray in the main hall, saying, "[We do not like it] because the bimah [in the main hall] is not in the center. Also, the architecture is like that of a reform synagogue, or a church in Germany. The altar is in front and there is a space on the third floor for a chorus, like in a cathedral. Also, no women are allowed in the small hall."

There was more to this choice of prayer space than a preference for an Orthodox Jewish architectural style. The elderly Russian Jews considered themselves to be the descendants of Avram Miller and Getl Vilinskii. Shmuel Berl, a sixty-seven-year-old Jew from a Lubavitcher Hasidic family, told me that he prayed in the small hall because "The Hasidim used to pray in the small hall. Not the Hasidim you see here today, but others." Shloimie sighed deeply several times when he overheard the conversation. He admitted that, despite his and Shmuel Berl's faults, they "tried to follow them [the Hasidim]" in their religious conviction and knowledge. Shloimie in particular related to how his religious faith and knowledge gave his life meaning and happiness. He told me that he was a cantor because "I sing, because I know. When I read, I understand what I am doing and therefore I love it. I put all of my soul into my voice. I serve the Almighty and will serve him forever."

By placing themselves within the line of Hasidic descent, the elderly Russian Jews asserted their right to pray in the small hall on Shabbat. Rabbi Silverstein's project put a new twist on the former small hall/main hall dichotomy; it strengthened the Russian Jews' view that they were a group of "old people" who could rely only on one another to make sure that the younger Jews did not get rid of them. As Yurii said, "The old people have prayed in this small hall for seventy-five years. The leaders said that we should all go to the big hall. They [the old men] refuse to go." They implied that leaving the small hall would cause them to lose touch with their identity and religious practices. They insisted that they continue to pray in the small hall so they could see themselves as descendants of the great Hasidim. However, while the elderly members of the congregation saw their old age as a sign of their adherence to Judaism in spite of the Soviet government, the administration of the synagogue categorized these old men as impediments to modernization.

By April, the rumors about Rabbi Silverstein's plans to renovate the small hall had grown. I asked him if the stories were true. "Yes, I want to make it look like a modern prayer hall in Jerusalem," he said to me.[15] I must have looked disappointed, because he asked, "What? You don't think that it's a good idea?" "Well, I feel bad for the old men, and I really like the way it looks now."

Rabbi: All anthropologists want things to stay the same. Listen, there is no need for the men to pray there on Saturdays. Do you know why they started doing that?
Sascha: The times of the service?
Rabbi: No.
Sascha: Because the bimah is in the front?
Rabbi: No.
Sascha: Because men and women . . .
Rabbi: Right. Because men and women sat together. Listen, the small hall was where the real religious men prayed. Men gathered there to pass on knowledge. I dedicated my book to three of those men—Shalom Taubin, Avram Miller, and Getl Vilinskii.
Sascha: And now, all those men have emigrated?
Rabbi: No, they died. The last died in 1989. Those men there [in the small hall now] are just the leftovers. They drive on the Shabbat [and thus break the Jewish law]. They come [to services] because they are used to it, or because they want to get to work earlier. I want to redo the small hall for the youth. Without the youth involved, there will be no one left in the synagogue in ten years or less. [Giving the youth the small hall] will start a chain reaction. The Georgians will see that the small hall was fixed up for the youth and that they are gathering there, and then the Georgians will organize more. Just like in business, we need competition here.

Competition in the religious market has become commonplace in post-Soviet society where former state religions (like Russian Orthodoxy and Romanian Orthodoxy) feel threatened by the onslaught of missionaries representing a myriad of Christian, Muslim, and other religious groups (Verdery 1999, especially chapter 2). In fact, Russia has a strict law about which religions are indigenous to Russia and thus allowed to exist within its borders: Russian Orthodoxy, Judaism, Islam, and Buddhism. This cuts down on "the competition for souls" because it is difficult for other Christian denominations to get a foothold in the country. After the arrival of Western Jews, an antagonism developed between the *Mitnaggedim* (Orthodox Jews, such as Rabbi Silverstein, who do not consider themselves Hasidim) and the Lubavitcher Hasidim; both groups have been vying for the attention of the same Jewish population. Perhaps, then, Rabbi Silverstein implemented his plan to modernize the synagogue to attract more Russian Jewish youth in order to counteract the various youth programs run by the Lubavitchers. [16]

Rabbi Silverstein's interpretation of the old men's presence in the small hall on Shabbat draws on a conceptualization of the synagogue as a business venture and thus reflects the pro-capitalist discourses typical of modern-day Russia. The Soviet state had condemned market behavior as anti-Soviet and blamed the "greedy" Jews for engaging in such activity. Then, in the 1990s, Yeltsin's administration, as well as many Russian and foreign businessmen, actively supported the development of the free market economy in Russia. They wanted to transform Russia from a socialist country into a capitalist one. Rabbi Silverstein too believed that business meant progress, and he modeled the synagogue's administration on this idea. The elderly Jews aligned themselves against Rabbi Silverstein and his plans to "improve" the synagogue, choosing instead to place themselves symbolically within the heritage of those Hasidim of the small hall who had challenged the Soviet government and synagogue administration. In the process, the elderly Russian Jews also re-identified themselves with Soviet values.

Yehuda Levi, a middle-aged Russian Jew, considered himself to be Rabbi Silverstein's main adversary and an advocate for the ideals embodied in the history of the small prayer hall. He called himself a rabbi and an academic since he descended from a long line of Byelorussian rabbis and taught engineering. He was a longtime participant in morning ritual, and Yurii Isaakovich introduced me to him during my second week of fieldwork. "You really should meet him," Yurii said to me one morning after services. Yehuda was sitting near us at the green table. Turning to Yehuda, Yurii said, "She wants to know about all the Jewish organizations here and where all the money goes." "Oh, I cannot answer that," Yehuda laughed. "No, she really wants to know. It's okay," Yurii said. Yehuda leaned in toward me: "Just between you and me, there are two professions that are really in style now: being a Jew and being religious." I had heard this statement before. "You mean that people make money by being religious and Jewish?" I asked. He looked surprised, turned to Yurii, and said, "She has learned it so well already!" He continued, "The Jewish organizations have a mafia structure." I asked, "Who is at the top? The rabbi?" "Everyone is at the top. I'll tell you about it later," he replied, making a gesture as if to say that there were too many people in the room, and writing down his name and phone number.

I went to visit him a month later. It was November, and already I was freezing. My hands began to feel numb even though I was wearing gloves. His street was icy and bumpy, but children attempted to sled on its slight incline while their parents watched. There was just enough light from the street lamp to catch my breath as I exhaled, looking up at the blackened sky above his apartment building.

At Yehuda's apartment, I took off my coat and shoes, as is the custom so as to not get the floor dirty, and put on the pair of *tapochki* (slippers) he handed me. He then led me to the apartment's main room, which had shelves of books from floor to ceiling. There were piles of newspapers in each corner. Above one bookcase hung pictures of his late father and mother. He and his father had lived together for thirty years after his mother died. His father passed away seven months ago, and Yehuda was saying Kaddish for him. Apologizing for the mess in the room and the meager meal of cheese, salad, and wine, he said that he lived alone, *po kholiastke* (as a bachelor). He remarked that he had been married but that his children and wife no longer kept in contact with him.

During our conversation, he told me that foreign Jews, like Rabbi Silverstein and Yose, were "false Jews" because they used their Jewish heritage to make money off the synagogue, pocketing contributions made to the community. However, he said that the elderly Russian Jews "have been Jews all their lives." He continued, "It is easy to be religious, and now false people use this [their newfound faith] to make money. No one was in the synagogue when it was not advantageous. But now when it is free [to be religious], they gather around it [the synagogue]."

Yehuda explained the relationship between foreign Jews and local elderly Jews through their varying attitudes toward ritual objects, specifically prayer books and Jewish religious calendars. He said:

Jews back then were real heroes. They risked their lives for a cause. The religious men during communism would take the covers off the prayer books in order to carry them in their breast pockets where no one would see them. If you are to understand Russian Jews, you have to understand our mentality and how it has changed. I remember this one rabbi from Canada. He came to Russia. We had a Jewish [religious] calendar issued here with the government's permission. The circulation was limited to five thousand. This rabbi quietly took one of the calendars back with him to Canada. He photocopied it there and sent it back to us with visitors. We did not know about photocopy machines then. Americans, they don't understand this. They say, "Well, it only cost him twenty dollars to photocopy the calendar." But he risked his life to do it! Americans don't understand this mentality. Now, they treat us as less than human. At morning prayers foreigners come, and they only talk to each other. They never say hello to us. They don't respect us.

The path of the calendar and prayer books details the way "believing" Russian Jews dealt with the shortage of religious items resulting from government policies aimed to curtail "cult" activities. The dearth of ritual items was similar to the deficit of goods in general in the Soviet Union. Nancy Ries, in her book *Russian Talk*, discusses how her Russian friends saw the challenges of finding food and goods in Moscow as a way "to celebrate their own highly developed but impromptu coping skills" (Ries 1997:36). Similarly, Yehuda proudly told me how, by hiding the coverless prayer books in their pockets and secretly exporting the religious calendar, Russian Jews creatively obtained items they needed for worship and outwitted state authorities.

Yehuda suggested that the value of a ritual item lay not only in its subversive quality, but also in its use value. He said that Russian Jews saw the value of an object in the effort it took to make and distribute it, and in the way it served the community. This statement relates to the Russian notion that only poor people have the capacity to create a truly "soulful," and thus "Russian," community of equals (Pesmen 2000, especially chapter 6). According to Yehuda, "Americans" (that is, all Westerners) calculated the value of an object according to its market value. For them, the calendar was only worth the twenty dollars it took to copy it. Extrapolating from that argument, Yehuda stated that, because they did not value objects the way Russian Jews did, "Americans" did not value Russian Jews and treated them as backward and childlike.

I found myself growing to like Yehuda during my visit with him. His words were passionate, and he had a strong sense of morality. I admired how he felt that he had a duty to defend the honor and rights of the elderly Jews. And yet, he had a soft side as well. His eyes were large, and they filled up occasionally with tears when he talked about his deceased parents. When he walked me out to the bus stop, he said that there was not much reason for him to continue living. Leaning on his cane as we made our way over the ice, he admitted that he was ready to die. "How old are you?" I asked. "Fifty-six."

In the light of the street lamp at the bus stop, I could see that his eyes were tearing. Was it the cold or his feeling of loneliness? He told me that Israel should train the young Russian Jewish youth to lead the

Moscow congregation. The bus came. He asked me to call him when I got home. I kissed him on the cheek, and he did the same. We waved goodbye.

As I spent more time with Yehuda both inside and outside the synagogue, I noticed how the elderly Russian Jews at the synagogue highly respected him. He had a solid religious knowledge, and his father had been an important member of the small hall *minyan*. Yurii Isaakovich was especially fond of Yehuda and his father; he had taken care of Yehuda's father when he was dying.

Although I was very happy that such a well-respected and outspoken member of the *minyan* was willing to share his experiences with me, I was concerned that our growing friendship would negatively affect my relationship with Rabbi Silverstein, who had recently begun to share information with me and to invite me regularly to have Shabbat dinner with his family. Yehuda and Rabbi Silverstein represented opposing economic systems and moral orders. Yehuda longed for socialist values in the synagogue while the rabbi was eager to implement capitalist reform there. Both men were convinced, although for different reasons, that business practices and the logic of the market would destroy the old ways of being religious at the Central Synagogue. Such concerns about the future of the congregation directly shaped morning ritual.

Morning Ritual in the Small Hall

The increased presence of Western and migrant Jews during morning prayer marginalized many Russian Jews at the Central Synagogue. In response, Russian Jews employed ritual to protect their prayer space. During morning prayer, the majority of elderly Russian Jews occupied the center of the small hall. Historically claiming this room as their own, they regulated and led the service. Both Shloimie and Moshe conducted the service according to an Ashkenazic prayer style, with a slight Lubavitcher Hasidic influence.[17] In contrast, Georgian and Mountain Jews stood along the peripheries of the room, and they were expected to follow the Ashkenazic liturgy. Yurii Isaakovich explained prayer to me this way: "On weekday mornings, all the groups pray here [in the small hall]. There is a Bukharan man named Isaak who prays here." He pointed to the chair next to his. "The Mountain and Georgian Jews congregate around the table" in the back of the room.

On the one hand, the separation of these Jewish groups mirrored the structure of Shabbat services, where each group had its own *minyan* in a separate part of the synagogue. This arrangement corresponded to the history of prayer at the synagogue. Valeri specifically mentioned that, during the Soviet period, the Bukharan Jews had their own *minyan* and cantor and that there were Mountain Jews at the synagogue: "Perhaps they [the Mountain Jews] did not have a big *minyan*, but they were there. Maybe they prayed with the *bukharskie* [Bukharan Jews]. I remember that on the holidays, we were in the large hall, and they [the Bukharan Jews] took out the Torah and brought it to their own room where the Mountain Jews are now. But recently, I think that more *gorskie* [Mountain Jews] and *gruzinskie* [Georgian Jews] have settled here."

The Bukharan Jews who attended Shabbat services during my research confirmed Valeri's statement. They claimed that they had their own *minyan* from the 1920s to the 1970s in the room now occupied by Mountain Jews. Tzvi, a Georgian Jew who had lived in Moscow for forty years, gave me a different interpretation. He said that three Georgian Jews used to pray regularly at the Central Synagogue: "Only after the Soviet Union fell apart did Georgian Jews come to live in Moscow. Before that, they came as tourists or businessmen. When we had enough for a *minyan*, we prayed under the steps" in the place where the Mountain Jews have their prayer hall.

On the other hand, Yurii's statement about seating arrangements during morning prayer epitomizes how he took the presence of his own group for granted, failing to mention the Russian Jews and the Western Ashkenazim. Despite the stories that Jews from the republics told about gathering in the Central Synagogue over the last seventy years, most Russian Jews recalled that only one or two individual Georgian Jews attended the synagogue. Russian Jews claimed that until 1991, "It was mostly us."

By placing themselves in the center of the room and in charge of the ritual process, the Russian Jews performed their identity as Russian and Ashkenazic Jews. This spatial mapping of morning prayer reproduced the order of the Soviet state; the dominant group was equated with the core of the nation (Moscow) with ethnics located at its borders (republics). Through prayer, the Russian Jews re-created a social and political order in which they occupied the main place of power.

Inherent in this process was the way in which Russian Jews characterized Georgian Jews as "loud" and "disruptive," supposedly like the Georgian people. At almost every morning service I attended during my thirteen-month stay in Moscow, there was at least one comment made about how noisy the *gruzinskie* were during prayer. During our interview, Valeri said that some of the Georgians are "quiet people" like Adom, and some are "hot-tempered people whom Shalom calls 'carbonated.'" Valeri told me how, at one morning service, "I heard how one honored Georgian Jew cursed out his own in Georgian. Well, I thought I was going to die! I thought that they all would start talking that way! But there is something common in all of us Jews. You can't get away from it." When I asked him what he thought about when he prayed, he said, "At that moment, one should not think about anything, not about one's work, but about with whom we are talking, to whom we address our words: to the Almighty. And it is irritating when people are talking around me."

Adom, a Georgian Jew, even had something negative to say about how Georgian Jews talked during services. Extremely mild-mannered, he was always ready with a shy smile and kind words. He was in his fifties and had originally come to Moscow from Oni twenty-five years earlier to study at an institute. When I asked him why he usually stayed in the small hall even when Georgian Jews had enough men for a *minyan* in the main hall, he said, "Why should I [pray with the Georgians]? I have been praying with the Ashkenazim so long now that I am used to it. Besides, the Georgians like to la la la la [talk loudly about nothing]." "Oh, you mean Aleksei and Zviad?" I asked. "Yes. When they talk to me, I don't answer them. *Mne stydno* [I am ashamed]. One is not supposed to talk while one is praying. . . . I don't want to say anything bad about people. Sascha, it depends on how they were raised at home."

The Russian and Western Jews followed the Ashkenazic interpretation of Jewish law, in which talking is prohibited during the recitation of the *Amidah*. Samuel Heilman (1976:144) writes, "The proper way to recite the amida [*sic*] is standing erect, feet touching one another in at the instep, and facing toward Jerusalem and the site of the former temple. Nothing is allowed to challenge one's involvement in the amida. . . . Openly defiant deviations (e.g., boisterous conversations) are both halachically (according to Jewish law) and socially illegitimate, for they publicly undermine the devotion to prayer called for by the occasion."

Accordingly, the Russian and Western Jews talked to one another before prayers and during some of the opening psalms, but, as soon as the *Amidah* began, they fell silent. This was not so with the Georgian Jews. A few weeks before the fight, three Georgian Jews—Mordechai, Aleksei, and Zviad—sat around the table in the back of the room. Throughout the whole service, they talked in hushed Georgian. Their voices filled the prayer hall during the long and silent repetition of the *Amidah*. Only during the *Kedushah*, the third blessing in the *Amidah* that praises God's holy name, did they participate in the service. According to Ashkenazic tradition, the *minyan* recites the *Kedushah* responsively in a standing position during the repetition of the *Amidah*.

The Georgian Jews took it one step further. They stood up together in a line. Loudly, above everyone else, they recited the sanctification of God's name.

Scenes like this one occurred often, and they caused much consternation among the Ashkenazic Jews, both Russian and foreign. Yurii Isaakovich told me that after constantly telling the Georgian Jews to "Sha!" he gave them his newspaper to read. "Now, they talk about what they read in the paper," he sighed. Yose complained about Zviad and Aleksei to me early on in my research stay: "I try to tell them to be quiet, but they refuse. Their talking is a slander against God. There are certain times when one is permitted to talk and times when one is not. They would better serve the memory of their mother by not coming at all. This way, they would not disturb others."

Closer to the fight on May 6, Yose told me about how he and Aleksei almost hit each other recently:

You really missed a good one. He [Aleksei] and his brother were talking as usual, so I turned around and told them to be quiet. I said, "Shhh!" Aleksei came up to me and said, shaking his fist, "I will show you how to be quiet after the service." After the [Georgian Jewish] Torah reading, Zviad came in [to the small hall] with the Torah scroll. He said something to me, and I said, "Go back to Georgia!" Well, a fight almost broke out. The rabbi [Silverstein] came over and told us to calm down. He said that I had to apologize for telling Zviad to go back to Georgia. I said that I would apologize only if Aleksei apologized for wanting to get into a fight with me. We never apologized to each other, and by now, we have basically forgotten about the whole thing.

The Ashkenazim blamed the Georgian Jews' loud behavior on what they saw as the "typical" "Georgian mentality," which supposedly revealed their low intelligence. For instance, Yehuda commented to me that, although the *gruzinskie* kept the religious laws during the Soviet period, they were not aware of the specificities of Jewish prayer and ritual behavior. Rabbi Silverstein said the Georgians were religious, but they did not know how to pray correctly. He commented that they were accustomed to repeating after their rabbis because they did not have any prayer books of their own. Yurii once conveyed to me his general disappointment with the Georgian Jews, saying that first, he thought that they were good people, judging from the way they kept the religious laws during the Soviet years. "But," he sighed, "then I found out that they are *vspylchivye liudi* [hot-tempered people]. That means you think they are nice, and then op!"—he made a face as if he had been pinched—"they do something that bothers you. They say something bad, et cetera."

Because he was the small hall administrator, Yurii was responsible for maintaining an appropriate atmosphere for prayer. Not only did he tell the Georgians to be quiet, but he also fined them for talking at unacceptable times. In such a way, he affiliated the Georgian Jews' higher economic status with their negative "Georgian" traits. One of his job requirements was to take the old metal *tzedoka* box around to each *minyan* member during the opening psalms. He was not above shaking it loudly to remind the noisy worshipers of the *mitzvah* (good deed) that is *tzedoka*. Using this formula, Yurii devised a way to make the Georgians "pay"—literally and figuratively—for disrupting prayer. He explained: "The Georgians have a lot of money. When those two brothers [Aleksei and Zviad] came here last year, they put in five thousand roubles [one dollar] for charity [every day]. Now, they only put in two hundred roubles. I ask them to put in money because they talk. *Shtraf* [It is a fine]. . . . Beniamin [another Georgian Jew] too. When he comes in, he pays money right away and says, 'Here, I know that I will talk.' "

Georgian Jews symbolically protested the structure of prayer in the small hall not only by talking but also by decreasing the amount of money they gave for collective charity. It was common knowledge in the synagogue that the Georgian Jews gave their rabbi, Khakham David, *tzedoka* during their separate service, and several non-Georgian Jews said, "It costs a lot of money to get an *aliyah* [the privilege to be called up to the Torah] in the Georgian *minyan*." In contrast, it was the tradition in the small hall to make *tzedoka* on a voluntary basis according to one's material situation. By giving large amounts of charity only to their own rabbi, the Georgians sent the message that they preferred to help Georgian Jews specifically, and that they were not willing to spread their wealth to members of the small hall *minyan*. According to Yurii, "We have never had that tradition" of paying to be called up to the Torah in the small hall.[18] "If a person wants to give *tzedoka* out of the goodness of his own heart [that is okay]. But the Georgians do it all for money. Before the Khakham came, the Georgians gave a lot of money. This [the charity box on the desk] was just full from them. When Khakham David came, he told them to give the money to him. Why does he need so much? Now for *tzedoka*, I see what the Georgians put in the box—a one thousand or a five hundred-rouble note."

Yurii used *tzedoka* as a tool of ethnic differentiation, and yet, by taking money from Georgian Jews, he reincorporated them back into the small hall collective, turning their divisive behavior into a positive act that supported the small hall *minyan* as a whole. Because they made up about half of the worshipers on any given day, Georgian Jews lent the most critical kind of support to the aging Russian Jews. Russian Jews needed the Georgian Jews; and Yurii made it clear that, while ethnically different, Georgian Jews had a rightful place within the Jewish people.

Georgian Jews among Their "Own Kind"

In the small hall, the Georgian Jews dealt everyday with the way the Russian Jews categorized them as rude and noisy businessmen. But instead of playing down these supposed ethnic traits, they enhanced them. For example, in January 1996, I commissioned a local photographer to make a video of the morning service. At the start of the *Amidah*, he placed the video camera on a line of Georgian Jews standing at the back of the room. At first, they talked among themselves in Georgian, but then they suddenly formed a single line and began loudly repeating the *Kedushah* along with the cantor. They stood up on their toes and raised their arms up high—a movement none of the Ashkenazim did during prayer. Once they had finished, Aleksei mumbled sarcastically, "Well, good job, guys."

The Georgian Jews purposefully showcased their differences during ritual to reproduce the stereotypes of themselves as noisy and hot-tempered, as well as to contest the Ashkenazim's control of the service. The Georgian Jewish style of praying loudly and gesticulating in the small hall challenged the spatial and social order there. These acts brought them into the center of prayer from the periphery and also proved their desire to read the Torah separately.

Out of the core group of twelve Georgian Jews who attended services regularly, I talked extensively with six. Two, Adom and Tzvi, considered themselves to be religious Jews, having prayed in the small hall for many years. The other four, Beniamin, Mordechai, Aleksei, and Zviad, ranged in age from thirty-three to forty-one. Beniamin was the only one of this younger generation who had been raised in Moscow; the rest emigrated from Georgia in the 1990s. Unlike the core group of elderly Russian Jews who prayed in the small hall out of an attachment to those who worshiped there before them, these four young Georgian Jews came to morning services for one reason only, to say Kaddish for their dead relatives. As Aleksei put it, "I go to the synagogue every morning to say Kaddish for my mother. My parents raised me to respect them. As a good Jew, I respect my parents." Once they finished their obligation, they attended services only on the holidays.

Young Georgian Jews like Aleksei used the synagogue as a way to fulfill their family obligations, and they needed the prayer community in order to do so. Although they laughed and joked with one another during the service, they rarely formed strong friendships. These Georgian Jews knew that as soon as they were no longer obligated to come

to the synagogue, they would cease to be a part of the *minyan*. Beniamin stated this idea during an informal interview, telling me at first
that he came to say to Kaddish for his mother "because one has to."
When I tried to get him to compare his situation to that of other Georgian Jews, this is the conversation that followed:

Sascha: It seems to me that a lot of men come here just to say
               Kaddish. Aleksei told me that he comes here only to
               say Kaddish for his mother.
Beniamin: I do not know about that, and I will not find out about it
               either.
Sascha: But, aren't you friends? I see you talking to him all
               the time.
Beniamin: No. We just say hello.

Despite the differences in their upbringing and their unwillingness
to get to know one another, Beniamin and Aleksei did share a sense
that it "feels good" to pray together. The first time I saw the Georgian
Jews leave the small hall to read the Torah separately happened to be
the day Khakham David returned to the synagogue after a long stay
in the hospital. Shloimie led the service as usual. After the repetition
of the *Amidah*, a large group of Georgian Jews talked very loudly in the
back of the room. Yurii walked up to the ark to get the Torah scroll as
he did every Monday and Thursday. He immediately handed the
scroll to Shloimie. Mordechai followed Yurii to obtain another scroll
from the ark. As Shloimie stepped up on the bimah to start the Torah
reading, Mordechai handed his Torah scroll to Khakham David. About
fifteen to twenty Georgian Jews followed their rabbi as he walked out
the door into the big hall, nearly tripping over me as I sat watching
services from the doorway.

Confused at what was going on, I asked Beniamin to explain why
he and the Georgian Jews were in the big hall. "Because we are," he
responded matter-of-factly. "But up to now you've prayed in the small
hall," I said. "Today there are many of us," he replied curtly.

Beniamin's statement that the Georgian Jews were in the big hall
"because we are" might seem tautological, but, on a second look, it
shows an emotion that he assumed everyone should know—that it
feels good to be with your own people. More specifically, when I asked
Aleksei to tell me if he liked to read the Torah with the Georgian Jews
or the Russian Jews, he answered, "With the Georgians." "Why?" I
asked. "It is better to be *sredi svoikh* [among your own kind]."

More than pure sentiment was at work here. Reading the Torah together allowed the Georgian Jews to enact a shared way of practicing

ritual. Their reading of the Torah differed from that of the Russian Jews; and they held up the Torah scroll to show it to the congregation before the reading, while the Russian Jews showed the scroll after the reading. Khakham David auctioned off three *aliyot* and the privilege to look after the Torah while it was on the bimah. Aleksei explained: "When you are at the Torah, you are supposed to take some money out of your pocket. Not to give it to the rabbi for personal use, but for charity. This is our custom."

Reading the Torah together with their own rabbi also allowed the Georgian Jews to have their preferred prayers said for their success in business, the health of their loved ones, and the entrance of their deceased parents into heaven. There were several prayers that fulfilled such goals. The Ashkenazim said the *Mi Shebayrakh* ("He who is blessed") prayer after the Torah reading for each person and for those who requested the prayer to be said for a sick person or a woman who has given birth.[19] Khakham David followed the same formula, except that he also said a *Mi Shebayrakh* in Georgian for the Georgian Jewish congregation as a whole before the Torah reading. He prayed that "God give money, all the sick become healthy, all the children lead happy lives, and all those in jail be released soon."[20] Khakham David also recited upon request part of the *Haskhavah* ("laying to rest") prayer for the deceased.[21] Because he came primarily to say Kaddish, Beniamin conceptualized the whole service in terms of how it benefited his deceased mother. He said, "When we are at the Torah, we talk with God. *Eto velikoe delo* [This is a great deed], especially for the dead." He commented that the three Torah portions were all important, but the third one was especially desired, because after it, one said the Kaddish, in which "We ask God through the Torah for the soul of the dead, so that it has a place in heaven."

When the Georgian Jews went to the main hall to read the Torah, they all gathered on the bimah, transforming this space into a tiny sanctuary in which they occupied the central positions as the leaders and followers of a Georgian Jewish ritual. This was in contrast to their position in the small hall, where they stood along the back wall of the room. Their peripheral position in the small hall signaled their marginality in Ashkenazic prayer; it also enabled them to leave the room easily when they had enough men to form a *minyan* in the big hall. When they completed the reading, they went back into the small hall to finish the morning service with the Ashkenazim. This movement signified how a Jewish national identity and practice allowed a space for Georgian Jewish ethnicity within it.

In fact, despite the differences between Georgian and Russian Jews, some Russian Jews insisted that both groups could pray successfully together. In formal interviews, I asked Yehuda and Yurii how they differentiated among the various Jews at the synagogue, and how they evaluated the relationships among these groups. Yurii Isaakovich responded, "We have a good relationship. Everyone respects one another. We fulfill the prayers, but the language is different. The only difference is that we pray in different places. There are differences in how we worship according to traditions." Yehuda Levi answered this way: "There are religious differences and different customs. I pray just fine in any company. The problem is really a question of language. We talk in Yiddish, and they don't understand us. But there are no problems. It is normal."

According to Yurii and Yehuda, Georgian Jews and Russian Jews could pray together because they were Jews at the most basic level. This acknowledgment allowed the Georgian Jews to move back and forth among the *minyans* depending on their personal preferences. For example, Tzvi and Adom—the Georgian Jews who had attended morning prayer at the Central Synagogue the longest—prayed more often in the center of the small hall. However, they left the room to help form a Georgian *minyan* if they were needed. Although he said that it was better to be *sredi svoikh* (among your own kind), Aleksei claimed that he preferred to stay in the small hall on several occasions because he had "just gotten over a cold, and it is too cold in the big hall." In addition, even though Beniamin attended the Georgian Jewish Torah reading on Mondays and Thursdays, he did not like to pray with the Georgian *minyan* on Shabbat. He explained that since his family lived in Moscow, his father attended services in the small hall. When his father died, the worshipers who gathered in the small hall brought the body to the synagogue to pay their last respects. "I know all the men who come here [to the small hall] to pray. I respect them because they respected my father."

These ties of common identity were not strong enough, however, to hold these separate communities together. Issues of power and difference bubbled up to the surface when Yose challenged Zviad. I believe that Yose told Zviad to leave the small hall to join the Georgian Jews for two reasons. First, Yose considered himself to be very knowledgeable about how to pray correctly, having grown up in an Orthodox Ashkenazic family in Israel. Like the Russian Jews, he complained that Georgian Jews were noisy. He commented that Georgian Jews said the Kaddish with the cantor "because they all want to be the cantor. They all want to lead the service." Second, by wanting the voluntary segregation of Georgian Jews to become something mandatory, Yose attempted to take control of prayer. He accomplished this by voicing his assumption that Georgian Jews always read the Torah separately; Georgian Jews themselves said they preferred to pray together when they had the chance. But Yose took these statements one step further. By stating that the Georgians should "go there," to the main hall, he essentialized the ethnicity of the Georgian Jews in terms of a separate and bounded prayer space: he placed them outside of what he saw as correct prayer and, by association, on the periphery of the Jewish people. With one comment, he not only highlighted the creation of ethnicity that took place during morning prayer, but he also offended the Georgian Jews and endangered the status of the entire small hall *minyan*.

By the time the fight broke out, both Russian Jews and Georgian Jews were fed up with Yose. Yurii Isaakovich complained that Yose actually made more noise than the Georgians, and he expected all members of the congregation to accommodate him when he was late. Yurii's comments set the scene for the alliance of Georgian and Russian Jews against Yose.

The Fistfight Revisited

When he was taking off his phylacteries in order to fight Yose, Zviad yelled loudly at him, stopping prayer. Zviad shouted, "What do you want? 'Get ready for a fight,' you [Yose] say. What is wrong with you? Rabbi, Rabbi. Every day he says this. Now I will hit you. Rabbi, Rabbi, once he told Lyonia to get ready for a fight. Then he tells the old men to get ready for a fight. How much can one tolerate?"

Rabbi Silverstein stood silently and did not move when Aleksei pushed Yose over the pew. Most of the old men had also tried to stay out of the conflict. They gathered on the bimah and read the Torah in stops and starts, forming an island of prayer in the middle of the storm. After Yose had gotten up from the floor, Zviad started to lunge at him again. Rabbi Dubinovich held Zviad back. Finally, Zviad and Aleksei returned to the main hall. Yose followed them, looking to continue the conflict. Zviad and Aleksei ignored him, and Yose left in a huff after services.

By appealing to Rabbi Silverstein, Zviad took his conflict with Yose to the level of the entire small hall *minyan*. He knew that the rabbi would listen to him now because excluding the Georgian Jews jeopardized its existence. Zviad cited the way that Yose bullied everyone—from the Georgians to the defenseless Russian Jews. Yose himself admitted to me that he once told Lyonia to be quiet during prayer. Yose said: "Lyonia told me that I act like a woman. After services, I went up to him and dragged him into the big hall. I got him in a headlock and asked him to apologize. He said that he did not really mean it, and he was sorry. Beniamin and Zviad came into the room, and they split us up."

Zviad acted as if he had the right to claim that Yose was a threat to the whole *minyan* and the health of its individual members. Zviad took on the role of the hero, prepared to fight the dangerous outsider in order to protect the others. Zviad's words, backed up with Aleksei's show of strength, now placed Yose on the periphery of the *minyan*. After the incident, Rabbi Silverstein explained Yose's actions to everyone present by saying how Yose was "crazy. He is not right in the head." The rabbi's words further disempowered Yose, delegitimizing his claim to control the services. Rabbi Silverstein refused to mediate the conflict because, he said, "Yose needed to be taught a lesson. They were both looking for a fight."

Yose's conduct and the rabbi's passivity created a Georgian-Russian alliance that superseded perceived differences between these two groups. This alliance questioned the influence of foreigners who were a threat to Russian citizens. Although elderly Russian Jews did not want Zviad and Yose to fight in the synagogue, they agreed with Yurii that Yose "needs to be shown that he is not so strong." Zviad knew that he had Ashkenazic support when he asked Rabbi Silverstein to solve the problem. Russian and Georgian Jews allied themselves against Yose, the Israeli, and thus all "foreigners." Accordingly, Beniamin said later that even Rabbi Silverstein was to blame for Yose's misconduct:

He [Yose] has no respect for us. I am a guest here. I come here for forty-five minutes in the morning to pray and then thirty minutes in the evening to pray. I give my life to this synagogue. Why should I have to deal with Yose? What I cannot understand is the passivity of the administration here. The head rabbi does nothing, Dubinovich does nothing, the administration does nothing. When someone points a finger at you, you speak up if you do not deserve it. If you do not speak up, that means that you deserve it, that you do not respect yourself. He thinks that we Jews [Jews of the former Soviet Union] are second class. What? Does he have a better education than me?

Russian Jews too described foreigners as having no respect for local Jews. In opposition to Yose and Rabbi Silverstein, some Georgian and Russian Jews were able to forget their differences because both groups considered themselves to be *rossiiskie evrei* (Jewish citizens of Russia) at that moment.

Other members of the congregation, however, reflected differently on the situation. Yurii insisted that the rabbi was really showing his alliance with the Georgian Jews: "The rabbi does not say hello to me when he comes in. He says hello to them." He pointed to the table in the back of the room where the Georgian Jews sat during prayer. "I am going to tell him that he should tell them to be quiet. I have told him this a hundred times. He is the rabbi."

Yurii saw the fight as another outcome of the Georgians' noisy behavior and the marginalization of the Russian Jews in their own prayer space. According to Yurii, the rabbi preferred the Georgian Jews over the Russian Jews because the former had more money. In addition, Zviad's and Yose's display of physical strength reinforced the image that the Russian Jews were a disenfranchised, weak, and elderly group. The new heroes of the small hall were now those with money and muscle. This situation undermined the temporary alliance forged between the Georgian and Russian Jews against Yose.

Tensions between the Center and the Periphery

The fight that pitted Zviad and Aleksei against Yose shows how post-Soviet ethnicity is constructed upon divergent relations to, and opinions of, capitalism. It also highlights the contextual and performative nature of Jewish identity. While Jews at the synagogue were able to draw on their universal Jewish faith and practice to traverse ethnic boundaries, they were not able to overcome the emerging class categories that were rapidly transforming Russian society due to the expansion of the market economy. Post-Soviet Jewish identity is thus not monolithic; it corresponds to the creation of "Russian" Jewish and "Georgian" Jewish ethnicities that reflect each group's perceived successes or failures in new business opportunities. Russian Jews' statements about "us" or "the Georgians" and Georgian Jews' evaluations of themselves were also comments about the Russian state and the place of Jews within it. The Jews at morning prayer envisioned citizenship in the new Russia as based upon access to finances and networks, a concept that reverberated well beyond the walls of the synagogue.

In the past, Russian Jews relied on the West for material and spiritual aid. While some scholars might argue that the fall of the Soviet Union led to the independence of the Russian Jewish community from foreign money, the reality, because of generational differences, is not so simple. Elderly Russian Jews, unable to invest in the new economy, still need Western sponsors. At least during communism, many religious Russian Jews felt that their small hall community gave them a sanctuary against the regime. Now, due to death, emigration, and political and economic transformation, they have no place to call their own. The fight between Yose and Zviad elucidates the tensions between the center and the borders, showing that Jewishness in the former Soviet Union involves both a physical and a symbolic fight for economic and spiritual resources, and ultimately for a sense of belonging on a national scale. But the lesson of the *minyan* is clear—Russian Jews cannot survive without the Georgian Jews in the same way that Russia cannot survive without its ethnics.

Chapter 2
Georgian Meatballs and Russian *Kolbasa*

Why are the Georgian Jews so beautiful? First, they have beautiful wives. Second, they eat such tasty food, that it must make them beautiful. But more importantly, the most beautiful Georgian Jews live with God. . . . They have always observed the wonderful tradition of remembering their close relatives, so that they could be in the family circle. The family is very important for Georgian Jews, and it is important for us [Russian Jews] as well. I am glad that there are those people who respect and value our laws. That always inspires us with optimism and gives us hope for the future.
—Rabbi Dubinovich at a Georgian Jewish *Yahrzeit* meal at the Central Synagogue

Morning services in the small hall lasted until 9:30 or half an hour later if the Torah was read that day. Ordinarily the majority of the congregation dispersed soon after prayer, but there were times when the men stayed behind in the small hall to take part in a *Yahrzeit*,[1] the anniversary of the death of a congregant's close relative. They sat at the table at the back of the room to share the food and drink provided by the mourner in memory of his loved one. These meals ranged from the standard elderly Russian Jewish fare of crackers and a bottle of vodka to spectacular Georgian Jewish feasts: steaming kettles of kosher beef, fish, and poultry; bowls overflowing with spicy vegetable dishes; a variety of fresh fruit; and bottles of vodka and soda. The meat provided by the Georgian Jews was too expensive for the average Russian Jew to buy, and Georgian Jewish wives and daughters painstakingly prepared all the dishes at home. The gorging and continuous toasting at these meals reversed the hierarchy established between Georgian Jews and Russian Jews during prayer.

Unlike during morning services where Russian and Georgian Jews conceptualized their different ethnicities through a negotiation of synagogue space, at the Georgian Jewish *Yahrzeits* they evaluated one another's ethnicities according to what they saw as each group's either shameful or honorable practices. Russian Jews said that Georgian Jews were "holy" and "moral" because they kept the Jewish sanctity of the home and family throughout the Soviet period. In contrast, Russian Jews talked about themselves as "immoral Russians," referring to their assimilation into Russian culture.

These declarations of ethnicity reveal a new trajectory in post-Soviet Jewish life: as Georgian Jews increasingly reproduced their social world within the synagogue, Russian Jews had to adjust to the possibilities of living an openly religious life in Moscow. The prestige of being religious indicates the growing influence of the upper classes in connecting the act of consumption with perceived morality in post-Soviet Russian society.

My investigation into this phenomenon also provided me with the opportunity to reflect on the advantages and disadvantages of being a female ethnographer of a male community. I realized that Georgian Jewish men acted one way inside the home and the synagogue, and another way when outside the confines of such holy spaces. In this chapter, I explore what those different behaviors meant to them personally and as members of the Georgian Jewish ethnic group.

Mordechai's *Yahrzeit*

Out of all the Georgian Jewish *Yahrzeits* I witnessed at the synagogue, Mordechai's *Yahrzeit* for his mother in April was the most lavish in terms of both food and cultural meaning. Mordechai was in his mid thirties and had been born in the same Georgian town as Adom, Aleksei, and Zviad. He attended morning services regularly in the small hall, and, like several of the Georgian Jews at the synagogue, he was reluctant to say more than a few words to me in front of the congregation. He had first addressed me in January when he brought me some food during a *Yahrzeit*, but it was only in early April that I had the chance to speak with him at length.

He stood in the dark hallway, waiting to buy some wine at the synagogue kiosk for the upcoming Passover holiday. The kiosk attendant was on break, so Mordechai stood alone, smoking a cigarette. When I asked him if planned to have the Passover meal at home, he said that he was. "I cannot go out to listen to music or to a restaurant because my mother died recently. I am in mourning." He came to services so that he could say Kaddish for her. She died in Moscow, but they buried her in Israel. His father died years earlier in Georgia. "It must be hard for you without your parents," I said. "Yes," he responded and looked out into the hallway, taking a drag from his cigarette. He had mentioned briefly in January that he would invite me home for Shabbat dinner, but he never brought it up again. I was hesitant to ask him now. We were silent. I said, "I saw your son here one day." Mordechai smiled, "Oh, really? He is a fine boy. I have two daughters and one son." The kiosk opened and he went in, leaving me alone in the hallway. After buying the wine, he said goodbye and drove off in his white car.

A week later, Mordechai sponsored a *Yahrzeit* meal in honor of his deceased mother, thus marking the end of his year of mourning. At the Georgian Jewish Torah reading, he was given the highest honors. He had the final *aliyah* and then said Kaddish. After services, people helped him bring into the small hall what seemed to be an endless supply of food from his car: bowls of kosher meatballs and meat cutlets, plates of roasted chicken and fried fish, oval loaves of *lavash* (Georgian bread), and containers filled with puréed eggplant topped with pomegranate seeds. While Aleksei and Zviad stood at Yurii Isaakovich's desk scooping food onto paper plates, Shloimie, Berl, and Moshe placed newspaper as a makeshift tablecloth on the table in the back of the room. The scene was electric. The whole *minyan* was involved in carrying plates of food, opening bottles of vodka and soda, and setting out cups and silverware. I had never seen Aleksei and Zviad take such an active role in any *Yahrzeit*. They usually took some food while standing, said a quick, kind word to the mourner, and then rushed off in their cars to various business appointments.

Aleksei asked Yurii for some sturdy plates on which to serve the meatballs and the other juicy items. Yurii went to the cabinet by my usual spot in the corner and took out some stoneware plates and shallow bowls from a cardboard box on the second shelf. Bringing them back to the table, he said, "These need to be washed." "Sascha can wash them," Aleksei said, looking at me. "Oh, sure," I said eagerly, wanting to get involved. Evgenii Moiseivich, the Russian Jewish administrator of the Mountain Jewish community, gave me some soap, and I washed the plates in the hallway sink.

I handed the clean dishes to Aleksei and Zviad, who used them to serve the rest of the food. Mordechai oversaw the whole process while standing between the table and the last pew. When the preparations were finished, he faced the ark. Grasping the back of pew, he chanted the mourner's Kaddish. His voice was melodic and loud, and he rocked his stocky body back and forth, pushing himself off the back of the pew and pulling himself toward it again. The men stood behind him, saying "Amen" at the appropriate times. After he finished, they crowded around the table. Aleksei and Zviad sat at the head of the table, and Mordechai stood beside them throughout the entire meal. At the other end of the table sat Khakham David, the rabbi of the Georgian Jewish community, who gave several speeches in Georgian. Then, Aleksei and Zviad toasted Mordechai in Georgian. The Russian Jews, even though they did not understand the Georgian language, raised their glasses in solidarity with the mourner.

I sat next to Yurii. Aleksei filled up a plate for him, and Yurii offered to share it with me. Aleksei then handed us what he called "homemade" bread *(lavash)* that he said was "better" than the usual "Russian bread." I ate the bread but avoided the variety of kosher meat dishes on the plate, because I had not eaten meat for years. Yurii advised me to have some meat anyway, saying, "It is good for you. What is wrong with you that you don't want to eat some meat? Here!" He held a meat patty up to my mouth. I took a small bite to appease him, but Yurii snickered at me and then finished the rest himself. Yurii then dug into the eggplant salad on his plate. Leaning over the trash can down by his knees, he spit out de-fleshed pomegranate seeds.

It was just then that Yaakov, the beggar, wandered into the room. After receiving a plate of food from Zviad, Yaakov stood across from us and began to eat voraciously. Mordechai asked Yaakov to get the rest of the bags of food from his car outside. Yaakov agreed, warning us not to touch his plate of food, especially the meatball. Just after Yaakov left, Yurii turned to me, and, putting a finger to his lips, he reached over the desk to take the meatball that Yaakov had saved for later. Yurii ate it quickly with a smile.

Yaakov returned to place several bags of green apples and bananas on the desk. I stood up to help Mordechai distribute the fruit. He smiled approvingly at me when I gathered a bunch of apples and followed him to the table. I walked behind the old men and leaned down between them to place an apple on each of their plates. My hair fell slightly forward and brushed up against their dull and worn out suit jackets, making me feel awkward and out of place. Mordechai smiled, saying, *"Molodets"* ("Well done"). Everyone was quiet now, concentrating on eating and drinking.

When I returned to my place, a second elderly Russian Jewish beggar, whose back was bent and hands were permanently bunched up in fists, entered the small hall. Zviad handed him a plate of food and told him to eat it. The beggar sat down next to me, eating with his twisted hands and talking to me, or perhaps in my direction, about the past holiday. His words were slurred as they came out of his heavy-tongued, full mouth.

During the meal, I noticed Semyon staring intently at an apple near Yurii's plate. I held the apple out to him, assuming that he would come to take it, but he continued to look at me without a change of expression. I walked over to the table and handed it to him. He placed it in his pocket. Several men stood up to make toasts to Mordechai, and he accepted each one with a smile and a nod. When I sat back down, the beggar next to me asked for some more food. Semyon walked over to him and gave him the apple. Several seconds later, the beggar shouted, "Give me a banana!" I started to hand him one, but Yurii extended his arm between the beggar and me, yelling "Get out! You have had enough! Get out! Eat outside!" The man took his food and left.

Having eaten their fill, Zviad and Aleksei got up from the table. The others slowly followed. As soon as the room began to clear, Mordechai sat down and began to consume the remaining food with his hands. He ate ravenously. His passion at the table completely contradicted the self-restraint he had exhibited earlier throughout the meal.

Zviad walked to the desk to use the phone. He talked to me for the first time since he had asked me to sit in the small hall six months ago. Standing over me as I sat in my chair, he asked, "Sascha, did you like the food? Wasn't it tasty?" I agreed.

Not wanting to get in Zviad's way, I got up to help Yurii clear the table. We placed the dirty dishes and glasses on the desk to clean later. This was not an easy task since we had to make our way around Berl, the elderly Russian Jew who had survived Hitler's concentration camps, who was now staggering drunkenly around the room. He had a tendency to drink too much at *Yahrzeits*. He walked up to Yaakov, who was standing near the desk, and shoved his fist in his face. Yurii pulled Berl away from Yaakov, but as soon as Yurii's back was turned, Berl swung a punch at Yaakov. Yaakov hit back, sending Berl falling backward, his outstretched arms taking the stack of glasses and plates down with him onto the floor. Yaakov quickly fled the room as Yurii helped up an unharmed but dazed Berl. Mordechai, Zviad, and Aleksei shook their heads in disbelief.

Most of the men had left by the time we had finished cleaning up the mess. Mordechai was getting ready to depart as well, and he gave me a bag of bread and apples, insisting that I take it. I asked him if I could have his phone number so that I could call him to arrange for a time that I could meet his family. He answered with a smile, "I come here every day. We will see each other here." "All right, thanks," I said. He then flipped through a stack of bills in his hands, giving Yurii some money, and then he handed me a fifty-thousand-rouble note (ten dollars). "What is this for?" I asked. "For the road," he said as he walked out the door, having paid Yurii and me to finish cleaning.

Kosher Meat and "Holy" Jews

Mordechai's *Yahrzeit* contained three Jewish "key scenarios" (Ortner 1973:1342): (1) the production and consumption of kosher food, (2) acts of charity, and (3) paying respect to one's parents. Ultimately, all three are variants of charity in the Jewish tradition. *Tzedoka* ultimately means "social justice" in Hebrew. According to Jewish law, the rich must give to the poor, and "the poor are not to be patronized but given the assistance they need because they have a just claim on the wealthy" (Jacobs 1995:71). In principle, the rich store up good deeds in "a spiritual bank in order to draw on them in the future," and the poor receive financial and material aid (Jacobs 1995:71).

Russian Jews relied on Georgian Jews to keep the morning *minyan* going, and Russian Jews exhibited their authority by gathering money from Georgian Jews. In contrast, Georgian Jews at their *Yahrzeits* gave charity to Russian Jews and thus had a moral power over them (see Zborowski and Herzog 1952:199; Douglas 1984:10; Gregory 1982:17). The Georgian Jews took center stage, dictating the ritual, while the Russian Jews were passive, taking what they received. Homemade Georgian Jewish kosher food was "evidence" of how Georgian Jews were "Jewish" and how Russian Jews were negatively "assimilated" into Russian culture. As Yurii told me, "To be religious, one must observe kosher." He later remarked, "The Georgians observe all the laws. They are holy. Everyone can eat the bread they bring. But ours, the Ashkenazim, don't always keep kosher. Many of them are old, in their nineties, so why bother them with that stuff? Many of those who come here don't keep kosher."

Both Russian and Georgian Jews talked as if kosher food embodied the code of Jewish morality. Georgian Jews were thus the most religious and observant Jewish community in the former Soviet Union because they kept kosher, while most Russian Jews did not.[2] Joseph, a Georgian Jew who recently arrived in Moscow, told me succinctly, "We keep kosher. We eat kosher meat." Kosher meat is slaughtered and then prepared in a specific way as outlined in the Torah. In addition, the Torah names only certain animals as "right" or "fit" to eat because they conform to certain categories, and Jews should thus not mix different categories of food, such as milk and meat, in one meal. By eating in such a way, Jews maintain a holy or pure status. The kosher laws highlight a central idea in Judaism about the holiness of God—God told the Jews to be holy because He is holy (Leviticus 11:44; see Douglas 1970). As Khakham David simply put it, "We were the first in the world to keep kosher."

A Brief History of Georgian Jews

Georgian Jews refer to their history to explain their higher Jewish morality.[3] Their legends state that they first came to Georgia after they were exiled to Media when the Assyrians destroyed Samaria in 721 B.C.E. They again arrived in Georgia after Nebuchadnezzar, the king of Babylon, conquered Jerusalem in 586 B.C.E. While present-day Georgian Jews like to tell this early part of their heritage, they are not as willing to discuss how many communities were destroyed in the thirteenth century by Genghis Khan's Mongols, because, as a result of Genghis Khan's victories, Georgian Jews were forced to work as serfs for the local royalty, churches, and estates for the next five hundred years. With the abolition of serfdom in Georgia from 1864 to 1871, the majority of newly freed Jews moved from villages into cities, where they established communities and worked in petty trade and craftsmanship.

Georgian Jews commented to me that their late-nineteenth-century communities were strong. Each one had its own khakham who served as a rabbi, cantor, ritual slaughterer, *mohel* (a man who does circumcisions), and Hebrew teacher. When Georgia came under Soviet rule in the early 1920s, the "eastern politics" of the Communist Party, which stressed letting the locals engage in their own activities so they would be more likely to cooperate with the new Soviet government, allowed Georgian Jews to gather at synagogues and organize Zionist activities. Then, in 1924, the government outlawed Zionist activities and aimed to increase industrial productivity by organizing Georgian Jews into cadres of factory workers, placing them into cooperatives of Jewish craftsmen, and relocating them onto Jewish *kolkhozi* (collective farms). These programs were not successful. Until the end of the Soviet Union, Georgian Jews continued to prosper in trade, and, with the silent agreement of local authorities, they developed small factories under the cover of state trade and manufacturing enterprises.

The Soviet government in Georgia eliminated Jewish cultural institutions in the 1930s and late 1940s and closed synagogues in the 1950s. Many Georgian Jewish towns successfully fought to keep their synagogues open, however, and Georgian Jews continued to visit the synagogues throughout the Soviet years. From the 1960s onward, communist authorities in Georgia were lax about implementing restrictions against Jewish religious practices and education, and they even allowed many Georgian Jews to attend the Soviet Union's only yeshiva (Jewish institute of higher learning) at the Central Synagogue. In fact, the majority of students there came from Georgia, and Khakham Eliahu received his education as a ritual slaughterer there.

Keeping Kosher in Moscow

In contrast to Georgian Jews in Georgia, observant Russian Jews in Soviet Moscow could not explain Judaism to their children since teaching religion was illegal and they were so close to the center of Soviet power. Yurii claimed that many old Russian Jews who came to pray at the Central Synagogue had been jailed for trying to teach their sons Hebrew. The shortage of kosher meat in Moscow was another reason why Russian Jews had trouble keeping their religious traditions. In the late 1920s, they bought kosher chickens at the synagogue and the Central Market. But by the end of the 1940s, the government tightened the surveillance of those persons selling kosher meat, to make sure that they were not profiteering. As Inspector Tagaev explained to the Council: "This archaic ritual [keeping kosher] has been resurrected by Jewish clerics in recent times. The selling of kosher meat is of equal interest to the Jews as is their own spirituality. Those involved in the business [of selling] are affiliated with the synagogue in order to make a personal profit. Until 1947, religious communities illegally performed the slaughtering ritual. In 1947, the Tsentrosoiuz allowed the sale of kosher meat by trade organizations, but it did not establish special stores for this goal. Today, believing Jews can buy kosher meat in almost all cities."[4]

Correspondingly, I heard many stories from elderly Russian Jews about how a store or a marketplace in Moscow suddenly stocked kosher meat and how this information spread among observant Jews. However, the availability of kosher meat never lasted very long, perhaps due to both the Soviet anti-religious policies and the inefficiency of the centralized distribution system (Matthews 1986; Alexeev and Sayer 1987; Millar and Clayton 1987). In 1956, Rabbi Shliefer complained to the Council that a store in the Zhdanovskii region had recently stopped selling kosher meat.[5] He asked the Council to open a special store to sell this highly needed item, but the Council never approved his request.[6] To persuade the West that there were good relations between the Soviet government and Jews, Rabbi Shliefer repeatedly told foreign visitors that a government kosher meat store existed, but that it was not working due to "technical problems."[7]

Religious Jews in Moscow thus had to come to terms with not being able to eat kosher foods on a regular basis. Shmuel Berl, an elderly Russian Jew from a Hasidic family, told me how he compromised his religious beliefs with the material and ideological situation in the Soviet Union. He said, "I served in the army, and I observed Shabbat when I could. I told people at work that I could not work on Saturdays." "Did they say anything against you?" I asked. "No, I am lucky that I did not have to experience that. . . . We did what we could. We could not do what we wanted to."

In order to avoid breaking the religious laws, some Jews did not eat meat, or they tried to obtain kosher meat through reliable personal networks; they procured kosher food the way most people obtained regular food and consumer goods during the Soviet period. These practices continued into the 1990s, but by then people were no longer concerned with its availability, since the new market economy in Russia had brought many kosher products into Moscow. The synagogue's food kiosk sold kosher dairy, meat, and wine products imported from Israel, Europe, and America. The Hasidic synagogue located near Bolshaia Bronnaia Street had its own butcher and provided a small selection of kosher goods. I even saw Khakham David slaughter chickens on request in the parking lot next to the Central Synagogue.

Although kosher products were now easy to find, they were often too expensive for most Russian Jews, even synagogue workers, to afford. As Yehuda Levi told me at his apartment during the dinner of cheese, salad, and wine, "Before, it was difficult [to keep kosher], now it is just expensive. I eat local cheese; I am not that strict."[8] He added, "Before, my father and I would go without meat. Now, sometimes I go to [the yeshiva at] Kuntsevo where they give me some free meat. They know that I am experiencing hard times." Yurii blamed high prices, as well as corruption in the synagogue, for his inability to keep kosher: "I became kosher five years ago. Before that, I did not keep kosher all the time. We needed [food] products, but they were twice as expensive. They [the synagogue administration] give out the kosher products only to those who come here. They do not give them to the workers. We have to pay for it."

Yurii was aware that most Georgian Jews regularly purchased kosher meat because of their business contacts and good profits. This is not to say that all Georgian Jews were rich; I met several refugees from Georgia who were surviving on meager salaries, but they, unlike the Russian Jews, were able to appeal to the Georgian Jewish community for assistance. For the most part, Russian Jews talked about Georgian Jews as rich businessmen, and their displays of generosity at the *Yahrzeits* only solidified this impression. In this case, their money allowed them to increase their own holiness in the post-Soviet context. By buying and distributing their food, Georgian Jews helped Russian Jews to share this status, if only for a short time.

Kosher Bread and Georgian Jewish Families

Although keeping kosher is a traditional Orthodox Jewish practice, when Mordechai gave the *Yahrzeit* meal at the Central Synagogue, he purposefully distinguished himself as a *Georgian* Jew, as opposed to a Russian Jew. The food he served was the vehicle for the expression of his ethnicity, allowing him to re-create a Georgian Jewish social order within the space of the small hall.

The abundant amount of food presented at the *Yahrzeit* signaled Mordechai's success in business. It also allowed him to enact a very Georgian scenario. In Georgia, women are supposed to take care of the household, while men have to do well in business to provide for their families. Georgian men show off their wealth by hosting extravagant displays of consumption that exhibit their manliness and establish and reinforce social networks (Mars and Altman 1987:271). As Ernest Gellner observes, Georgians "virtually never eat or drink, unless it is to establish, enhance, affirm, and sacralize a human relationship" (Gellner 1990:283). Feasts have been such an important part of Georgian life that they hold them at the end of the funerals of relatives, and they visit graves at every feast day to toast the dead (Dragadze 1988:152).

At Mordechai's *Yahrzeit*, Georgian Jewish food functioned as artifacts of Georgian Jewish religiosity and lifeways. Mordechai served typical Georgian Jewish dishes such as eggplant, *lavash,* and meatballs. Georgian Jews were proud of their food as mixing the culinary traditions of the Georgians and the Jews. By eating and offering such items to Russian Jews, Georgian Jews re-created and reinforced their ethnicity as Georgian Jews and thus reaffirmed their ties as a community distinct from Russian Jews. Not only did Aleksei and Zviad serve everyone, but Aleksei said that homemade Georgian Jewish bread was much "better" than Russian bread, a comment that showed his belief that Georgian Jews have a higher morality than Russian Jews. By talking about bread in particular, Aleksei expressed his approval of the way that Georgian Jewish women continued to stay in the home, as compared to more "assimilated" Russian Jewish women, who generally worked outside the home. His praise of homemade *lavash* related to a remark he made to me later: "We Georgian Jews do not like our women to work. They have to take care of the family."

Georgian Jews who migrated to Moscow tried to retain the parameters of the lives they left behind by stressing the sanctity of the home. The division of labor among the sexes and the maintenance of a strong family loyalty have been essential components of the Georgian Jewish value system, and the *lavash* (bread) symbolizes those standards.[9] Georgian eating habits are comprised of specific preparation and cooking techniques that reflect a specific view of the domestic economy (Bourdieu 1984:185). Historically, the Georgian Jewish family was "grounded in traditions of loyalty and moral behavior of the spouses, particularly the wife. Raised in strict accordance with ancient traditions, she was to be modest and discreet in relations with men. . . . Among the personal responsibilities of the mistress of the house were the baking of bread and the preparation of food" (Dzhindzhikhashvili 1994:127).

I encountered these aspects of Georgian Jewish life when I had Shabbat dinner in the apartment of Adom and his wife Leah in May. Adom's business had done well, and he was able to fully support his wife and children. Russian Jews at the synagogue thought highly of him. Yurii lovingly called him "Adomchick," and said that he was an honest and quiet man with a good family. Yaakov once even called him *svetlyi*—pure and bright.

Adom began the Shabbat meal with the traditional Jewish blessing of the bread. Standing up, he raised two halved loaves of round bread and, putting them together, said the prayer. He cut off the first piece, dipped it into salt that was in the middle of the bread plate, said another blessing, and then took a bite. He cut off another piece, and said the blessing again, as he dipped the bread into the salt. He gave me that piece. He repeated the process at least four more times, putting the pieces of salted bread on top of the loaves. After he sat down, he told me that I could start eating, but I was not sure how to eat the bowl of thick spicy meat and rice soup without a spoon. All I had was a fork. Leah went into the kitchen to get me a spoon, and Adom pointed to the bread and proudly said to me, "My daughter made this bread." Leah explained as she returned that the bread was Georgian. Adom broke off a piece of bread, put it on his fork, and dipped it into the bowl. He then put the soaked piece of bread in his mouth. I dipped my spoon into the soup to taste it. It was spicy, oily, and delicious. Watching Adom, I remembered the advice of a Tamara, a Georgian woman I had met several weeks before at the huge meal in honor of the bar mitzvah of Niko Aleksandrovich's son: "Georgians eat food with bread."[10] I said to Adom, "So, do you do it like this?" as I ripped up a piece of bread, stuck it on my fork, dipped it into the bowl, and ate it. He did not respond but continued to eat. Leah asked me to watch how she ate the dish. She ripped up pieces of bread and dropped them into the bowl with an authoritarian air. I did the same. She speared the bread with her fork. Soon, my soup was a solid mass. By the time I had finished, the back of my throat was smoldering from the hot spices.

While we were eating, I asked Adom if he helped out in the kitchen. Leah let out a short laugh, "He does not know how to make anything or find anything. I never let him in there. I like to do everything my way. When my son went to Switzerland on some business for the synagogue, he said that everyone ate out of plates you can throw away and that the food is already prepared." Adom added, "I never eat food on the street. I don't even drink on the street. When I was in Israel, I had food with me that Leah had made and packed. I would stop somewhere for lunch and invite friends to sit with me."

Adom had a definite pride in his wife's cooking and his daughter's baking. Anchoring him to his ethnicity, his wife's food helped Adom navigate his way through the non-Jewish world, keeping him tied to his Georgian and Jewish traditions when he was far from home.

Leah brought out a long rectangular plate of cabbage with ground nuts and pomegranate seeds and a round plate of marinated beets and red cabbage. She then returned to the kitchen. Adom leaned in toward me. "I wanted to invite you many times to dinner here, but I did not want people to start thinking. Well, you know how some people start to talk. You remember at Niko Aleksandrovich's?" "Yes." "You know, if I had seen you, I would have walked over to you to say hello. But I did not see you before you tapped me on the shoulder. I wanted to talk, but I did not know who that woman was sitting next to you. Usually we have a lot of guests over. I like having guests. I invited Rabbi Dubinovich to come today but he said that he was too tired." Leah came back to the table with two more dishes—a plate of fried meat patties and a bowl of what she called *solianka*, beef stewed with vegetables, pickles, and spices.

Niko Aleksandrovich's son's bar mitzvah highlighted a problem I had not foreseen regarding getting to know Georgian Jews outside of the synagogue. Although Niko never attended services, he had his son's bar mitzvah at the synagogue. After the ceremony, he loudly invited everyone to come celebrate that evening at a banquet in his restaurant. Joseph, a Georgian Jew who occasionally came to the synagogue, was there that day, and he promised that he and his family would escort me to the event. He never showed up, and I was the only unescorted woman in the room. Fortunately, I got to know Tamara as we waited to eat while the men played cards and smoked. She insisted that we sit together at the end of the long banquet hall. During dinner, I recognized Adom at the other end of the room. I gathered up my courage to walk up to him to say hello. He seemed surprised to see me. We shook hands. His hand was puffy and soft, and his handshake was light. The man to his right turned to me as well, and I recognized him from the synagogue. His face brightened immediately, and he grabbed my hand tightly, saying, "Where have you been?" "Working," I said. I pulled my hand away. I could not remember if I had ever talked to him before. I then turned to Adom and asked him how he was. He said, "Fine, thank God." The other man grabbed my hand again, but harder this time, and said, "How are you?" staring into my eyes.

At that moment, I remembered who he was. His name was Albert, and he had called me at home several months earlier. I had given out my phone number to congregants, asking them to get in touch with me regarding interviews. On the phone, Albert said he wanted to *gu-liat'* with me, which I thought meant "to take a stroll." I told him that I was not sure what he intended. "How could you not know what I mean? You, a young girl and an American," he said on the phone. He wanted to "have a good time"—the other meaning of *guliat'*. I told him that I was not that kind of woman. He ignored my comment and said that I could stop by his work since there was a sauna there. I was polite, telling him that I was really busy. Luckily, by then he no longer came to the synagogue, as the official period of mourning for his deceased mother was over, and he never called me again.

At the bar mitzvah celebration, he continued to smile up at me as Adom said, "Where are you sitting?" "Over there," I pointed back to my table. He stood up on my left side, put his arm lightly around my waist, and walked me back to my seat, as if he were guiding me through an ocean of sharks. As we got to my chair, he said, "Thank you for coming over to say hello." He smiled, and I did too. I thanked him as well, and he returned to his seat.

After we finished Shabbat dinner at his apartment, Adom insisted that he walk me to the bus stop. Along the way, he said that he was worried that I was dating a non-Jew back home. When we arrived at the bus stop, he leaned toward me, his head coming up to my shoulder, and said, "Tell me, have you had relations with him?" "What?" I asked. "I can't say. . . . I am a man. . . . You are a woman," he mumbled, embarrassed. I told him that I did not want to talk about it, that it was none of his business. He said, "It is just that if you have, it would be harder to throw him away." He was probably referring to the Georgian Jewish custom of a woman marrying the first person with whom she has had sex. He said, "When I first saw my wife, I said, 'I will break her.' I was standing with my friends, and she was walking home from music school. When I saw her, I joked about it to my friends. Later, my father said, 'If you want a tall woman, go to Moscow.'"

I commented sarcastically, "Well, she didn't break." He did not smile and said in a serious tone, "Understand, it did not matter if she were short or tall, I just did not want to marry. I was eighteen at the time." We stood looking in the direction of the approaching bus.

He said, "Sometimes, we lock up the synagogue to talk and drink. We have a good time. I'll invite you." The bus arrived, and he kissed my hand and told me to call him to let him know that I had reached home safely.

Back at home, I thought about dinner, the bar mitzvah celebration, and Albert's phone call. It seemed that because I was a young, American Jewish woman, I was privy to a side of Georgian Jewish life that no one at the synagogue was willing to discuss, let alone acknowledge. Russian Jews did not mention Georgian Jewish sexuality, and this stood out especially since they often commented about how Mountain Jews were lascivious and thus "immoral." Russian Jews said Adom was a "good" man, yet his kind words and hospitality were laced with sexual innuendos that implied he was gauging his own opportunity while looking out for my well-being. Needless to say, I was confused, wanting to trust Adom at the same time that I worried about my safety if we were left alone. My mind was full of questions. Did Mordechai and other Georgian Jews refuse to invite me home because they saw me only as a possible mistress? Did Albert and Adom make passes at me because they thought that I would not tell anyone at the synagogue? Would anyone have believed me, or would they have blamed me if anything went wrong? Finally, how could I judge if Georgian Jewish men sincerely wanted to participate in my ethnographic research? In the end, it seemed inevitable that men at the synagogue would position me with regard to my gender, age, and perceived sexual availability (Kulick 1995:19). Even Yurii made jokes about marrying me from time to time. I decided that I should try to anticipate what might happen next because I needed to interview more Georgian Jews.

As it happened, much of the information I obtained on Georgian Jewish ritual practice and family life came from a conversation with Aleksei in which he expressed interests in other things besides my research. The incident provided me with an insight into how male sexuality is a key ingredient in Georgian Jewish morality. As winter arrived, Aleksei told me that he wanted to give me a pair of boots as a *mitzvah*. He owned a clothing and shoe store, and he said that my hiking boots were not suitable for Moscow winter weather, nor were they "feminine" enough. I asked Yurii and some other men at the synagogue what they thought about this idea, and they all agreed that Aleksei was helping out a fellow Jew. Aleksei and I agreed that after services he would take me to his business. After I chose a comfortable pair of boots, he drove me to the metro. The following conversation took place in the car:

Sascha:	No.
Aleksei:	Oh, come on. [He put his hand on mine.]
Sascha:	No.
Aleksei:	I bet you would with a Jew. Then, that would be okay.
Sascha:	No. I really don't want to *guliat'* in general. [Silence.] So, you bought me the boots because you wanted to *guliat'* with me?
Aleksei:	That is not true. You have really insulted me. I like to do *mitzvahs* for people. I am a good Jew. I am a good man. Aren't all men who go to the synagogue good men? I saw that you needed a good pair of boots made of leather. If I wanted to *guliat'* with you, I would have taken you somewhere first. Why waste time? You have really offended me.

We were silent. I looked over at him. His black suit fit snuggly over his wide shoulders and back. Dark stubble covered his chin and cheeks, and his black hair was thinning at the top of his head.

Aleksei:	When I first saw you in the synagogue, I wanted to talk to you, but *mne bylo stydno tam* [I was ashamed there]. [There were] so many people around. I knew that you were a good person. I told my brother that I would take you to get some new boots.
Sascha:	Why were you ashamed?
Aleksei:	It is not the place to talk to a woman. If I could, I would take you now to a restaurant. But, I can't. In the year of mourning, I have to eat at home. It is a Georgian Jewish custom.
Sascha:	Why don't you just invite me to your house for dinner?
Aleksei:	If I brought you home, my wife would think that you were my lover.

In between his asking me if I was sure that I did not want to "have fun with him" (questions to which I always answered, "No"), I managed to interview him about why he went to the synagogue and why he thought Georgian Jews have held to their Judaism so strongly during socialism. He said:

Each time a Georgian Jew lands in Israel, he says that Georgian Jews had a more religious life in Georgia, where the Jews lived together. *Mne bylo by stydno* [I would have been ashamed] if I did anything wrong in front of my father. I learned Hebrew at home. We had a tutor teach us secretly. I did the same for my children—a boy and a girl age twelve and eight. That is the way my parents raised us. I respect them. I say the Kaddish for them everyday. They put us on our feet. I don't know what the world will be like when my children get to be my age—they will have grown up here—but I hope that they will respect me as well. . . . There is another reason why we keep the traditions. I don't know if I should tell you. You might get offended. We make sure that our fiancées are virgins.

Through a strong sense of honor, Adom and Aleksei obeyed their fathers. Their fear of shaming their families made them keep the Jewish traditions. This honor/shame scenario extended to the synagogue and other religious occasions because the male community acted as a surrogate kin group. The men were "ashamed" to speak with me there since they saw me first and foremost as an object of sexual desire. This reason became clear to me only when we were alone. Georgian Jewish men saw themselves as having insatiable sexual appetites, and they divided their sexuality into two spheres—the home and the street. At home, they had sex with their wives to perpetuate the Jewish family and its traditions. They expected their wives to be chaste before marriage and faithful after. The wives expressed these qualities in their ability to make delicious kosher meals at home. The street was for secret, lustful encounters that contradicted the "Jewish"—and perhaps drew on a more "Georgian"—model. However, as Adom indicated, carrying homemade food had the power to distill such passions. When I questioned him if it were okay for a married man to *guliat'*, Aleksei said, "There is no problem with being married and doing it. I do. Russian women are easy to get. I don't like them very much. Nowadays, it is hard to tell if someone has a disease or not. They stand on the street—down by that hotel—and say that they are clean. They lie. It is not fun anymore."

By hitting on me, an American Jewish woman, the Georgian Jews mixed their metaphors. As an American woman, I represented to them the stereotype of Western sexual liberation. As a Jewish woman, I was part of their extended family. Aleksei and Adom vacillated from one image to the other. That would explain Adom's behavior at the bus stop and why Aleksei wanted me to sit inside the small hall. Perhaps Aleksei was more interested in looking at me during the service than he was in cutting down on the draft; I often found him staring at me during prayer. But, although he was adamant about having an affair with me, he never forced himself upon me, saying that all the men at the synagogue were "good" men. He was waiting for me to say "yes." These contradictory interpretations point to how Georgian Jewish men have certain ideas as to what kind of sex is acceptable in what kinds of situations, but these categories blurred easily when honor for the Jewish tradition was mixed up with lust for a Jewish woman in the synagogue.

In dividing their sexuality this way, Georgian Jewish men saw no conflict between being Georgian and being Jewish. For them, being a "good" man was not anathema to "having a good time," as long as the two did not obviously intersect in the same space. Georgian Jews managed to blend their Georgianness and their Jewishness into what appeared to Russian Jews to be seamless whole, a symbol of Jewish morality and holiness. Russian Jews never acknowledged Georgian Jewish sexuality beyond the family, and I never told them about the incidents with Albert, Aleksei, and Adom, because I was concerned about how that information would affect their opinion of Georgian Jews and myself. When comparing themselves to Georgian Jews, Russian Jews often perceived their Russianness and Jewishness to be at odds with one another. They had to work hard to reconcile these two ethnicities, to fuse them into a legitimate Jewish identity in the face of the new post-Soviet religiosity.

Becoming a Religious Russian Jew

If, in 1996, the mark of being a "true" Jew was keeping kosher and honoring one's parents by saying Kaddish (a practice that led to giving charity and regularly attending services), then Russian Jews were at a disadvantage due to their history of assimilation. Not only did many Russian Jews at the synagogue worry about their inability to keep kosher, but they also complained about the loss of family unity due to state surveillance. As Yurii told me, "We [Russian] Jews have lost our Jewishness. Our children do not even know our traditions." This break between the generations produced silence and a feeling of loss among Russian Jews. Musia, a twenty-six-year-old Russian Jewish woman who recently "returned" to Judaism, regretted how her observant grandparents never taught her about their religion:

Mama was a late child. Her parents were already old when they had her. Because they died when I was ten, they did not give me a Jewish education. They did not talk much about Judaism. However, they did do Jewish rituals. I believe that for a child to grow up to be a Jew, he needs to be told about his traditions. He must be aware of them. My grandparents did not explain what they were doing. Maybe they did not tell me how and why because it was dangerous, and they were scared that I would talk about it outside the home. It was dangerous to say, but it was not dangerous to do. It was dangerous to say, because the child might talk about it openly in a country where there was anti-religious propaganda.

Unlike Georgian Jews who could turn to their parents and relatives for religious guidance, Russian Jews in Moscow had to learn about Judaism from peers searching for their Jewish roots. In the 1970s, during the refusnik movement, Russian Jews studied Hebrew and Judaism in groups of close friends. Lyonia became involved with Judaism in his mid-twenties, when his university friends introduced him to refusniks and took him to the synagogue despite his family's disapproval.

Lyonia: I remember when my stepfather and I listened to the Voice of Israel to hear the political news. He had many friends in Israel and he wanted to know what was going on there. When the broadcaster announced the Hanukkah program, father smirked and turned it off. He saw his Jewishness as an annoying and disappointing circumstance of life; it was his unpleasant origin.

Sascha: How did you feel when your father turned off the radio?

Lyonia: I did not protest because I was not interested in Judaism yet. It became interesting to me only when my friends explained it to me. Then, I started to come to the synagogue. Later, I brought my daughter to the synagogue, and in 1988, she attended Sunday school there. I bought all religious and non-religious Jewish books that I could find. I celebrated all of the holidays the best that I could. I began to read the *International Jewish Gazette* [a local Jewish newspaper] in 1991. I learned about the Reform Jews in Moscow. I went to them in the fall of 1991. But I felt that I still did not have enough knowledge. They did not teach me enough there. So, I decided to study with the Orthodox to see things for myself. I studied with a rabbi in his apartment, and then I studied at the Jewish University of Moscow for two years after it opened. I also went to seminars.

Sascha: You decided to become an Orthodox Jew?

Lyonia: The Orthodox suited me better. Because I studied, I now understand the meaning of the Jewish commandments and how they are tied to the deep culture and genius of the Torah. All of that really fascinates me! I evolved through my education. Now, I think that it is important to be a Jew. However, Judaism is not close to the Russian intelligentsia. I am a scientific worker, so I am used to research, but I feel that I must get to know Judaism and the Talmud, even if I cannot understand them. They must be close to me, because I am a Jew. In order to be a Jew, I have to understand Jewishness. Many Jews are not comfortable thinking this

way because they don't want to, but I want to. This is all unusual for me. I am closer to Christianity because I am a Russian intellectual. Right now, it is worthwhile to be a Jew;
being a Jew is prestigious. When I became aware of the Jewish religious tradition, my tradition, I had to honor it, even
if it was not close to me. I am conscious of the fact that my
place is in the synagogue. You must do a religious ceremony
out of honor for your ancestors. If you understand that
you and your children must be married to other Jews, then
your children will be Russian Jews. There will always be
a certain percentage of religious people in the world. And
that is Jewishness.

Lyonia's narrative about becoming religious rests on the notion that
being a Russian intellectual impedes one's ability to "come closer" to
Judaism. In fact, many Russian Jews referred to their "Russianness" as
a driving factor in how they approached Judaism. Irina Maksovna, a
Russian Jewish woman who worked as the administrator of the women's
section of the main hall, delineated a connection between Russian
Jews and Russian culture when she said, "Jews pick up the characteristics of the people around them." Russian Jews explained these characteristics in terms of mentality and ways of being. For example, Lyonia
said his Russianness was the reason he decided not to immigrate to Israel with his friends in the 1970s: "My friends did try to talk me into
it. I began to be obstinate. I am a very stubborn person. I don't like to
satisfy the enemy. The Soviet power wanted me to live badly, so I tried
to live well. [I did not emigrate to Israel] because I understood that I
love Russia. I am good here. I am used to this land, the Russian language, and my life here. [I am used to] the mentality of Russians and
Russian Jews. I will always consider myself a Russian Jew."

Unlike Lyonia, Irina stated that her affection for Russian culture allowed her to become more involved with Judaism. She was also a scientific worker and considered herself an intellectual. In an interview,
she talked about the similarities between Russian culture and the Jewish worldview:

[Living i]n Russia, I came to God through my soul. Since Russia is a Russian
Orthodox country, and Russian Orthodox churches are the great creations of
Russian culture, I was attracted to that kind of beauty in childhood. I learned
about religion through Christianity. I understand all religion to be a monument to culture, architecture, and history. And God was in my soul, and so
there came a time when I was forced to think about what I believed about my
own religion. In 1982–1983, my husband was killed, and it was difficult for
me, so I started to go on all kinds of excursions. . . . I liked to talk about

church history and icons. One Russian woman said to me, "You are so good at explaining things. Why don't you tell us about your own religion?" I was scared. I thought that she was some kind of anti-Semite. But she really helped me. Next year during Passover, I told my friends about the Passover Seder. I got some information from my father and from what I read. By the 1970s, there were many small books in the Russian language about the history of Judaism, the Torah, and the Jewish people. During Passover, I brought some matzah to work to share with my colleagues. On Orthodox Easter, I baked the special cakes and brought them to work too. I can say much about Russian culture and Russian traditions. But I also understand how Christianity came from Judaism. When non-Jewish visitors come to the synagogue, I can explain Judaism to them, as well as show them my respect for their own people and beliefs. They always say a big "Thank you" to me when they leave. And they leave with much respect [for Judaism].

Lyonia's and Irina's stories point to the paradoxical nature of being a Russian Jew. A Russian Jew's identification with Russia can either obstruct her ability to become more Jewish or provide her with a path through which she is able to obtain a better understanding of Judaism.

Being "Russian": Drinking, Stealing, and Hoarding

In relation to the "holy" Georgians and religious Orthodox Western Jews like Rabbi Silverstein and his family, Russian Jews tended to conceptualize their "Russianness" as negative—a mark of their failure to be "true" Jews. When Irina said that Jews become like the people around them, she went on to emphasize how "Jews lost their national character. This is an internal assimilation. They say, 'They did not teach me, and I do not want to know.' This is the tragedy of the Ashkenazic Jews."

She blamed this situation for her inability to eat only kosher products: "The hardest thing for me to do is keep kosher. The hardest [foods] for me are milk and *tvorog* [cottage cheese], *kolbasa* [sausage] and meat. We have kosher meat, but it is three times as expensive. Milk and *tvorog* are two times as expensive. I make *tvorog* myself. Sometimes, I really want *kolbasa*." This self-proclaimed sliding into "negative" Russian practices and desires structured how Russian Jews sometimes talked about themselves as having become "Russian," engaging in the harmful Russian habits of drinking, stealing, and hoarding.

Despite the centrality of toasting in Georgian feasts, Russian Jews considered excessive drinking of alcohol to be a Russian trait, and they used drinking as a way to talk about the differences between Jews and Russians. One day in November, I arrived at the synagogue wearing a new skirt. Yurii told me that we should celebrate the new purchase with an *obmyvanie* (a "wet," the slang word for a "drink"). He explained, "I am telling you this because we Jews live among Russians, and it is their custom." Before the Revolution, Russian workers frequented the pubs to "wet" (celebrate with a drink) all different kinds of events such as new jobs and farewells (Sidorov 1995:238). Throughout history, Russian men—peasants, workers, landlords, and clergymen—imbibed copious amounts of alcohol according to a rigid frame of traditions and customs that required drinking on fixed occasions (Sidorov 1995:239).

Russian Jews at the synagogue said that excessive drinking contributed to Russian men's "immoral" character. Russian Jews told me many times how Russian women liked to marry Jewish men, since they, unlike Russian men, did not get drunk and beat or cheat on their wives. These stories relate to the larger reputation that Jews throughout Europe are able to moderate both food and drink. In Russia, there is even a folktale about the "Immortal Golovan," who went to the Jews to find out how they were able to drink without getting drunk (Keller 1979:406). This reputation is based on the Jews' ritual attitude toward drinking alcohol, namely that they drink only to sanctify important rites (Keller 1979:406).

When Berl and Yaakov fought at the *Yahrzeit* sponsored by Mordechai, they stepped beyond the usual parameters of *Yahrzeit* drinking. On the one hand, Berl was known to be confrontational, due in part to his experience in a concentration camp in Poland, where he lost many of his family members. Talking about his youth, he once told me, "There was anti-Semitism in Poland. If they gave us a hard time, we would punch them." He showed me his fist to make his point. His anger increased when he was drunk. Yurii warned me, "You can only talk to Berl when he isn't under the influence." Yurii felt sorry for Berl's alcoholism and begged him several times to see a doctor. On the other hand, Berl's drunkenness articulated the ways that Russian Jews talked about themselves as having become more *beznravstvennye* (immoral) and *russkie*.

In general, the narratives of Russian Jewish *beznravstvennost'* (immorality) focused on the hoarding, stealing, and begging of food at synagogue meals. Russian Jews agreed with Georgian Jews that those attending *Yahrzeit* meals should eat as much as possible, in order to honor the deceased. They also remarked that taking food from the table to eat later was a "shameful" and "greedy" act, unless they were specifically asked to do so by the host. Evgenii Moiseivich said, "They [the elderly Russian Jews] say that they are doing a *mitzvah* [by attending a *Yahrzeit*], but then they put food in their pockets." In addition,

Yurii said he was ashamed of how the elderly Russian Jewish men stuffed food in their jackets, pants, and bags. "Just the other day, Semyon, who lately has not been talking to me, actually came up to me and said that he got a raise in his pension. Now he receives a million [roubles]. But still, at a *Yahrzeit*, he puts food in his bag. It is shameful." Yurii also complained about Moshe, saying that he "puts food in his pocket after *Kiddush* [the small meal served after Saturday morning prayers]. I say to him, 'What? You don't have enough bread?' "

Discussions of hoarding complemented larger narratives about Russian stealing since, at the synagogue, the phrase "to put something in one's pocket" functioned as a metaphor for stealing. Russian Jews had the impression that Russians were prone to thievery. Yurii once said, "When a Russian is born, stealing is in his soul. The Jews do not do that. Jews should be a cultured people." Accordingly, Russian Jews said with certainty that Jews had higher values and intellects than Russians. At times, they referred to having an *evreiskaia golova* (Jewish head). By taking food, Russian Jews thus performed the idea that they had "lost" their Jewish culture to become more "Russian." Russian Jews said there were two categories of people who took food: those who were too poor to afford the basics and had no qualms about stealing, and those who had enough money but were so greedy that they wanted to take food home with them. Yurii and others alleged that both types of Jews had no "self-respect" and thus "shamed" the Jewish people. So, while being sexual in public shamed Georgian Jews for destroying the image of them as honorable Jewish men, stealing food shamed Russian Jews for pointing out their high degree of assimilation into Russian culture.

According to Yurii, hoarding not only violated normal *Yahrzeit* conduct, but it also gave the impression that Russian Jews were so poor that they had to pocket food items. Even though he admitted that many Russian Jews were poor, including himself, Yurii chastised men like Semyon and Moshe for their conduct. He tried to make them change their ways; their performances of poverty, whether financially motivated or not, created the "facts" of overall Russian Jewish poverty and of their reliance on donations from others. Perhaps he told me these stories because he was worried that I too would see these acts as real.

Irina also complained about the conduct of Russian Jews during synagogue meals. She said to me: "We [Russian Jews] live poorly, but we are not so destitute that we do not have money for a piece of bread with butter and a glass of tea. We are not that destitute. So, those who are greedy and who come here to eat *na khaliavu* [for free]—*na khaliavu* is a Russian saying—cut us off from our *natsional'nogo dostoinstva* [national dignity]." According to Irina, even though the majority of Russian Jews were destitute, they still had their "national dignity," which for her meant pride in their intellectual heritage, professional achievements, and high culture. Irina said that when Russian Jews obtained food *na khaliavu*, they enacted a Russian scenario to become more "Russian" and less "Jewish." She implied that these actions cast Russian Jews to look like an uncultured people, hurt Jewish self-esteem, and depleted the resources of the Jewish community at the synagogue.

Interestingly, Russians say that *na khaliavu* is a *Ukrainian* expression, which means "to freeload" or "to eat something at others' expense" (Pesmen 2000:246). This saying criticized the Soviet system in which the bureaucratic elite benefited from the work of the common people. And yet, by calling it a Ukrainian expression, Russians depicted foreigners as self-interested. Correspondingly, Russians have accused Jews of caring only about themselves (Pesmen 2000:247). Similarly, Irina considered the Jewish beggars, who gathered on the steps outside the Central Synagogue, as epitomizing Jews who were interested only in their own welfare. She called them *karmushki*, playing on the word *karman* (pocket). She told me that the beggars were a sign of how Russian Jews had moved so far away from their traditions that they began to exhibit *beznravstvennost'*. She said, "There is a saying here [at the synagogue]. *V sinagoge, odin chelovek molitsa, a drugoi kormitsia* [At the synagogue, one person prays, and another person eats]." According to Irina and others, these Jews were professional beggars, freeloading off the synagogue and making it difficult to build a moral religious community there.

Valeri stated, "Unfortunately, Russian Jews are used to taking more often than not." Berl complained that the synagogue has changed in the last two years: "People come to the synagogue who would not even think of coming to the synagogue to pray. They come only for the *Kiddush*. Did you notice that?" Irina whispered to me:

Greed is the fundamental nature of the Jews. Take Yaakov for example. The beggars are genetically like this. He is by all means a rich person. But just look at the way his face changes when he sees a rich person come into the room. He just cannot help himself. He has to beg for money when he sees that person putting bills in the *tzedoka* box. . . . Our national characteristics are to be prudent, not give away money, and be greedy. That is a scary thing. Jews turn into monsters! Don't you agree with me that Jews can be like this?

Irina's tale reversed the stories that blamed the Russian Jews' lack of Jewish character on their assimilation. Speaking from a Russian perspective, she insisted that greed was a genetic Jewish trait that had the power to turn Jews into monsters, to make them think of themselves before the welfare of the Jewish community at large. This story pointed to how Russian Jews had internalized the stereotypes of themselves that existed in Russian society (Gilman 1986). According to Russian folktales, the Jew is greedy and stingy. In Russian, the word *zhid* (kike) means both "Jew" and "stingy," and the slang verb *zhidit'sia* means "to be stingy" and to "show stinginess," like the English slang "to Jew" (Dreizin 1990:3). For example, according to Felix Dreizin (1990:28), Nikolai Gogol's book *Taras Bulba*, published in the mid-1800s, portrays Jews as "humanistically inferior not because of what they do . . . but because of what they are. Pathological greed and the pursuit of gold are presented as the main moving force of the Jewish nation as a whole. Jewish men are ugly and dirty. Jews do not know what loyalty and ideals are. [The Jew] is motivated by bourgeois individualism."

Correspondingly, there was a common belief among Russian Jews that displays of Jewish greed incited anti-Semitism. For example, my Russian Jewish friend Natasha warned me not to stand like everyone else in line at the synagogue for matzah, when it was distributed a month before Passover. She told me that her father, Evgenii Moiseivich, told her, "Last year, the line was all the way down the street. People pushed and yelled at each other. Standing in line would not be worth the aggravation and tiredness you would feel after. When he [Evgenii] passed by them, he said out loud, 'I would be an anti-Semite if I were not a Jew.' " While these Jews enacted the old Soviet strategy of standing in line for scarce goods, Evgenii interpreted it as a performance of Jewish greed—their "worst national characteristic"—that gave Russians cause to hate them.

During the Soviet period, the presence of beggars questioned the prevailing socialist ideology that the state was able to provide for all of its citizens. On a visit to the synagogue in 1955, an American doctor commented to Rabbi Shliefer that the high numbers of beggars outside the Central Synagogue indicated that Jews lived poorly in Moscow. Rabbi Shliefer told him he was incorrect and assured him that no one in the Soviet Union was in need of food or shelter: "Those [people] who you saw around the synagogue are professional beggars who, taking advantage of the humanitarian feeling the worshipers have before they pray, gather around the synagogue during the holidays. Because of our religious conviction, we cannot take any repressive measures against the most professional beggars."[11]

The rabbi's words pointed to how the beggars disrupted the state's narrative of maintaining adequate living standards throughout the Soviet Union. The state even outlawed charity organizations on the grounds that they were not necessary, since the state supposedly took sufficient care of all its citizens. As a result, anyone who was begging for money was supposedly doing it "professionally"—that is, not really needing the help but making a living off of it. Rabbi Shliefer also said that it was the Jewish way to give money to the poor, even if they were "professional." This difference of opinion led to a conflict of Jewish and state interests. In 1948, Tagaev wrote in his report to the Council: "Almost all Jewish religious communities have a widely developed organization of charity, and the Council has expended a lot of energy to hinder this illegal activity. Today, this action is officially stopped, but nonetheless it continues to exist in veiled form."[12]

These opposing views about charity continued to affect the way Russian Jews conceptualized beggars at the synagogue. On the one hand, Russian Jews who visited and worked at the synagogue felt they had a responsibility to provide for those Jews less fortunate than themselves. Yurii sponsored several elderly Russian Jews, giving them about five thousand roubles (one dollar) when they came to see him every month at the synagogue. He also tried to deliver food to several bedridden elderly Russian Jews once a month. Visitors and worshipers at the synagogue voluntarily gave money to the beggars, especially on the holidays. The front of Yurii's desk had three slots for charity money, and there were several *tzedoka* boxes throughout the synagogue. On the other hand, Russian Jews had little tolerance for those who took "too much"—a supposed sign of "professional" begging status. Echoing Soviet dogma, Irina said these Jews really did not need the charity, because they were not really as poor as they seemed. She complained how the old people stood in the hallway during Shabbat services, so they could be the first ones in the small hall to "grab food" at the *Kiddush*. She commented, "They are just plebes and lumpen proletariat." She constantly tried to get these *nekul'turnye* (uncultured) people away from the tables lined with snacks. She even instructed several of us who helped set up the *Kiddush* table one morning, "If beggars come in, you have the right to tell them to leave because it is Shabbat." Even Yurii had little patience with these "professionals," as evidenced by his telling the crippled old man to leave Mordechai's *Yahrzeit* because he had asked for too much. Many congregants shared Lyonia's opinion that "Right now, it is worthwhile to be a Jew; being a Jew is prestigious." As mentioned in the previous chapter, Yehuda also ascribed to the view that people can make money off of being Jewish. For many Russian Jews at the synagogue, being Jewish had become a way of life, a response to an increased religious faith or a need for money—or both.

Reenacting *Tzedoka*: Performing the Russian Jewish Soul

Integral to these stories of Jewish greed is the notion that it is possible for Russian Jews to get rid of this "bad" Jewish quality; they could develop a "good" Jewish characteristic to help them gain acceptance within the new religious atmosphere of the Central Synagogue. After saying how Jews are genetically greedy, Irina commented, "I also see goodness [and] righteousness [in the Jews]. This means that a person is naturally good. This person cannot be greedy because he has a strong *chelovecheskoe chuvstvo* [humane feeling]. He lives by the rule of not leaving a person in distress. That means that he always helps a person. I cannot be greedy. Maybe to myself, but not to others. One must have ethics and morals."

Irina insisted that some Jews have a strong genetic Jewish moral sense that overrides their impulse to be greedy. Irina's term *chelovecheskoe chuvstvo* expresses how many Russian Jews used their "Russian" characteristics to resist the negative image of assimilation. The noun *chelovek* means "man" or "human" in Russian, and *chelovecheskii'*, an adjective constructed from the same root, means "human" or "humane." The phrase *chelovecheskoe chuvstvo* (humane feeling) creates a link between the Russian soul *(dusha)* and Russian culture *(kul'tura)*. *Kul'tura* connotes more than just high education; it is "simple, fundamental kindness" that shows the existence of a person's soul (Pesmen 2000). Through humane feeling, they performed a positive Jewish identity in the Russian and Soviet traditions.

Throughout their discussions with one another and me, Russian Jews occasionally made reference to the Russian soul or the Jewish soul. The soul concept is a multifaceted one in Russian culture because it is full of literary allusions and historical significance. Russian Jews used the notion of the soul in the synagogue to refer to a feeling of national identity and communal belonging (Pesmen 2000). Having "soul" compelled a person to do good deeds for other Jews and to care about the well-being of the Jewish collective. Giving did not spring from greed (giving to get something in return) but from a "genuine," "soulful" compassion for others. Such "pure" motives could lead to one's own happiness since the good of the community benefited the self.

The concept of *chelovecheskoe chuvstvo* also corresponds to the Yiddish word *mensch*, which is a decent person who has a sense of what is right (Rosten 1968:237). This scenario of "humane feeling" combined Ashkenazic traditions with Russian culture to create a Russian Jewish perception of themselves as *veruiushchie* (believers) and not *reli-*

gioznye (religious). The distinction between the two terms is the difference between religious belief—holding Judaism close to one's soul—and religious action—performing religious law and rituals. This re-categorization of themselves allowed many Russian Jews to salvage some pride in what they thought had been lost to assimilation, fear, and poverty.

Judaism in Soviet Moscow was one of belief rather than practice; the state's anti-Semitic and anti-religious policies banning the enactment and teaching of religious rituals made practice too much of a risk for many Jews. Lyonia told me a story about how, after much prodding on his part, the old men at the synagogue advised him how to set up a Passover Seder in 1978:

> I did not know what else to do but to come here [to the synagogue] to find out how to conduct a Passover Seder, and we wanted to learn how to do it. Well, understand, the old men thought that each person who came here was a spy. And they did not tell me a word. They thought they would have trouble at work because the Soviet powers forbade them to lure the youth. They thought I was a provocateur. They told me the following: "It is extremely difficult. Do you have wine?" We said we had bought it. And they said the wine must be special, a specific kind. They said we needed to get red wine. And one of them said, "If you want to celebrate Passover, then celebrate well, because you remembered it."

These elderly Jews implied that the act of remembering a Jewish holiday was a legitimate way of celebrating it. This emphasis on remembering—an act that can be invisible to others—over the performance of religious rituals and laws—an act that can be seen by others—shaped how many Russian Jews understood Jewishness as a private matter of the soul. Avraham, an elderly Russian Jew who attended Shabbat services, told me, "Yes, I was afraid, but I observed. But, thank God, God pardoned us. I can say one thing. From the depths of the heart, the Jewish soul stirs, and while it stirs, they are Jews." What the Russian Jews could not do in observance, they made up in belief within the soul—a place that preserved individual identity and national consciousness. As Irina once explained, " 'Next year in Jerusalem' does not mean to walk there on your legs. It means to be in Jerusalem in your heart." In these statements, the heart is connected to the soul, and the soul, in Russian discourse, is the locus of a person's humanity. Russian Jews acted like Jews not only when they followed religious rituals, but also when they displayed *chelovecheskoe chuvstvo*. As Berl put it, *"Byt' veruiushchim znachit byt' chelovekom* [To be a believer means to be human]. . . . [That means] don't mess in other people's business. Don't look at what is going on over here and over there. Don't offend anyone, be attentive, go to synagogue once in a while, explain things. See these women waiting? I could walk by them with my head held high, but I help them. I told them to wait here for Yurii."

When I asked him how one could be a decent person *(poriadnochnyi chelovek)*, Valeri had a similar idea:

A decent person is decent . . . in family relations and in the global sense. One must not steal and do vile acts. One must never, let's say, on the one hand come to the synagogue to pray and on the other hand put money in your pocket. A person works at the synagogue. People come to him. He starts to take money to light candles on Shabbat, or he sells yarmulkes. The most important thing is to maintain good relations with people. I try [to do it right], but I know that I have offended many people. I try not to offend them. I try to give back the money I borrowed. Well, I try. But I am not holy. It is a shame, of course, when you have not offended a person, but still he stops calling, and it seemed that everything was fine. Well, what can one do? That's life.

Reciprocity in Charity

Through acts of kindness emphasizing community instead of relational hierarchies, *chelovecheskoe chuvstvo* celebrated the moral responsibility Russian Jews said they had for one another. Berl helped synagogue visitors and did not expect anything from them in return. Valeri said being a good Jew means maintaining excellent relations with others, an integral part of which is to refrain from taking from those in need. As shown above, the act of charity at the Georgian Jewish *Yahrzeit* created an unequal power relationship between Georgian Jewish givers and Russian Jewish receivers, where the latter owed the former respect and deference. However, the scenario of *chelovecheskoe chuvstvo* worked at Russian Jewish *Yahrzeits* to create a path of immediate reciprocity through a circular pattern of giving and receiving. Russian Jews gave not because they wanted something in return, but because they wanted to give from their "soul" *(ot dushi)*. As Myerhoff writes (1979:129), "Every Jew wants above all to be a giver. To give is a mitzva [*sic*]. It comes back to you in Paradise. It is said, 'The one who makes the life of the poor man longer by charity, when his time comes to die, he will have his own life lengthened.' Even if you don't believe in Paradise, doing good deeds does you good in this world. And naturally among Jews it also gets you respect. But always the one who must take, he is ashamed, so he fights it off or tries to find someone himself he can give a little something to."

When Semyon, the elderly Russian Jew, gave the beggar the apple at Mordechai's *Yahrzeit*, he became the giver and not the receiver, thus slightly balancing out the power relationship between Georgian and Russian Jews at the meal. Whether they knew the Jewish law or not, their actions corresponded to it: "Even a poor person who obtains his support from the contribution of charity . . . is obliged to give charity from that which is given to him" (Zborowski and Herzog 1952:197).

However, unlike the meal at the *Yahrzeit* given by Mordechai, Russian Jewish *Yahrzeit* meals made everyone a giver and a receiver because the gifts were small in size and low in cost. In general, the host of a Russian Jewish *Yahrzeit* distributed food as an act of sincerity, giving away to others what little he had for himself. Thus, in opposition to the Georgian Jewish *Yahrzeit* ritual of massive consumption and promotion of Georgian Jewish status, Russian Jewish *Yahrzeits* re-created the Russian and Soviet scenarios of obtaining and distributing scarce food items. These meals reproduced neither the old Soviet hierarchy of bureaucratic elites nor the new market hierarchy of the haves and have-nots. Instead, it created another Soviet Russian social order—a sense of community against the powers that be. By handing out small edible items in circular patterns among themselves, Russian Jews equalized their relationships, so that no one had more status than anyone else. The Russian Jew who sponsored a *Yahrzeit* meal gave to others "from his soul" and thus acted like a *chelovek* who had a moral responsibility for others like himself.

In September 1996, I attended a Russian Jewish *Yahrzeit* after Shabbat services. During the *Kiddush* meal in the back of the big hall, several old Russian Jews set up a makeshift table to the left of the bimah by placing a board on top of two pews. As I stood in the crowd surrounding the *Kiddush* table, drinking some juice from a plastic cup, I watched Avraham, an elderly Russian Jew, take a plate of matzah from the table and walk up to the small gathering by the bimah. I followed him to join the nine Russian Jewish men who stood around the table on which were two cans of sardines, a can of gefilte fish, two bottles of vodka, a large bottle of Fanta (orange soda), a loaf of store-bought bread, and a plastic shopping bag half full of oranges and apples. Avraham encouraged me to find a place, and I decided to stand next to Shloimie. The men cut up bread and distributed food while Avraham opened the cans of sardines. The men talked and joked among themselves in Yiddish.

When the food was prepared, Shloimie held up a cup of vodka. He drank a bit and then grabbed the hand of a bearded man in his fifties who was sponsoring this *Yahrzeit* for his father. Shloimie asked the man for the name of his father and then said a blessing in Yiddish. He told me later in Russian that he gave a blessing for the father, the son, and for all gathered at the table. Shloimie then used his pocketknife to extract two sardines from a can. He gave one sardine to me and put the other one on his plate. The men passed the bread and sardines back and forth.

As soon as I finished the food on my plate, Avraham told Shloimie to look after me. Shloimie said he knew perfectly well how to take care of a woman and gave me a piece of gefilte fish. This little scene produced some chuckles from all those present. Izzi, a tall man in his sixties, took out a flask from his jacket pocket, announcing that it contained some homemade wine. He offered me some. Even though I declined, saying that I had already drunk some vodka, the men insisted that I try it. Izzi poured me a glass, and I sipped some, feeling it burn all the way down my throat. Izzi smiled with pride when I told him that the wine was very strong. He said again how he made it himself from syrup he got from Israel. After we finished eating, Avraham commented to me, in a slightly slurred voice: "All we had was an open bottle of vodka, and we did not finish it. Such are the Jews!" (Russians supposedly will never leave a half-empty bottle.)

At this meal, these men reinforced their ties with one another by talking in Yiddish, the *mama loshen* (Yiddish for "mother tongue"). All of them were born in small towns in Ukraine and Byelorussia where Yiddish was the "Little Tradition" of Judaism, embodying the everyday language and culture of the small Jewish towns. For many Ashkenazic Jewish elders brought up in such an environment, Yiddish was the central source of their identification as Jews. As Myerhoff writes, "It was the warp and woof of what held them together, the stuff of their common childhood in Eastern Europe, in it they were *equals and equally comfortable*" (Myerhoff 1979:96, emphasis added). At the Central Synagogue, Yiddish was one of the ways Russian Jews produced a vision of themselves as equals, and it reinforced their common experiences and historical heritage. The circular distribution of the small food items also placed these Jews on equal footing. All the participants provided something to make this ritual into a meal. There was no status seeking here, only the wish to *byt' chelovekom*.

Defining Jewish Morality

At the *Yahrzeit* meal for Mordechai's mother, Georgian Jews exhibited an ethnicity that combined "Georgian" and "Jewish" traits via metaphors of family honor and shame. Georgian Jews used their business practices and high-class status as the basis of good Jewish religious practice by buying, producing, and consuming kosher foods, which

not only identified them as moral Jews but also helped them to perpetuate the Jewish people by providing sustenance and charity. The
sexuality of Georgian Jewish men was implicit in their ethnic identities
and rituals. Their wives' cooking symbolized honorable Jewish sex at
home for the continuation of the Jewish people, while the men's
carousing on the street was a more Georgian scenario, a shameful
practice within a communal Jewish context.

During their *Yahrzeit* meals with the spicy and hot smells of eggplant
purée and *solianka*, Georgian Jews controlled synagogue space, dis-
placing the Russian Jews as leaders of the small hall. The Russian
Jew's Russianness changed from being an identity of authority to one
of assimilation, as symbolized by their yearning for non-kosher *kolbasa*.
Russian Jews had to adjust to the increased presence of influential Caucasians, as well as to the new status of being religious, which stressed
engaging in expensive Jewish practices more than maintaining Jewish
belief. To compensate, Russian Jews drew on a notion of *chelovecheskoe
chuvstvo* to create their own inner circle of reciprocity that attempted
to level class differentiation.

Jewish identity in Russia today is quite fluid, opening up a space for
the assessment of value systems through food practices and sexuality.
The various meanings of "Jewish" rely on the ethnic adjectives that
come before it, namely "Russian" or "Georgian." These labels are full
of cultural content, demonstrating the complications involved in creating a post-Soviet sense of self.

Chapter 3
Renovating the Small Hall

When I go into the small hall, I have the impression that I am once again walking into a Soviet synagogue. It is dim and black. It smells horrible. There are iron gates on the windows. . . . And you want young people to come here? I think that if there is a possibility to make it better, so as to preserve our traditions, we need to do it. Let us listen to those who will do it. They will tell us what needs to be done. What are we arguing about here? Do we want to fix what will break again? Time goes on. Life goes on. Let us make a new and beautiful synagogue. *Dai Bog* [May God grant it] that people, and not just furniture, will be in the synagogue.

—Viatcheslav Yurov at a synagogue board meeting on June 28, 1996

In the spring of 1996, Mr. Feldman, the president of the Moscow Jewish Religious Community (MERO), donated several thousand dollars in the name of his deceased mother to renovate the small prayer hall. Several years earlier, the *dvadtsatka* (the synagogue board) had elected Mr. Feldman to be its "representative" (chairman) and the president of MERO. Feldman was a Belgian diamond dealer who had business in Russia and the West, and his international market ties were supposed to bring money and resources into the synagogue. His charitable gift sparked a long debate among congregation members, the board, and the administration about who had the power to decide the future of the small hall and the synagogue. Russian Jews worried that rumors about the renovation signaled the end of their small hall community. Rabbi Silverstein was clear with me about his intentions. In April, he said that he aimed to "modernize" the small hall to attract the young Russian Jews and bring "business"-like "competition" into the synagogue; he hoped other Jewish groups at the synagogue would increase their congregations as well. The rabbi wanted to guarantee the future of Russian Jewry in Moscow, and he saw no reason why the old Russian Jews could not join the other Ashkenazim in the main hall on Shabbat.

Unlike in their dealings with Georgian Jews, Russian Jews faced a more formidable adversary in the administration because it had both local bureaucratic power and international authority. After the fall of the Soviet Union, there was no longer a state organ directly supervising synagogue affairs,[1] and synagogues started independently negotiating with Western and Israeli Jewish agencies, like the American Joint Distribution Committee, for the majority of their funding. Every Jewish organization in Moscow had to have such financial support if it were to survive.[2] However, in order to gain access to these funds, post-Soviet Jews had to have connections with religious leaders, rich Russian Jewish businessmen, and/or foreign organizations. In the post-socialist world, "ties and accounts" were the key to success (Stark 1994), and Rabbi Silverstein was the only one at the Central Synagogue who was able to make such extensive contacts. As the chief rabbi of Moscow and head of the Central Synagogue, he facilitated the majority of the synagogue's financial transactions and controlled the distribution of funding.[3] He also relied on the international Orthodox religious community and others to pay his salary since he did not receive one directly from the congregation.[4]

The dispute over the future of the small hall brought the conflict between Yehuda and Rabbi Silverstein to a head, and it drew on a prime issue facing Russian society as a whole: how to move from a socialist past into a capitalist future. The synagogue administration and congregation saw this as an either-or situation—either living in the old socialist way of being or striving for new market values. The rabbi saw the old men as impediments to progress, and the congregation often repeated the statement "Everyone who has power or money is corrupt" (Ries 1997:198).

Russian Jews talked as if Rabbi Silverstein was personally responsible for their problems with the synagogue administration. They postulated that the rabbi's connections with foreign accounts helped him keep his position of authority. One frequent visitor to the synagogue explained it to me this way: "Simcha is the head [of the synagogue] because he has financial support from the West. Western religious institutions back him up." Valeri, who like Yehuda was a strong critic of the rabbi, said that Rabbi Silverstein was able to keep his position at the synagogue because he "counts on the fact that he is the only one here who knows what is going on."

This discursive dichotomy of us versus them (the people versus the elite) reproduced a historical Russian and Soviet image of the poor and powerless as morally and spiritually superior to the politically and financially powerful. Nancy Ries writes that this model is one of the reasons Russia has failed to become a democracy; the present system gives common people no faith in the government's ability to enact positive changes, making it easier for officials to get away with corruption (Ries 1997). In the synagogue context, this discourse produced an image of Russian citizens at odds with Western infiltrators, a common Russian nationalist image. Coming into such an environment, Rabbi Silverstein was at a clear disadvantage in his attempts to connect with congregants. Although they respected him for his high learning and religious lifestyle, they constantly suspected him of wrongdoing because he had access to money (Graeber 1996).

Definitions of "us" and "them" were confusing, sometimes blurring the lines between foreigner and local, spy and friend, market economy and Soviet bureaucracy. During my stay at the Central Synagogue, I saw evidence of how modernity in Russia consists of reformulations and re-articulations of Soviet practices in the name of both "progress" and "tradition." Congregants and I had to make compromises in order to contest, as well as to survive in, this post-Soviet world.

New Economies, Old Bureaucracies

As the administrator of the small hall and a member of the *dvadtsatka*, Yurii Isaakovich was responsible for maintaining synagogue property. He was concerned about the leaking roof, the bursting pipes, and the mysterious disappearance of synagogue funds earmarked to fix these problems. He wanted to raise these issues at the next board meeting; however, Mr. Feldman, the board representative and the only one who could call the board to order, was out of town. Feldman's constant traveling made it very difficult for board members to contact him, and his absence was one of the reasons why the board rarely met.

Yurii Isaakovich expressed his frustration to Rabbi Mark Dubinovich: "Can we get the *dvadtsatka* together?" The rabbi responded, "We will have to wait for the representative to get back. What questions do you have?" Yurii took a deep breath and said, "I would rather address them during the *dvadtsatka*. I really want to know, please do not get offended, where does all the money go? I cannot understand. Why do we have to wait for the representative? We have a lot of questions. We chose him like a sponsor. Where is he?"

Yurii took his responsibilities very seriously because he believed the synagogue was central to the lives of Moscow Jews. He was fond of telling me, "The synagogue stood, it stands, and it will stand. Governments and rabbis will come and go, but the synagogue will stand." He was perfectly willing to tell others and me what he found wrong with the synagogue administration. He frequently remarked, "I do not like the way the *rukovodstvo* [leadership] does not understand who is leading. *Poriadok net* [There is no order]. Who answers to what? The synagogue must be beautiful and clean." His complaints pointed to a concern about money shared by many congregants—they wanted to know who was taking it, how they were taking it, how much they were taking, and who (and what) was suffering because of it.

In 1995 and 1996, Muscovites repeatedly told me that Moscow was like "Chicago in the 1930s," a city plagued by mafia killings. Newspaper stories abounded with detailed pictures of mafia rings and the bloody murders of local and foreign "businessmen" on the streets and in dimly lit apartment entranceways. An article entitled "Death of a Fishtrader," in the newspaper *Moskovskii komsomolets*, begins with the statement, "Moscow, it seems, has become the place of massive shootings of businessmen, who have come to the capital on official business from other cities."[5] The same paper also discusses a "typical apartment entranceway contract murder."[6]

Such incidents gave the impression that Moscow was in a state of *dikii kapitalizm* (wild capitalism). One friend of mine repeated a common post-Soviet metaphor that Russia was "*bespridel, bez granits* [without boundaries, without borders]. Because it is *bespridel*, it is easier to make money here than anywhere else."[7] A young Russian Jewish businessman confirmed my friend's comments by saying: "America is not the land of freedom. Russia is. Why do you think that all these foreign businessmen come here? They come here to get rich. They cannot do that in America. The American dream is a myth. America has too many laws."

The flip side to this discourse was how foreign businessmen supposedly came to Russia to make money and then take it away with them, leaving Russia poor and underdeveloped.[8] It seemed as if everyday experiences in Moscow proved how the new market economy was making a small number of people richer and the majority poorer.

Katherine Verdery writes that talk about corruption shows the anxiety people have over the redefinition of what is acceptable and what is prohibited in post-Soviet society: "From a system of production in which the state was clearly the exploiter of labor . . . there has emerged a chaotic system in which it is completely unclear who owns what, who is exploiting whom, why there suddenly seems to be not enough money to go around, and why nothing is as it was expected to be in the first flush of postrevolutionary enthusiasm" (Verdery 1996:219). She also notes that talk specifically about the mafia expressed the difficulty many people had with the transition to a market economy in which goods moved among invisible horizontal connections rather than being guided by the socialist government vertically toward the center (Verdery 1996:219, 1995:38). In my research at the synagogue, I found that talk about corruption and the mafia did signal an anxiety about transition. But more importantly, this kind of discourse indicated how congregants reproduced the Soviet past within the post-Soviet present.

Several Russian Jews at the synagogue equated Rabbi Silverstein's actions with both the evils of foreign capitalist investment and local mafia-like practices. Because Rabbi Silverstein is a French citizen, they said he "comes here to make money and take it away with him." In a twist of a narrative about *na khaliavu*, Russian Jews were sure that the rabbi's "selfish" actions were destroying the synagogue building. Yurii said, "Simcha is here on a business trip. . . . He is here to make money. He gets it from donations to the synagogue. He set up schools. That brings in money. He will leave soon. Because all of this, the synagogue is falling apart." This kind of talk about the rabbi as a foreigner portrayed him as having no sympathy for, or understanding of, Russia and its Jews. For instance, some Russian Jews said Rabbi Silverstein could not speak Russian well and that he thus did not understand the "Russian mentality." Other Russian Jews remarked that he could not comprehend what Jewish life was like in the Soviet Union, and how hard it had been because "he was not born here. He is not one of us." Yehuda summed up all of these statements when he told me, "Rabbi Silverstein came here to set up his own mafia. Do you know how he got this job? His wife's father bought him this position. It is unheard of to have a foreigner as the chief rabbi of Moscow. Simcha does not know anything about life here. That is why he has Dubinovich around."

It is important to note that hardly any local member of the congregation faulted the age of the building and the poor care it received during the Soviet years as the reason for its present state of disarray. In contrast, Western visitors blamed the sorry state of the synagogue on the bad treatment it, and Jews, received in the Soviet years. Like Viatcheslav Yurov, the Russian Jewish entrepreneur and synagogue board member, they felt that they were entering a place of decay and destruction whenever they stepped inside. Rabbi Silverstein's aunt told me:

The synagogue is like a mammoth. It is an extinct architectural design that has too much space and no real usable space at the same time. When I walk into the synagogue, it smells like death. Half of the old people I saw there when I first came [to Moscow five years ago] are no longer around. Either they died, or they are too old to leave their homes. [Rabbi Silverstein's wife] said that, in the beginning, she did not have the strength to come there [to the synagogue]. She said that she felt like their [the old Russian Jews'] questions and stares took out all of her vital fluids.

In her view, Rabbi Silverstein needed to renovate the synagogue with foreign support to renew the faith among Russian Jews. Thus, while the visitors decided the past administration and current Russian Jewish torpor were responsible for the synagogue's sorry state, the Russian Jews felt that Rabbi Silverstein and his foreign associations were at fault. Interestingly, working in the archives on the Central Synagogue, I found remarkable similarities among the comments congregants made about Rabbi Silverstein in 1995 and 1996 and about Rabbi Levin, who served as chief rabbi of the synagogue from 1957 to 1971. In both cases, congregants blamed the neglect of the synagogue on the rabbis, saying they had taken synagogue funds for themselves; mafia talk in the mid-1990s clearly echoes dissident discourse about "corrupt" Soviet bureaucratic absolutism (Simis 1982; Lewin 1995:69).

Konstantin Simis, a Soviet intellectual who aimed to debunk Soviet propaganda, revealed how the government was essentially one big "mafia," noting that the district elite were tied to the ruling bureaucrats through a system of "never-ending tributes and bribes" that flowed in a constant stream from the district centers to the regional centers (Simis 1982:85).[9] Simis commented that the elite were financially corrupt because they hoarded money and goods, and they were immoral because they violated their obligation to take care of Soviet citizens. This last opinion reflects the Russian peasant mentality that anyone who amasses material goods limits the amount available to others (Foster 1967; Kon 1996; Ries 1997). Russians (and Russian Jews) said that such hoarding signals a person's lack of soul, since having a soul means showing kindness toward others, a kindness manifested in a person's willingness to share his/her last piece of bread (Pesmen 2000). The idea that financial dishonesty indicates spiritual and moral debauchery was still prevalent in the 1990s; thus, despite differences between market and socialist systems, Russian Jews sometimes saw both as "conspiratorially and effectively mastering social resources and power to the detriment of the people 'down there' " among the masses (Ries n.d.:32).

In the field and at the archives, I never found any proof of wrongdoing on the part of the rabbis. I did not see Silverstein take money, nor did I see any reports filed by Council members about Levin's taking what might not have belonged to him. I decided not to ask Silverstein point blank about such accusations either; the reasons for this will become clearer later in the chapter. But I did trace how both Levin and Silverstein clearly used patterns of Soviet-style bureaucracy as a way to gain and/or maintain control over the synagogue as an institution. These strategies and related activities from the 1950s to the mid-1990s produced three specific Soviet-style reactions from the congregation: moral opposition, denunciations, and spying.

The Soviet *Dvadtsatka*

In 1995, even though the Soviet government had collapsed, its statutes regarding the structure and responsibilities of the *dvadtsatka* at the Central Synagogue remained intact.[10] The new Russian state continued to recognize the board as the core of any religious institution, and according to Soviet law, the representative of the *dvadtsatka* was the one who had to call the board into session—even to resolve issues about the misuse of synagogue funds. Accordingly, Yurii's concern was not that there was no board in place within the synagogue, but that the representative and the rabbi, two foreigners who espoused "market" ideals, attempted to keep the board from meeting, thus making it difficult for congregants to influence synagogue affairs.

Yurii expressed his nostalgia for the past, for the days when the synagogue was "orderly and neat." He blamed the people in power now, not the structure of the *dvadtsatka* itself, for the synagogue's current state. He assumed that the problems would be solved if only he could air his opinion at the board meeting. During the Soviet period, many congregation members used the synagogue board as a socialist institution to cure financial corruption among synagogue officials. When they did not get the results they wanted, congregants appealed to the Council to reinstate what they saw as "proper" synagogue administrative and board practices. Therefore, Yurii's call for the enactment of Soviet bureaucracy to cure the errant ways of current synagogue officials articulated how *dvadtsatka* members in the 1950s looked to the Council for help.

According to statistical information collected by the Soviet state from 1945 until 1985,[11] there were four kinds of official positions at the Central Synagogue: (1) registered *sluzhitely kul'ta* (servers of the cult—the rabbi, the cantor, and the ritual slaughterer); (2) *obsluzhaiushchii personal* (personnel); (3) *chleny ispol'nitel'nogo organa i revizionnogo komiteta* (members of the executive organ and auditing committee); (4) *uchastniki khora* (participants in the choir). The people who fell into the first two categories were paid, and some who were part of the second were given salaries. All in all, however, the rabbi was the most important position because, until the 1970s, he implemented Soviet policy in the synagogue.

The *dvadtsatka* was created in 1918 when the People's Commissariat of Justice issued an ordinance separating church from state. The ordinance read that all religious property was to be turned over to local soviets (governing councils), all funds from such properties were to be confiscated, and "the property could then be given to the worshipers for free use provided that a group of twenty *(dvadtsat')* persons would assume responsibility for the property" (Rothenberg 1971:8). At the Central Synagogue, the *dvadtsatka* was in charge of maintaining synagogue property and insuring that the synagogue's funds were used for making repairs, performing religious rites, and paying the staff. The *dvadtsatka* handled these duties by electing a representative, an executive body *(ispol'nitel'nyi organ)* of three members, and an auditing committee *(revizionyi komitet)* of no more than three members to keep track of the funds collected and distributed (Rothenberg 1971:51). If a *dvadtsatka* failed to fulfill any one of these obligations, the synagogue property would be returned to the local soviet.

The Council made sure that the *dvadtsatkas* were working according to religious policy by sending state officials to survey *dvadtsatka* meetings, make routine inspections of synagogue accounts, and obtain personal reports from individual *dvadtsatka* members. Because of the government's suspicion of illegal profiteering activities at the synagogue, the Council paid special attention to synagogue finances. In 1948, Officer Tagaev wrote a report describing the synagogue as the center of Jewish greed due to how synagogue officials supposedly hid from the state the profits they made by providing ritual services: "Religious communities painstakingly hide the number of people who have observed this ritual (of the mikvah) with the goal to hide from the financial organs (of the government) the income from these operations."[12] He also stated that Jews continued to illegally sell ritual goods, noting that although Soviet policy decreed the cessation of the official sale of seats in the synagogue, "nevertheless, the communities continue to sell *aliyot* and places in hidden form."[13]

The state's obsession with controlling the procurement and distribution of ritual goods limited the authority of the *dvadtsatka*. Part of Soviet ideology was "socialist paternalism," which promised that the Communist Party would take care of everyone's needs by collecting the total social product and then allocating it to people as the party saw fit (Verdery 1995:32). Therefore, the state control forced the rabbi of the Central Synagogue to apply to the Council in order to make matzah, print a prayer book, or even receive items necessary for holiday as well as everyday worship.[14] In addition, up until 1971, the rabbi was the only official association between the synagogue and the Council. He occupied the position of the chairman of the Moscow Jewish Religious Community and served as the head of the *dvadtsatka*. In this way, the rabbi ran daily synagogue affairs—and he did so following the Soviet state's model of paternalistic redistribution.

During the Soviet years, the rabbi himself kept track of ritual goods and handed them out when he deemed it necessary. A synagogue worker once told me that the first time he came to the synagogue was when he needed some matzah for his family. He went directly to Rabbi Levin, who gave him a packet of matzah from his special office storage area. I heard other stories as to how Jews secretly sold scarce religious items for personal profit. One eighty-year-old man stands out in my mind as an example of this phenomenon: he showed up in the spring of 1996 from Australia, where he had immigrated with his family several years earlier. The members of the congregation told me that he came back every spring to sell yarmulkes—an activity he did throughout the Soviet period. They joked that, since he did not make a profit now, he did it "out of habit." The old man was part of the black market, a sort of second economy, that existed in response to the centralization of ritual goods at the Central Synagogue. Sometimes people bought these items on the black market because there was no other way to obtain them; at other times, they utilized this illegal system so they did not have to wait in line or search for the items themselves.[15] In this way, the synagogue functioned like a microcosm of the larger Soviet state's official and unofficial economies. The black market was an essential part of the Soviet system. Without it, the Soviet economy could not provide goods that people needed to survive and materials needed to run heavy industry, the mainstay of Soviet production.

The rabbi's role as the mediator between the government and the members of the congregation created a precarious relationship between the *dvadtsatka* and the government. The *dvadtsatka* was a legal body whose members elected their own executive board and auditing committee. If they had a problem with the way the rabbis or the executive body ran the synagogue, they turned to the Council. Specifically, members wrote *donosy* (denunciation letters) to the Council to complain about synagogue officials who supposedly took funds for personal use. If the Council found the grievance to be substantial, it sent a representative to investigate the situation.

These "abuse-of-power" letters were common in the Soviet period. Shelia Fitzpatrick writes about how they came from many sectors of the state, especially from the *kolkhozi* in the 1930s (Fitzpatrick 1996). She theorizes that these communications provided Soviet citizens with a certain amount of agency in their society (Fitzpatrick 1996:866). But these letters also provided a way for the state to control its citizens; through voluntary citizen reportage, government organs knew what people were doing and, in turn, they were better able to get citizens to conform to the state ideology in a short amount of time (Holquist 1997:419).

Even though board members had the means to shape synagogue life via their participation in synagogue administration and their ability to write denunciation letters, the board had as much power as the Council and the rabbis gave it, and both kept a close watch over synagogue affairs. Both the Council and the rabbis appointed their own men to observe the *dvadtsatka* meetings and to serve on its executive and auditing committees. The Council, in turn, used rabbis and *dvadtsatka* members as sources of information (willingly or unwillingly). Not only did government agents write reports on synagogue affairs, but rabbis, staff, and members of the congregation also submitted reports to the Council about interactions with foreign visitors in the synagogue.[16] Rabbi Dubinovich said that members of the congregation denounced him to the Council for spreading anti-Soviet propaganda. Therefore, it was difficult to tell when rabbis (and even *dvadtsatka* members) worked for the state, their own interests, or the interests of the congregation. These ambiguities produced a level of fear and mistrust in synagogue life, a situation that was prevalent, to varying degrees, in many Soviet institutions.

Two Denunciation Letters

Letters written during the Soviet years by board members to the Council claimed that synagogue officials abused their power by stealing synagogue funds and/or misappropriating synagogue property. Out of all the letters I read in the archives, the following two written by S. S. Virtser in 1958 and 1959 about Rabbi Levin provide the most insight into synagogue culture.[17] These years saw great transformation in both the synagogue and the Soviet Union at large. Rabbi Levin had just replaced Rabbi Shliefer, who had died after serving the Central Synagogue for fourteen years. In addition, members of Soviet society began to openly criticize Stalin and his regime. In 1956, Khrushchev gave a speech in which he attempted to end the cult of Stalin. He exposed Stalin's crimes of extending party and state control into every facet of Soviet life and eliminating all pockets of autonomy and criticism (Shatz 1980). For the intelligentsia, this speech was the "end of silence" (Cohen 1982), encouraging the liberalization of intellectual life (Alexeyeva 1985). Intellectuals began to publish their opinions freely in journals and magazines, as well as hold important open discussions on matters such as improving the Soviet state.[18]

It was in this atmosphere of growing criticism of the state that S. S. Virtser, a self-described *prikhozhanin* to the synagogue, wrote in 1958 to Rabbi Levin in the name of twenty-five other "frequent visitors" ("five to seven" of whom were *dvadtsatka* members).[19] In his letter, Virtser complained that Rabbi Levin, declaring himself to be the chairman of the *dvadtsatka*, took control of synagogue funds without consulting the *dvadtsatka*. Furthermore, Virtser wrote that Levin's actions had undermined the authority of the *dvadtsatka* to elect its own officials and to keep track of money donated to the synagogue.

Virtser listed the following complaints: (1) Levin decided that only *dvadtsatka* members could attend *dvadtsatka* meetings and ask questions, as opposed to Rabbi Shliefer, who had allowed all members of the congregation to come to the meetings; (2) Levin said that the members of the *dvadtsatka* did not have to know what was going on; (3) Levin did not let the representative of the auditing committee finish a report about how a synagogue official took money for his own use; (4) Levin refused the *dvadtsatka* permission to pick its own candidates for the auditing committee; (5) Levin took keys that opened *tzedoka* boxes in order to take the charity money for himself; (6) Levin handpicked members of the *dvadtsatka*; (7) Levin barred the auditing committee from carrying out an inspection of the yeshiva for the past two years. In conclusion, Virtser wrote that it was "not right that you [Levin] . . . sat at the table and took money and put it in your pocket."[20]

Virtser also asked Rabbi Levin to resign as the chairman of MERO, writing that the new chairman "will deal with household and financial issues, and it will be easier for you [Levin], and all discussions will be finished [about this issue] since you will no longer be in contact with any money."[21] Virtser also asked the rabbi to nominate a new auditing committee, noting that it, as well as the *dvadtsatka*, should be purged of men who were "employees" of Levin and replaced with men "really suited" for the job.

Virtser's complaints about Rabbi Levin correspond to a general pattern of denunciation letters in the 1930s. Fitzpatrick found the two most popular complaints to be about officials in local state organizations misappropriating funds and chairmen of these organizations suppressing criticism and forcing members or workers to do activities against their will (Fitzpatrick 1986:847). Virtser's letter suggests that Levin practiced surveillance because he obtained sole access to synagogue accounts containing important financial information and that he engaged in paternalistic redistribution by placing all synagogue funds under his own control. Levin further consolidated his power at the synagogue by placing his own candidates on the auditing committee, surveying the flow of information from the auditing committee to *dvadtsatka* members, limiting the membership of the *dvadtsatka*, and cutting the *dvadtsatka* off from the rest of the congregation.

While denunciation letters of the 1930s usually called for the official's dismissal or arrest (Fitzpatrick 1996:845), Virtser suggested separating Rabbi Levin from the synagogue's finances in order to make him a better spiritual leader. Perhaps this recommendation identifies how Virtser, like many Soviets, saw money as having the power to corrupt a person both morally and spiritually.

Despite his criticisms of Levin, Virtser did not delve into the ways in which the Soviet state was ultimately responsible for corruption at the synagogue. He blamed the rabbi instead of the state for the decrease in the *dvadtsatka*'s authority. It was not clear whether Virtser realized that Levin's accumulation of power was a product of the Soviet government's bureaucratic policies. But, if he did realize it, there was no way that he could have protested it without putting himself in danger. In general, those who wrote letters to the Council placed themselves at risk of surveillance. All "believers" were suspect in the eyes of the state, but also most letter writers gave their names, addresses, and phone numbers to the Council, so that they could be contacted later for questioning if an investigation ensued.

More than a year later, on August 3, 1959, several members of the *dvadtsatka* and the congregation wrote a letter to the Council complaining that Levin did not respond to Virtser's request.[22] The group reported that, at the end of December 1958, they sent another delegation to see Levin, who told them that there would be a *dvadtsatka* meeting on April 10–12, 1959, to evaluate the synagogue accounts of 1958. However, Levin never called the meeting to order. The authors cited Soviet law to appeal to the Council to take action against Levin. They wrote:

Levin's conduct is against the Soviet directive. At the Twenty-First Party Congress when Khrushchev gave a speech, he said, "We—the Soviet people—are proud that in our country the people and only the people are the masters of every happiness."*Pravda* 12.II. 58, page 2. But, at the beginning [of the meeting], Levin did not let us—fifty to sixty men—cross the threshold. When we [finally] came in, he deprived us of our right to vote, and then he completely kicked us out. This is truly not the Soviet way.

At the Twenty-First Party Congress, the chairman of party control and the former chairman of the High Soviet, N. S. Shvernik, said: "We must presently and quickly look over all the letters and applications of the workers. We must keenly and attentively take account of their inquiries in order to satisfy the legal demands of the masses and to correct the appearance of deficiencies at separate party, economic, soviet, and social organs." *Pravda* 3.II. 58, page 6.

That is how the Soviet authority teaches us, but Levin has not given us an answer to our letter for nine months. [H]e has not keenly and attentively re-sponded to our demands. [He] does not want to satisfy our request and does not want to correct the deficiencies at the workplace. The people do not exist for him, he does everything himself, he decides himself, [and] he does what he wants.[23]

This letter was like other denunciations in that it accused Levin of going against the people's will. It also reflected the anti-Semitic image of the Jew as an enemy of the people by presenting Levin as possibly driven by pathological greed and bourgeois individualism. Perhaps those who wrote the letter believed that calling Levin a "traitor to the people" might give them a better chance of persuading the authorities to correct Levin's behavior. As such, resistance to synagogue bureau-cracy involved both a critique of the abuse of power within the syna-gogue, as well as support of the Soviet state that created the unequal power relations at the synagogue in the first place. This meant that re-sistance in the Soviet context was inherently partial; when it protested one aspect of a power structure, it simultaneously reinforced another part of it (Abu-Lughod 1990; Ortner 1995; Berdahl 1999).

After Rabbi Levin's death in 1971, Yaakov Fishman became the rabbi at the Central Synagogue. However, by that time (perhaps in re-sponse to the charges against Levin), the Soviet government had sepa-rated the positions of rabbi and chairman of MERO. The government directly appointed the chairman, who replaced the rabbi as the inter-mediary between the community and the government. The rabbi now functioned as a figurehead. In the 1970s and 1980s, members of the *dvadtsatka* wrote letters to the Council to denounce the activities of the new chairmen. In 1975 and 1976, letters to the Council complained about the appointment of a man named Tandetnik to the position. Sup-posedly, he earlier had served as the head of a labor camp in Siberia. G. M. Manevich, a synagogue board member, wrote to the Council, "None of the members of the congregation know him [Tandetnik] [and] it is unlawful [to] name him the chairman by force and against the will of the community."[24] Complaints about subsequent chair-men and their misuse of synagogue funds continued well into the mid-1980s.[25] The Council intermittently led investigations into these charges, but it is not clear as to the specifics of how and why these men left their posts.

In 1988, the Soviet government allowed the American Joint Distri-bution Committee (JDC) to work in the Soviet Union, after it had been banned from entering the country thirty years earlier. The JDC helped create a position at the Central Synagogue called the chairman of the Union of Jewish Communities throughout the Soviet Union, which included the job of "executive director" of the Central Synagogue. As a result, the *dvadtsatka* no longer monitored the executive branch of the synagogue. The executive director was also the chairman of the community and thus had most of the administrative power. Anton Rizovskii, who used to be the synagogue's bookkeeper, took on this position.

In 1990, Rizovskii hired Simcha Silverstein to be the new rabbi of the Central Synagogue. Rabbi Silverstein was twenty-seven years old at the time. As a result of this hire, Rabbi Mark Dubinovich, who had served the community since Rabbi Fishman's death in 1983, left his post to fill the new chief rabbi of Russia position. In turn, Rabbi Silverstein became chief rabbi of Moscow and head of the new Rabbinical Court of Russia.

Post-Soviet Bureaucracy at the Synagogue

Soon after he took his post, Rabbi Silverstein fired Anton Rizovskii for misusing synagogue funds and property, and he named Grigorii Sharogradskii as executive director. This action placed Rabbi Silverstein in a very advantageous position. Although the community hired him (through Rizovskii), it could not fire him, since it did not pay his salary. In addition, Yurii Isaakovich complained to me that Rabbi Silverstein "brought Sharogradskii to the *dvadtsatka* to elect him to the executive director position without anyone knowing him." His words echoed the denunciation letters written against Tandetnik in 1975.

Rabbi Silverstein also created the office of the president and nominated his influential acquaintance Mr. Feldman for that position. The president's job was to appoint the executive director and to call the *dvadtsatka* together for a meeting. Feldman was hardly ever in town due to business trips, and since he could only speak to the members of the congregation in Yiddish (he did not know Russian), Rabbi Silverstein had de facto administrative power at the synagogue. He oversaw most of the administrative decisions and decided when to call the *dvadtsatka* to order. By restructuring the administration in this way, Rabbi Silverstein stripped the *dvadtsatka* of any real power to shape synagogue affairs.[26] In a comment reminiscent of Virtser's criticism of Rabbi Levin, Valeri told me, "He [Rabbi Silverstein] does everything that he wants. Everything, even down to the remodeling [of the small hall], is done the way Simcha wants it."

Stories abounded about Silverstein's practice of what looked like Soviet paternalistic redistribution. Members of the congregation talked about how Rabbi Silverstein used synagogue funds and ritual items to make money for himself, accusations that mirrored the denunciation

letters but were updated to the current situation. The two most prevalent tales were about the synagogue's kiosk and Rabbi Silverstein's
"mafia" connections with Georgian Jews. Many members of the congregation complained about the high prices of kosher food sold at the
synagogue's kiosk. Valeri said that during Passover, the kiosk sold
kosher wine at seventy-five thousand roubles (fifteen dollars) and then
reduced it to fifty-five thousand roubles (eleven dollars), but it was still
more expensive than the wine sold at the Hasidic synagogue on Bolshaia Bronnaia Street, which sold it for forty-five thousand roubles
(nine dollars). Others told me that the kiosk sold food that had been
given to the synagogue specifically for distribution to the poor for
free. Others disagreed, saying that food sold in the kiosk was legiti-
mately there, but that, in the words of one Georgian Jew, "The kiosk
charges 10 percent more than the stores," and that the extra profit
"goes in their [the administrators'] pockets."

Rabbi Silverstein's favoritism of Georgian Jews was another frequently aired topic. He supposedly gave them first choice of ritual
items. Yurii even indicated after the fistfight that he thought the rabbi
was in cahoots with the Georgians. There were two renditions of the
rabbi's relationship with the Georgians: (1) the rabbi sold ritual items
to Georgian Jews in secret, so that no other Jewish groups could have
them, and (2) the Georgian Jews gave the rabbi ritual items as charity,
and he sold them to make a profit for himself and the Georgian Jews.
These scenarios articulate the view shared by many Russians that Caucasians were involved in the mafia, and that Rabbi Silverstein was
practicing a version of paternalistic distribution, in which the "the
mafia" had replaced the original Soviet bureaucracy.

These stories point to an underlying issue that concerned almost all
of the synagogue workers; namely, how to make a living in the new
Russia without losing one's moral integrity. Yurii complained constantly to me how Rabbi Silverstein refused to increase his (Yurii's)
salary of five hundred thousand roubles (one hundred dollars) a
month. Such a low wage supposedly forced many synagogue workers
to take money and foodstuffs in order to supplement their incomes.
Although Yurii never mentioned that he took items from the synagogue, it was "common knowledge" that those who worked in the
synagogue had to steal to survive. One young religious Russian Jew
told me, "Everyone is completely occupied with business, starting with
the rabbi and ending with the last cleaning woman who thinks about
what she can steal. How can one pay several secretaries two hundred
to three hundred dollars [a month] here in Moscow? It is clear that
they pay these people [so little money] so that they will steal. Why
keep on twenty to thirty people here and pay them *kopeks*? They steal

and work badly. Realistically, how can an observant person live here on two hundred to three hundred dollars?"

Rabbi Silverstein acknowledged that the synagogue staff stole money and material goods, but he condoned it. He said, "People are going to steal money no matter what. It is just a question of how much they steal." The centralization of goods and money at the top of the administrative structure made the rest of the staff fight over access to the leftovers. I believe the rabbi was not worried about how they worked it out, as long as they did not take too much from the synagogue funds—an act that would have challenged his authority.

Igor, the administrator of the main hall, also inspired stories. Staff members said he lured naive foreign tourists to his office, where he showed them shelves of tattered old Torah scrolls so they would donate money to the "poor" synagogue. He supposedly took that money for himself. Rabbi Silverstein told me that Igor and Yurii got into a fight over access to money from foreign visitors. In order to resolve the dispute, the rabbi made Igor the administrator of the main hall on the weekends, and Yurii the administrator of the small hall during the weekdays, so that they could divide the charity money. Such low-level tactics on the part of the synagogue staff reproduced the old Soviet positions of *nachal'niki* and *duraki* (bosses and idiots), in which people attempted to become bosses by monopolizing access to goods and services. In turn, they expected others to blindly follow their orders. As Yurii once commented to me about Natan, an assistant to the executive director who liked to yell orders, "Everyone here wants to be in charge. Natan came here a year and a half ago, and now he is a big boss and wants to show everyone that he is a big boss."

Some people considered this kind of maneuvering for money and power particularly endemic to the synagogue setting. Such a narrative echoed Soviet state discourse on the inherent capitalistic and bourgeois individualist nature of Jews and Judaism. For instance, Yehuda once declared that Yurii was not as honest as I thought he was. "At first," Yehuda explained, "a person gets money handed to him, then he asks for money, and then he takes it for himself. That's the way it works there [at the synagogue]." "But Yurii Isaakovich does not take money," I insisted. Yehuda responded: "He [Yurii] is on the sixth step. . . . Look, he does not have a pension yet. He could work somewhere else, in a factory [for example]. But he wants to work in the synagogue. It is easier. Yurii is an honest man, probably one of the most honest there. But, as the Yiddish saying goes, 'He is better than the ten plagues.' "

There were at least three interpretations as to why the synagogue was an "easy" place to work. First, the synagogue administration paid its workers so little that they were "forced" to steal. Second, synagogue workers practiced "normal" stealing. Evgenii Moiseivich loved to tell me the following *pogovorki* (Russian sayings) that condoned a little bit of stealing: "When you are standing by a running river, you are bound to get wet" and "When you hold a honey jar in your hands, what you get on your fingers is yours, but don't stick your whole hand in the honey jar." Thus if everyone is stealing, it is natural that you will too, but don't take too much.

Third, it was assumed that when staff members had personal access to money, they took much more than they should, thus transgressing the boundaries of "normal" stealing. In other words, frequent contact with money made a person dishonest, an argument similar to Virtser's. Irina Maksovna described to me the three kinds of people who worked at the synagogue's charity center:

The first gets handed one hundred dollars for charity, and he immediately thinks of the ways that he can distribute it among the poor. The second person thinks, "If I put the money in the bank, in one year it will double. Then I'll have one hundred dollars for me and one hundred for the synagogue." The third person puts half in his pocket and gives the rest to charity. I do not like to deal with money that is not mine. I would rather they give me things to hand out to people. I am a moral person. Do you know what moral is? Conscience. Well, I have a clean conscience. I washed my hands of the whole thing.

Interestingly, Yurii claimed that Irina herself took money from charity donations. He told me, "Irina Maksovna was honest when she came here [to work at the synagogue]. The other day, she came in here and put her fingers into the slots for charity money [that are in the front of Yurii's desk]. 'What are you doing!?' I asked her. She said, 'I saw you do this. You said we could.' 'What are you talking about?!' I yelled. I am telling you this so that you will reconsider your thoughts about her."

These stories are verbal denunciations in the tradition of the "abuse-of-power" letters. As discussed above, denunciations could both resist and reinforce bureaucracy. In talking about one another and the rabbi as engaging in activities that corrupted the soul and the community, Russian Jews positioned themselves as intellectuals who resisted government corruption by professing an ideology of "moral intelligence" in the Russian/Soviet tradition. Dmitri N. Shalin writes that, according to the intellectual Aleksei Losev, the intellectual is "never socially indifferent, is acutely aware of the world's inanities and is determined to 'transform reality'—'a person who takes the interest of humanity as his own.' Moral intelligence is 'conscious spiritual labor

to improve oneself and to make the world around us rational' " (Shalin 1996:86).

Accordingly, the contemporary Russian writer Andrei Sinyavsky
(1997:2–3) comments: "Traditionally, the intellectual's attitude must
be very sensitive. He must not succumb to temptation, and he should
not become part of power; rather, he should observe power from the
outside. . . . An intellectual is a person who loves the people. . . . In the
nineteenth century, the intellectual, even if he was absolutely wrong in
his thinking, was a critically thinking person."

At the synagogue in the 1990s, "intellectual" resistance criticized
synagogue bureaucracy and strived to reestablish socialist values. As
Yehuda told me, "During the Soviet period, being a professor was a
prestigious job. We valued intellectuals here. The Soviet Union had
the highest degree of intelligentsia, more than in America, pardon
me. In America, what counts is how much money you make, not your
job. Here it was the reverse. Now, I make only 330,000 roubles a
month."

Yehuda, Yurii, and Irina resisted this construction of themselves as
unworthy by larger state and local discourses. They labeled monetary
transactions as "immoral" and negatively evaluated the relationships
that local Jews had with rich people. They reproduced the image of
the corrupt Soviet administrators and placed themselves as their
moral opposition. They also associated Western ideas and money with
superficiality and materialism, thus considering themselves to be more
moral and more spiritual than Westerners. They created their own
ethnic identity in opposition to the West.

However, in the absence of a state organization like the Council,
who was responsible for eradicating synagogue corruption? The influx of large amounts of Western money into the synagogue and the
presence of Rabbi Silverstein in Moscow placed local resistance on a
global scale. In order to protest the rabbi, Jews at the synagogue appealed to Western agencies, those same agencies that they claimed
were corrupt. These agencies were now in the same structural position as the Soviet Council. There were many times when Jews at the
synagogue told me a story about how "corrupt" Rabbi Silverstein was,
because they thought that I, as a Westerner, had connections to such
agencies that would publish an article about it in the West. They said
that when Jews in the West heard "the truth" about what was "really
going on" at the synagogue, they would be compelled to take action
against Rabbi Silverstein.

The "[Wo]Man and the Mirror": The Ethnographer as Spy

On his trip to the USSR in 1959, B. Z. Goldberg, the American Jewish writer and son-in-law of the famous Yiddish writer Sholom Aleichem, repeatedly heard stories that spies surrounded him in every synagogue. In one particular synagogue, a man broke up a conversation between Goldberg and several members of the congregation. Goldberg (1961:131) writes:

"Look here," I said to him, "why did you break it up? There was no reason whatever. First, I was telling nothing wrong; second, people are free to talk now—'they' (the KGB informants) don't bother anybody for talking; third, we were by ourselves, Jews in a synagogue." The man replied in broken Hebrew phrases clipped from the prayer book—you never could tell who was listening. Had I heard the story about the man and the mirror? A man was standing opposite a mirror, and observing his own image in the glass, pointed to it with his finger and said: "One of us will squeal."

Jews at the synagogue remembered spying practices, and that sense of fear and mistrust continued to shape their social relations long after the Soviet Union fell apart. They were thus very ambivalent about my writing. On the one hand, they wanted me to write well-informed articles in English about the synagogue, in order to combat what they saw as corruption in the synagogue. On the other hand, they were wary of my taking notes in front of them. Irina was very adamant about having me put down my pen and paper when she wanted to tell me something "important" about "real" relations at the synagogue. In addition, during my first month of fieldwork, Yaakov asked, as I wrote down what he had just told me, "Are you writing in English? [That is] so no one will read it." Even Shalom, the head of the Mountain Jewish community at the synagogue, commented to me, "You are writing everything down. What are you, a KGB agent?"

These expressions of anxiety indicated that the act of writing signaled a possible betrayal. Congregants knew that what they said in one context could be used against them in another. For even if I did not write anything down in front of them (I had ceased to do so several months into my fieldwork because my note-taking made people uncomfortable), they knew that I might write it down later, and they did not know to whom I would show it. Perhaps they remembered how, during the Soviet regime, people went to jail for making a seemingly innocent joke among friends about the state. And, as Valeri indicated in his story about visiting the military registration and enlistment office, intellectuals were forced to give out information on those who challenged the state's sovereignty.[27] Before I realized the depth of the power struggle between Rabbi Silverstein and Yehuda Levi, and partly due to Rabbi Silverstein's effective strategies for gaining power, I had become unknowingly entangled in the spy scenario. It all started with a simple fieldnote.

On December 2, 1995, I attended my first Shabbat service in the small hall with the elderly Russian Jews. I was struck by how central a role Yehuda Levi played in the ritual. He received the first *aliyah*, and on his way down from the bimah, the men gathered around him to shake his hand. He also read the Haftorah blessings to conclude the Torah reading.[28] Because this was my first observation of Shabbat in the small hall, and because he was a major figure in the ritual and professed to be a religious expert, I wanted to ask Yehuda a couple of questions about the organization of the service. I printed out my fieldnotes from that day and brought them to our meeting. After he answered my questions, he asked me if he could read over my notes, since he had a good working knowledge of English. After looking over the first page, he asked, "Why did you spell my name wrong?" "Sorry, but I write really fast. No time to make corrections," I said. He skimmed the pages. He gave them back to me, commenting, "I guess that you have to write everything down, or you might forget it."

Several weeks after that service, I had Shabbat dinner with the Silversteins. Afterward, Rabbi Silverstein and I sat at the table alone while his wife tended to the children. He suddenly said, "I heard that some people have told you something about my being a foreigner." I said that I had heard some talk about that topic. "Who told you that?" he asked me. "Some older people," I answered vaguely. The rabbi replied:

You mean Yehuda? Listen. There is a war going on between Yehuda and me. He married a religious Lubavitcher woman. Twenty years ago, she left him to go to Israel. He said that when she did, she put the KGB on him. He suffered for a couple of years. Because of that, he refuses to give her a *get* [a certificate of divorce]. You know that his children refuse to speak with him. He actually married again but in a civil ceremony and then got divorced. In the past, he would have been excommunicated. But now, we really do not do those things, especially here, where there is no solid community. In a real community, the men would have beaten him up or forced him out. . . . So, in order to force Yehuda to give a *get*, I barred him from reading the Torah.[29]

"But he does," I said, remembering what I saw in the small hall that Shabbat morning. The rabbi continued:

Only when I am not there. He is also not allowed to be the cantor, which is the tradition when a person's mother or father dies. Most of the old men here do not understand what a *get* really means, so they continue to let him take part in the services. I took his father's name off the list for humanitarian aid [to force him to give a *get*]. Some of the old men told me that his father was gravely ill, but I still took off his name. Someone told me that his father was going to die. I said, "Let him die!" He died three days later. The word got out about what I had said, and it was as if I had condemned him to death. When I first came here, I decided to try to get him to change his mind about the *get*. For the first years, I tried to be nice. I attempted to get his kids over here so that they could talk with their father. At the last minute, he said that he did not want to see them. So, you should really take what he has to say with a grain of salt.

My observation of Yehuda's actions during the Shabbat service became a key piece of information in the power struggle between Yehuda and Rabbi Silverstein. Both Yehuda and Rabbi Silverstein were fighting over who had the higher rabbinical authority to make decisions at the synagogue. This conflict was more than just personal. It was an issue of establishing a certain kind of social order at the synagogue. The only way one of them could win this conflict was by successfully deploying negative stories about the other. My work was central in their struggle, since, as an ethnographer of synagogue life, I had access to much needed information about both of them.

Contrary to what the rabbi told me, the old men did know what a *get* was, and yet they continued to support Yehuda. One elderly Russian Jewish *dvadtsatka* member put it this way: "Simcha is absolutely right, and Yehuda is absolutely wrong. But I side with Yehuda." In this case, Russian Jews valued their connections with one another more than their adherence to Jewish law. Although he represented the correct interpretation of the law, Rabbi Silverstein was considered by Russian Jews to be a "foreigner," whereas they saw Yehuda as "one of us."

Because the rabbi heard what people were telling me about him, I assumed that he probably knew, without my informing him, that Yehuda continued to read the Torah against his order. But my confirmation of Yehuda's actions showed the rabbi that I knew how Yehuda continued to challenge his authority at the synagogue. It seemed to me that Rabbi Silverstein wanted me to take his side. He knew that I respected Yehuda and was going to write down what Yehuda said in my fieldnotes, but the rabbi wanted his point of view to be represented as fact.

Several weeks after our conversation, Rabbi Silverstein asserted his authority over Yehuda during morning services. Yurii Isaakovich told me that Rabbi Silverstein had threatened him that morning: "He said that if I call Yehuda to the Torah, I will be fired. I told Yehuda and he said, 'Don't you respect my father?' " "He was offended," I said. "Yes. What can I do?" "You need to work to live." "Take me back with you to America to work as a cleaning person. That would be better [than this]."

By barring Yehuda from receiving the honor of reading the Torah in front of the congregation, Rabbi Silverstein made it impossible for Yehuda to continue to worship at the synagogue, since he needed to have certain honors in order to correctly mourn his father's death. In addition, by forcing Yurii to make a decision whether to keep his job or to stand by Yehuda, the rabbi cut the strong ties that existed among Russian Jews in the small hall community, ties that allowed them to challenge the rabbi's authority to control their *Shacharit* service. Yurii had to subordinate the sense of loyalty and respect he felt for Yehuda, and Yehuda's father, in order to keep his job. In this way, Rabbi Silverstein began to separate the Russian Jews from one another, adding to, as well as reaffirming, their sense of mistrust.

That evening, I phoned Yehuda at home:

Yehuda: He [Rabbi Silverstein] hates me. That thief. He knows I know he steals money. I have lists to prove it.

Sascha: They say Silverstein is against you because you won't give your wife a *get*. Is that true?

Yehuda: Who told you that?

Sascha: Silverstein.

Yehuda: Please, don't talk about me with him. It is true that I won't give my wife a *get*, but that has no relation to Torah readings, to remembering my father. . . . It is none of his business. Don't listen to what he tells you.

Sascha: He wants to force you to give a *get*.

Yehuda: He will not reach his goal. He is stupid. He does not realize that the more he pushes me, the more I won't give in. He offered me five thousand dollars to fill out the papers. I told him that I can't be bought. That was unheard of before, but now it is becoming normal. They [the members of the congregation] know that he steals, but they don't say anything. And, there is nothing we can do about it. We are stuck. You should write an article about Silverstein and his stealing. Let's set a time to meet [to talk about such an article].

By insisting that Rabbi Silverstein could not "buy him," Yehuda showed that he would not subordinate his own beliefs and actions to the rabbi's wishes. He would not reaffirm the rabbi's power at the synagogue; power that Yehuda insisted was based on mafia finances. In refusing the money, Yehuda positioned himself as a Russian Jew and an intellectual.

However, we never met to discuss composing that article. One week later, Yehuda cornered me in the big hall after morning services. "Who brought up my name when you were talking to Simcha?" he asked me. I told him that I was eating Shabbat dinner at the Silversteins when the rabbi mentioned his name. Yehuda said:

Now I cannot pray here. Understand? I have been coming to this synagogue for my whole life. Simcha, that son of a bitch, forbade me to be the cantor and the Torah reader. Now, he forbade me to be called up to the Torah on Saturdays. How did he find out that I was called up on Saturdays? You must have seen me. You were there on a Saturday. You did not have to mention me by name. You did not mention the other ones. You hear for yourself how they talk about him in the morning. He has no right to mess in my business. I got permission from one hundred rabbis to remarry. I am not married now, but I got permission to remarry. Who is he? . . . You mentioned my name.

Suddenly, I was no longer Yehuda's advocate but his enemy. His harsh words indicated that he believed that I was spying on him, or perhaps he was so caustic with me because it was at that moment that he finally realized that he had lost the battle with Rabbi Silverstein. Without Yurii's support, no one would back him. Either way, I had to confront my own reflection in the mirror. I had informed Rabbi Silverstein about Yehuda's participation in services. There was no denying it.

Standing alone in the big hall after Yehuda left, I worried that his allegation would jeopardize my fieldwork. How could people trust me if Yehuda told them that I had "squealed" on him to the rabbi? How could I even trust myself to figure out what to say to whom?

Upset with myself, I walked back into the small hall to see Yurii Isaakovich sitting at his desk. Yurii noticed that something was wrong and asked me to tell him about it. After I had summarized the situation, Yurii said, "You are not at fault. You are a good person. Simcha wrote an article a couple of months ago in the *International Jewish Gazette* that Yehuda would not divorce his wife. Everyone knows about it. The old people here tell Simcha [that Yehuda gets honors at the service]. They talk about him [Simcha] themselves but then tell him what other people say." Yurii's words assured me that I would still be able to work in the synagogue. And they also revealed an essential aspect of synagogue relations—any act of resistance could easily be caught up in larger strategies of domination.

From that day forward, Yehuda rarely came to the Central Synagogue, and hardly anyone mentioned his name in my presence. The next time I heard about him was the following spring, during a Shabbat dinner at the Silversteins'. Rabbi Silverstein had just told me about his plans to renovate the small hall. He said, "I want to kick out the old people in the small hall on Saturdays. I want to set up a student *minyan*. Now that Yehuda is gone, it will be easier."

Of Prostitutes and Pews: The June *Dvadtsatka* Meetings

When Rabbi Silverstein called the *dvadtsatka* meeting to order on June 11, 1996, it was the first time the board had convened in at least one year. Even though it was the president's job to get the *dvadtsatka* together, everyone said that Rabbi Silverstein was the one in charge. Rumors had been circulating as to the reasons why Rabbi Silverstein refused to call the board to order for so long; some said he was ashamed to call it because he would have to face charges of embezzling funds, others said he simply did not care about the synagogue and would rather go on business trips. Yurii Isaakovich, however, blamed Rabbi Dubinovich for the *dvadtsatka*'s inactivity. Yurii told me, "Dubinovich promised that we [the *dvadtsatka*] would meet soon. *On prodazhnyi chelovek. On ne derzhit slova. U nego net svoego slova* [He is a corrupt person. He does not keep (his) word. He does not have his own word]." "What does '*prodazhnyi chelovek*' mean?" I asked.[30] He answered: "It means that he is a *prostitutka* [a prostitute]. Just like a woman who sells herself, he sells himself to the highest bidder. Excuse me for using such a word. Dubinovich wanted to call the *dvadtsatka*, but Simcha did not want it to meet. He gave Dubinovich 235,000 roubles to shut him up. A person must live. . . ." "What do you mean by 'live'?" I asked. "Have enough money to eat, to walk around, to go to work," he said.

By calling Dubinovich a prostitute, Yurii echoed common contradictory opinions in Moscow about women who sell sex to foreigners for a living. The post-Soviet media has portrayed these women as immoral, treacherous individuals who threaten Russia's honor by bringing diseases like AIDS into the country (Banting, Kelly, and Riordan 1998:347). But, at the same time, because they are able to make enough money to live in style and fashion, such hard-currency prostitutes are respected as symbols of the new market economy. Yurii thus acknowledged a comparable, although slightly different, situation facing the Russian Jewish rabbi. According to Yurii, if Dubinovich did not take the bribe money, he could not have managed to live a normal life since his salary was so low.

Another aspect of the prostitution metaphor worth considering is the notion that a woman who sells herself compromises her whole physical and spiritual being. For example, Lyonia once told me about how he figured out that his friend had a niece who was a *zaderzhanka* (a kept woman). He said:

One day, he [Lyonia's friend] told me that he had a niece in Moscow. I thought that it was odd that he never mentioned her before. It is unusual for members of a Jewish family not to socialize with one another. Little by little, I found out why he did not talk with her. She is a prostitute. She came over for Passover one year, and I noticed that she had too much money. That was the first sign. Her uncle said this was because she was an only child. I saw a picture of her. When she was younger, she was very pretty. Now, she is all shriveled up, used up. She is a *zaderzhanka*. She has one client for a year or a couple of months. He puts her up in a nice place, pays for things. Then, she finds someone else after that.

Lyonia said he could tell that his friend's niece was a kept woman because her body was "shriveled up, used up," which was a sure sign of prostitution in Russia. Because she gave sexual favors for material goods, her whole physical being suffered irreversible damage. This image related to a statement Yurii had made earlier about how Rabbi Silverstein supposedly used up the synagogue's resources and, as a result, physically destroyed the synagogue building. In this way, the synagogue (the feminine *sinagoga* in Russian) became a prostitute to foreign money. This idea played a key role in the board meetings that occurred in June 1996.

When he called the first board meeting to order on June 11, Rabbi Silverstein had a clear agenda—the modernization of the small hall. He did not leave room for discussion about the synagogue's distressing physical state. He opened the meeting with the following words:

Dear friends, the small hall demands our special attention. We are there every day, except for Shabbat. The president of our community, Mr. Feldman, has decided to redo the small hall in the memory of his mother. We need good furniture—a good capital renovation from beginning to end, and we need to spend a lot of money. We need a good marble floor and panels. We need to repaint the room and change the windows. . . . We will not change the ark. It must be restored. The bimah is old. We need to change it. We also need to change the pews. They and the bimah will be made out of beechwood. The pews will stand in the same place as they do today. We will have a new table and a new cabinet in which to put the prayer books and holy books.

The majority of the members of the *dvadtsatka* took offense at the suggestion of a complete restructuring, especially when it came to the pews. They saw the pews as having an intrinsic spiritual value that could never be replaced by what they saw as "cold and boring" Western pews. Natan, the assistant executive director, said:

If he [Feldman] wants to do a good deed, he should look at what actually is in need of being fixed here. As for those old pews, to get rid of them, to spend his money on making new pews. . . . These old pews are museum pieces. And we should throw them out to make a *Dom Kul'turi* [a Soviet House of Culture that aimed to replace religious organizations]? Do you know what that is? These pews have *dukhovnost'* [spirituality]. Our synagogue is more than one hundred years old, and it looks like a trash heap. People from America, from Israel, they want to see something pretty, like they have in their own countries. We do not have that here.

Lyonia agreed: "When churches are renovated, their old roofing tile is restored because it has historical worth. When you plan the renovation, don't think there is nothing here [to work with]. I suggest that before giving the small hall a new interior, we should invite those people who are skilled at making renovations [to look at our synagogue]. They can look at the small hall and make an estimate. Then we can compare costs."

Anton Rizovskii, the former executive director, summed up the opposition to the replacement of the old pews: "We have renovated our small hall several times. It is very beautiful. It is historic. And that which we see in the picture [he held up a picture of the newly proposed pews made of light-colored wood] is a cold, modern, boring, and tacky hall. I think that the correct way is the path of restoration. If we do it this way, we will remember what was, and Mr. Feldman will know that he did a good thing."

The majority of *dvadtsatka* members voted to look into restoring the pews and to meet again to discuss price estimates. They did not heed Rabbi Dubinovich when he warned, "Feldman has been kind enough to offer his money to redo the small hall, and it is not up to us to tell him what to do." For the members of the *dvadtsatka*, the pews represented more than just seats. Russian Jews believed that the pews, like moral Jews, had a "historic worth" and "spirituality" that could never be exchanged or bought by Westerners. The elderly Russian Jews thus repeatedly talked about the small hall in terms of its use value (Kopytoff 1986:69). The Western administration, on the other hand, conceptualized the small hall in terms of its exchange value. According to them, the small hall could, with the proper amount of money, be redone into a newer and "modern" room (Polyani 1997:180). By using a use-value argument, Russian Jews, like Yehuda in his discussion of the value of prayer books in the Soviet Union, attempted to resist the marketization of synagogue life.

At the second meeting of the *dvadtsatka* on June 28, Rabbi Silverstein announced that "the restoration of the pews would take up most of the money that would be needed to fix up the rest of the synagogue in the future." The majority of those in attendance were still not convinced. Shmuel Berl, one of the oldest members of the small hall *minyan*, stood up to say, "This is a synagogue. It is a synagogue and a historical monument that has colossal meaning for the Jews of Moscow and the former Soviet Union. We must preserve elements while adding new features. . . ." But he was cut off by more discussion about the options. Finally, Rabbi Silverstein placed two proposals before the board: restoration of the old pews or purchase of new ones.

At the first meeting, the majority of the board, especially the older Russian Jews, voted unanimously in favor of restoring the old pews. But this time, many came out vocally in favor of replacing them. Moshe said, "It will be for the best if it is cheaper. I suggest that we go for the best option. Thank you, our rabbi [and] President Feldman, for giving the money, for being generous." Shloimie agreed: "I am very glad that the rabbi said that we will build something better here. You want to make it new, well, why not? What is the difference if we sit on this pew or that pew? But if we do it better, well, everyone wants it to be better. I will vote for it to be better."

In the end, thirteen members voted to buy new pews and eight voted to restore the old ones. After the meeting, Yurii, Shloimie, and Moshe gathered in the small hall. Yurii was visibly upset by the board's decision. He confronted Shloimie: "I cannot believe that you voted to change the pews." Shloimie answered, "I changed my mind." "Just yesterday you voted the other way," Yurii said. "I can change," Shloimie retorted. "For twenty dollars, you can be sold," Yurii angrily stated, believing that Shloimie and Moshe sold their votes to Rabbi Silverstein. "Don't say such a thing!" Shloimie gasped, looking offended. Moshe walked up to shake Yurii's hand, saying, *"Zai gazunt!"* ("life to you" in Yiddish). Yurii refused to take his hand, mumbling, "I don't want to." Shloimie declared, "What you said about prostitution was not correct."

Yurii accused Shloimie and Moshe, like Rabbi Dubinovich, of prostituting their word to Rabbi Silverstein. Shloimie disagreed, implying that he and Moshe changed their minds out of their own convictions. But Yurii's refusal to shake Moshe's hand showed that he was convinced that they had taken money from Rabbi Silverstein and thus allied themselves with him. It seemed that once again Rabbi Silverstein, who represented Western materialism and capitalism, destabilized the relationship among Russian Jews, further disabling the Russian Jewish *minyan* in the small hall to resist his modernizing and monopolizing plans.

Anton Rizovskii told me several months later: "Now the community is too weak to throw out the rabbi. It is well known that the *dvadtsatka* can be bought. Give each man ten dollars, and he is happy to change his opinion." This statement articulated one of Yehuda's and Yurii's worst fears—that the Russian Jews were now too frail, both morally and physically, to stand up for themselves.

The End of Russian Jewish Sovereignty

Russian Jews were not angry at each other for very long, due to the small number of them in the morning *minyan*. Despite his readiness to accuse others of prostitution and thus position himself as an intellectual, Yurii admitted in his discussion of Rabbi Dubinovich that it was not always immoral for a person to give in to the lure of money. During the Soviet regime, intellectuals were forced to collaborate with the government, and "most chose to compromise not out of conviction but out of necessity, yielding to the survival instinct, citing the need to protect children, family" (Shalin 1996:72). When Yurii acknowledged the hardships of life in post-Soviet Moscow, his corruption narrative lost its powerful and moralizing sting. In this way, he was able to forgive Moshe and Shloimie, and he later tried to reestablish the bonds that were broken that day.

Despite Yurii's efforts, those two *dvadtsatka* meetings marked the beginning of the end of Russian Jewish sovereignty at the synagogue. The Russian Jewish *minyan* could not withstand the death of its elderly members and the influx of young and virile Jews from Moscow, the republics, and the West. Events at the Central Synagogue indicate how Soviet-style paternalism, redistribution, and spying practices are crucial to the consolidation of capitalist resources in post-Soviet Russia (Wedel 1998). However, Yurii and other Russian Jews at the Central Synagogue were not yet willing to admit defeat; they still struggled to hold on to their place—and space—in the synagogue.

Chapter 4
The Savage in the Jew

The Ashkenazim think that they are better and smarter [than us].
They think of themselves as having *belaia kozha* [white skin] and us
as having *chernaia kozha* [black skin].
—Kostia, the treasurer of the Mountain Jewish community

The Russian Jews were extremely concerned about the establishment
and growing influence of the *Gorskaia evreiskaia obshchina* (Mountain
Jewish community) at the Central Synagogue in 1995 and 1996. Even
though they harshly evaluated the Georgian Jews for their loud and
disruptive behavior and because "they do everything for money," Russian Jews nonetheless conceptualized Georgian Jews as part of the
Jewish people. In contrast, Russian Jews had a troublesome time ac-
cepting Mountain Jews as Jews. They expressed this difficulty through
a racializing discourse about Mountain Jews as *chernye*, dark-skinned
"traders from the Caucasus" who threatened the Moscow synagogue
community.

Russian Jews at the Central Synagogue used metaphors of race to
place Mountain Jews outside the Russian and Jewish nations, providing evidence that race is a modality in which class is experienced and
contested in contemporary Russia (Gilroy 1987:30). Mountain and
Russian Jews conflated class with race; they made value judgments
equating the morality or immorality of money and commerce with the
"natural" characteristics of both groups. These racializing narratives
embody socialist and post-socialist notions of order, further elucidating how Russian citizens draw on the Soviet past to deal with present
business practices and profits made by "foreigners" in Russia.

By the mid-1990s, many Mountain Jews lived in Moscow, having
left their homes in Azerbaijan, Dagestan, and Chechnya due to political unrest and economic hardship. Similar to other traders from the

Caucasus, Mountain Jews had traveled to Moscow throughout the Soviet period to sell their homegrown produce and other goods.[1] Although the selling of products outside the state's redistributive economy was outlawed, Soviet citizens got the goods they needed from the black market where Caucasian traders played a fundamental role. The legalization of the free market in the 1990s caused a huge growth in the number and type of economic transactions transpiring in Moscow, coalescing in the construction of large bazaars and expensive grocery stores. Mountain Jews, as well as other Caucasians, have taken advantage of this opportunity to work in kiosks or open up their own commercial enterprises. Although Russian and Mountain Jews engaged with one another in the marketplace, it was at the Central Synagogue that they were forced to interact with one another as fellow Jews.

The categorization of Russian and Mountain Jews into "whites" and "blacks" functioned at the synagogue like other systems of race that work to fix and naturalize the difference between belonging and being an outsider (Hall 1992:255). "Black" is thus synonymous with the exotic "other," and "white" with the civilized self. Because notions of race are always gendered, the danger of the "other" often becomes a sexual one—the black man seducing the white woman (Stoler 1989; Gilman 1991). Thus, whereas Russian Jews hardly ever mentioned Georgian Jewish sexuality outside of marriage and Georgian Jews were "ashamed" to discuss it in the synagogue setting, Russian Jews constantly talked about Mountain Jewish men's supposed lasciviousness. Being a female ethnographer of Ashkenazic Jewish descent was a central part of this portrayal, since my presence in an all-male community catalyzed and crystallized many statements concerning race, sexuality, and gender. For example, Russian Jews at the synagogue continuously warned me how Mountain Jews are a *dikii narod* ("wild people," both savage and barbarous) like Chechens and other peoples from the Caucasus. Russian Jews also made the following statements to me about Mountain Jews: "They are all *chernye* and will cheat you on prices"; "They are *chernye*, [so] we don't associate with them"; "They are a *temnyi narod*" (a "dark" and "stupid" people); "They are *khitrye*" ("cunning"); they have "that certain Eastern mentality, cheating and dealing with goods, because that's the way they live"; "Their women are oppressed like in Asia"; and "They are from the Stone Age." These descriptions formed what Kwame Anthony Appiah calls "a sort of racial essence" (Appiah 1990:4–5); each trait—black, stupid, cunning, savage, barbarous—metonymically invoked the "other." They formed a set of inheritable characteristics and tendencies that Mountain Jews theoretically shared as members of the same race.

This racializing discourse permeated interactions between Russian and Mountain Jews, revealing a deeper layer to the issue of Russian citizenship. I was struck early on in my fieldwork by the fact that Mountain Jews accepted the notion that they were "blacks." They redefined the term to indicate how their savage capitalist nature made them better Jews—and better citizens of the new Russia—than the Russian Jews. I also noticed that, although Mountain Jews described the Russian Jews as "whites," Russian Jews themselves never used that term. Instead, they labeled themselves as "intellectuals," "civilized," and "cultured" in order to separate themselves from Mountain Jews, assimilate into Russian culture, and claim their place as part of the Jewish people.

That both groups wanted to be an influential part of Russian society is a product of the modern and global Jewish condition. The aspiration of Jews to blend into the dominant culture has been a common theme in post-Enlightenment history. In the 1880s, German Jews, living in Germany, which then advocated the values of rationalism and humanism, adamantly defined themselves as modern and civilized in opposition to newly arrived "traditional" immigrant Russian Jews (Aschheim 1982).[2] And American Jews since the 1950s have asserted their whiteness (and have been accepted as white) in a society which privileges whiteness (Roediger 1991; Brodkin 1998).

Russian and Mountain Jews also used two transnational, but contradictory, metaphors about Jewish nationhood and belonging. Since the Enlightenment, Jews have maintained that they are both "People of the Body" and "People of the Book" (Eilberg-Schwartz 1992). The former metaphor advocates the talmudic notion that Jewishness is transmitted through physical reproduction—Jewish mothers produce Jewish babies. The latter ascribes to the ideal that the Jewish nation is something separated from bodily desire. As Howard Eilberg-Schwartz writes, "In the modern period, the majority of Jews came to regard various parts of Judaism, particularly those having to do with the body and sexuality, as primitive and disgusting. These sorts of feelings and judgments partially explain why Jews have been so enthralled with the designation 'People of the Book' in the post-Enlightenment period" (Eilberg-Schwartz 1992:3).

These metaphors inform two essential issues about being Jewish in the former Soviet Union and the Jewish diaspora at large. The first investigates how post-Soviet Jews can substantiate their claims to be one people when they use at least two contradictory notions of national belonging. The second explores what happens to Jewish identity when membership in the Jewish nation hinges on being a full Russian citizen.

A Short History of Mountain Jews

The majority of Mountain Jews have lived in Azerbaijan, Chechnya, and the Dagestan republic of Russia. Their traditional language is Judeo-Tat, a mix of Hebrew and Farsi, and the main population centers in Azerbaijan were Baku (the capital) and Kuba.[3] In Dagestan and Chechnya, the largest populations were located in the cities of Derbent, Makhachkala, Nal'chik, and Grozny.

Like Georgian Jews, Mountain Jews claim to be descendants of those Jews captured by Assyrians and Babylonians in 722 B.C.E. and 589 B.C.E. respectively. However, there are three different versions of this legend. One states that in 387 B.C.E., Persian monarchs obtained the area of the Caucasus. As a result, Jews living in Media (Persia) were sent to the territory of modern-day Azerbaijan and southern Dagestan. Another variation of this legend has the Jews moving into the Caucasus only in the fifth century, to escape persecution (Murzakhanov 1994). A third narrative asserts that some Mountain Jews descended from the Khazars, a group of converts to Judaism who ruled the area known today as Dagestan and Azerbaijan from the mid-seventh century until the end of the tenth century, when they were conquered by Muslims.

According to historical record, the Mountain Jewish population grew and prospered in the seventeenth and eighteenth centuries, maintaining their own vineyards, growing madder and tobacco, and engaging in handicrafts. They lived in large extended families, and it was not uncommon to find Mountain Jewish men with more than one wife. Mountain Tats had problematic relations with their Muslim neighbors; Mountain Jewish folktales chronicle drawn-out vendettas between Jewish and Muslim families involving frequent murders of men in each group. These tales also highlight how Mountain Jewish heroes saved their villages from bloody destruction and forced conversion by the local Muslims (Kukullu 1995). Mountain Jewish men were known to carry long knives and, in later times, guns strapped to their waists as well as rows of bullets crisscrossed over their chests and backs. These stories help explain the existence of a warrior tradition among Mountain Jewish men.

From 1813 to 1828, Mountain Jews came under Russian rule. They established contact with European Jews, and some Mountain Jews sent their sons to study in Russian and Lithuanian yeshivas to become ritual slaughterers. When they returned home, these men served as rabbis in their communities due to the lack of local religious experts. Mountain Jews continued to cultivate grapes and tobacco, and they also engaged in petty trade.

The Bolsheviks took over Dagestan and Azerbaijan in the early 1920s. In accordance with the Soviet Union's "eastern politics," the state sponsored schools to teach Mountain Jews in Hebrew and Judeo-Tat, and it established Soviet youth clubs and magazines to develop Mountain Jewish literature and drama. The state also set up Mountain Jewish communal farms, although this endeavor was unsuccessful. After World War II, however, the government cracked down on Mountain Jewish culture, outlawing all teaching and literature in Judeo-Tat. Increased urbanization and education of Mountain Jews after the war made Russian and Azeri the primary languages among more Mountain Jews, adding to the destabilization of Mountain Jewish ethnic practices.

The ban on Judeo-Tat corresponded to the Soviet state categorization of the Mountain Jews as members of the larger indigenous Tat population of the Caucasus. According to the Soviet social scientist R. M. Magomedov, the Soviet authorities used the term "Tat" to refer to "the dispersed inhabitants of the Caucasus, the small ethnic groups who speak one language—Tat (with small dialectical differences)—that is related to the Iranian [Persian] language group" (Magomedov 1994:157). The groups included in the Tat population had different religious traditions (Islam, Judaism, and Armenian-Gregorian) that they abandoned for socialism. By calling the Mountain Jews Tats, the Soviet state denied the Mountain Jews' religious heritage and supported the idea that they had "lost" many Jewish rituals and knowledge about Judaism because of their intermingling with other mountain peoples (Magomedov 1994:157). The Mountain Jewish writer Amaldan Kukullu told me that being a member of the small Tat nationality allowed him to publish his books as long as he did not mention his people's Jewish traditions and beliefs.

In the 1970s, over ten thousand Mountain Jews (about one-quarter of the population) emigrated to Israel (Gitelman 1988:318). Mountain Jews continued to leave, especially in the 1990s because of the war between Armenia and Azerbaijan, and the conflicts between Russia and Chechnya. In 1995, the Jewish population (of both Ashkenazim and Mountain Jews) was thirty thousand in Azerbaijan and fifty-six thousand in Dagestan (Institute of the World Jewish Congress 1996).[4]

The Mountain Jewish Community and "Immoral" Commerce

Shalom Simanduev, the head of the Mountain Jewish community, gave me one of my first lessons about how Russian Jews used racial metaphors to describe Mountain Jews. It was a cold morning in December, and he sat in his prayer hall dressed in a fur hat and coat, with a scarf bundled over his Western-style suit and tie. His legs were sprawled out in front of him. He looked exhausted. He was in his mid-fifties, but he looked older than his age due to tired eyes and bad teeth. For several months now, he had been frantically renovating a large storage space at the end of the hallway leading into the *Gorskaia evreiskaia obshchina*. He wanted to accommodate the growing number of Mountain Jewish migrants coming to the capital; he himself was originally from Kuba, a large Jewish town in northeastern Azerbaijan. While Mountain Jews held services in their own room in the Central Synagogue on Shabbat, holidays, and special occasions (like bar mitzvahs), they, like Georgian and Bukharan Jews, did not have enough men to make a *minyan* there on weekdays, and thus prayed in the small hall. After services, several Mountain Jews always sat with Shalom in their community space to drink tea and chat.

In the first two months of fieldwork, Shalom had been reluctant to talk with me, so I rarely visited the Mountain Jewish prayer hall. This morning, however, Evgenii Moiseivich invited me to have tea with Shalom. I thought this would be the perfect time to talk with Shalom about his work.

"Can I interview you?" I asked eagerly. "You will know all you need to know about us *postepenno* [little by little]," he said, seemingly uninterested in talking with me. After a small period of silence, I tried a different approach. "How do the Mountain Jews differ from the Georgian, Russian, and Bukharan Jews who come to the synagogue?" I asked. "The Mountain Jews are *negramotnye i shumnye* [illiterate and loud]," he said. "Really, is that true?" I asked. "That is what they say about us and it is true. *My zanimaemsia biznesom* [We are involved in business]. We sell in the markets." He yelled "La kha la la la la!" to demonstrate how the Mountain Jews loudly hocked their wares in the market. "But the Georgian Jews sell goods too," I said. "Sure, but the Russian and Bukharan Jews are educated. They have stopped dealing in business."

Shalom pointed out (perhaps with a bit of sarcasm) how Russian Jews conceptualized Mountain Jewish market practices as the expression of Mountain Jews' "blackness." For example, when I asked Lyonia about the relations among Russian and Mountain Jews, he said:

Russians do not like the Caucasians because of the way they act and their different mentality. Ask any Russian, and he will tell you that Caucasians are insolent and impudent. They are like that because they mainly deal in trade here. They annoy everyone with their accent. Russians fear Caucasians because Caucasians are not able to stick up for themselves, so they are always walking around in small groups. If a Caucasian man is alone, he will try to prove his own worth. [As for the Russian Jews,] the farther they are from the Jewish traditions, the closer they are to the Russian mentality and the worse they will relate to the Mountain Jews.

And yet, even though he professed to be a religious Jew, Lyonia had commented to me on another occasion that the Mountain Jews are a *dikii narod* (wild people). Russian Jews called Mountain Jews uncivilized, uneducated, and lazy behind their backs, as well as to their faces. I remember one morning in particular when Shalom, Kostia, and Sergei (a Mountain Jewish friend of Kostia's in his mid-thirties) sat around the table discussing politics. Maria Abramovna, an elderly Russian Jewish woman who worked at the synagogue, came into the room. Upon seeing the steaming glasses of tea, the round silver tin of sugar cubes, and the plate of candies on the table, she said, "The Mountain Jews have it so rich in here. They wag their tongues half the time and work the other half."

The comments made by Maria Abramovna and Lyonia exemplify many Russian Jewish narratives concerning the "immoral" market and its "lazy" workers; they also show how Russian Jews talked about Mountain Jews as bringing their "uncivilized" nature and dangerous practices into the synagogue. Russian Jews viewed the Mountain Jewish prayer hall as embodying the character of the marketplace and its workers. Throughout my stay in Moscow, Russian Jews warned me to be careful not to get cheated on prices when I shopped *na rynke* (at the market). One woman I knew even brought her own scale to the market to weigh produce because she did not trust the vendors.

In Soviet times, the market was confined to a hierarchical state system of food stores; but the collapse of the Soviet Union dismantled the state's food distribution system, making all goods available to those who had money. Muscovites said that a market mentality had influenced and taken control of all sectors of society, and many felt disoriented and overwhelmed because they envisioned business as having a corrupting influence on society. Correspondingly, by talking about Mountain Jews as traders, Russian Jews attempted to isolate them from the synagogue, a process similar to diagnosing and containing a polluting object. Russian Jews tried to curb the influence of the new economy on synagogue affairs and reestablish the Soviet order of the separation between the market and everyday life. As part of their organizing, Russian Jews made a dichotomy between moral and immoral, order and disorder, synagogue and market, and Russian Jew and Mountain Jew. As Mary Douglas comments, "It is only by exaggerating the difference between within and without, above and below, male and female, with and against, that a semblance of order is created" (Douglas 1970:15).

In relation to the stories of prostitution, Jewish greed, and eating *na khaliavu*, Russian Jews commonly referred to money as contaminating and dirty—a substance that leads to immoral and illegal activities. For instance, many Russian Jews were upset on the holiday of Yom Kippur when Rabbi Silverstein decided to sell off the privilege to be called up to the Torah. Maiia, a middle-aged Russian Jewish woman, explained to me, "For us, money is dirt. This is a prayer service, not some kind of business arrangement." Angrily, she asserted that no Russian Jew could afford to buy this honor and that Mountain Jews probably obtained their money illegally through mafia and business contacts. "They probably lose more than this sum of money at the casino," she complained, "but for us Russian Jews, this sum of money is a lot."

Mary Douglas writes that "dirt offends against order," and by getting rid of dirt, people reorder their environment, making it conform to an idea (Douglas 1970:12). By describing money as "dirt," Maiia expressed her growing anxieties over the emerging class differences and the devaluation of Russian Jewish intellectual capital. Like Yehuda, she stated her disapproval of the service, hoping it would instead conform to her image of what synagogue activities should be, namely spiritual and ethical. This drew on a Soviet notion that market transactions had no place in the synagogue, since they were "illegal." Maiia reasserted the morality of Russian Jews who, in her opinion, rarely handled large amounts of money.

By differentiating themselves from Jews who dealt in "trade," Russian Jews produced a Jewish spatial topography reminiscent of their small hall maneuvers in which "moral" Russian Jews belonged in the "spiritual" Central Synagogue and Mountain Jewish "businessmen" belonged in "immoral" marketplaces. This process is similar to the one employed by the newly propertied middle class in nineteenth-century Europe which positioned its bourgeois identity in opposition to its imaginings of "exotic" fairs and markets teeming with the lower classes and petty traders (Stallybrass and White 1986). Creating a Russian Jewish identity against the market was not complete without the casting of Mountain Jews as the Jewish trader, who, in Russian folklore, served as the antithesis of Russian spirituality and communality. In this way, Russian Jews forged an image of themselves as more moral and civilized than Mountain Jews, who supposedly exhibited the Jewish "national characteristics" of greed and dishonest business.

The Jewish tradesman is one of the most popular anti-Semitic images in Russian folklore; he is a foreigner whose greed and stinginess threatens to undermine Russian society (Dreizin 1990:3). Recently, Russian nationalist discourse has expanded the stereotype of the "tradesman" to include the growing number of people from the Caucasus who sell food and merchandise in Russia. Russians have considered these *chernye* as the reason for Russia's economic and social problems. This view was so pervasive that in October 1993 the mayor of Moscow, Yurii Luzhkov, implemented a state of emergency to expel from the city several thousand Armenian, Georgian, and Azeri traders who did not have residence permits (Humphrey 1995:53). One Russian Jewish friend of mine, in his early thirties, explained this phenomenon to me:

[Anti-Semitism] has decreased because there is a large quantity of other social issues. [In the past,] people needed to have an enemy, and they saw it in the Jews. Now look, for the businessmen, it is the bureaucrats. For the bureaucrats, it is all higher bureaucrats, isn't it so? For the small merchant, it is the bandits, and for the bandits, it is the *menti* [policemen], and for the *menti*, the enemies are the other *menti*. At the same time, the government is the enemy of all these groups. But, most of all, the Caucasian is every Muscovite's enemy. I know many people who relate very sympathetically to Jews in those levels of society where earlier one would have found many anti-Semites.[5]

The presence of Caucasians in the marketplace has provided a new stereotype of "tradesman." He is *chernyi*, a member of the mafia, rich, and prone to cheat customers.

Russian Jews distanced themselves from the anti-Semitic image of the *Jewish* businessman by making him into a *Caucasian*. This casting of the Mountain Jew allowed Russian Jews to separate themselves from negative stereotypes and to accentuate what they saw as their more positive—Russian—characteristics. In this way, Russian Jews claimed to be the real soulful citizens of Russia and the rightful occupants of the Central Synagogue. I heard Russian Jews repeatedly describe themselves as "Europeans," "intellectuals," "assimilated—low in religion and yet high in culture [*kul'tura*]," "rich in soul and poor in money." Irina told me, "Russian Jews carry Russian culture all over the world. But they lost their national distinctiveness because of assimilation. Mountain Jews [on the other hand] are poor and wild. They lived in the mountains away from civilization. They are from the country. In Baku, they did not get an education, and if they did, it was not a good one. It was easier for them to preserve their national distinctiveness."

Through such narratives, Russian Jews denied their negative Jewish "national distinctiveness" of greed and business as portrayed in Russian folklore. By conceptualizing these traits as embodied in the "black" skin of Mountain Jews, Russian Jews produced an image of themselves at that moment as more "Russian" than "Jewish." At the same time, the emphasis that Russian Jews placed on their intellect provided a model for a positive Jewish identity, an identity that corresponded to the international image of Jews as People of the Book, a highly cultured and educated elite separated from bodily desire. In this way, Russian Jews maintained that they were more Jewish than the "savage" Mountain Jews. Russian Jews did not see a paradox in saying they were Jewish and Russian at the same time; instead, they viewed themselves as having the best characteristics of both peoples.

Russian Jews highlighted their intellectual nature by telling stories about the allegedly brutal sexual habits of Mountain Jewish men, namely, how they cheated on, mistreated, and abused their women. Russian Jews cited Mountain Jewish men's sexual nature to mark them as racially other. Russian Jews worried about my physical safety, describing the way that Mountain Jewish men, like all Caucasian males, slit the throats of women who disobeyed them. One Russian Jewish woman even warned me against being friendly with Sergei, Kostia's friend, since she thought that he would kidnap me for ransom money and then kill me. I heard similar accounts in the Russian media about Muslim Chechens' kidnapping Russians during the war in Chechnya.

Mountain Jewish men did not directly challenge this portrayal of themselves as overly sexual businessmen. They did contest, however, the cultural values associated with their sexuality and market practices. Instead of focusing on the "immoral" aspect of the market, Mountain Jews stressed how the market was a male space, thus redefining the meaning of their blackness. They said the market was too dangerous and wild for women. Concomitantly, Mountain Jews insisted that their prayer hall was no place for a woman, and, if she should enter, she would have to be more modest than in any other place in the synagogue so as to not inflame the "animal" passions of Mountain Jewish men.

The Savage Marketplace and Prayer Hall

In June 1996, Sergei took me to visit several of his relatives who worked at *Ismailovskaia iarmarka* (Ismailovskaia fair), a large clothing and houseware market in the northeast end of Moscow. Sergei had begun frequenting the Mountain Jewish community at the synagogue a month earlier. He and Kostia had been childhood friends in Baku, and he, like many other Mountain Jews, had come to Moscow seeking a better life. Tall and slim, he looked elegant in his black sports coat and pants. Unlike Shalom or Kostia, who always seemed too busy to talk with me, Sergei took an instant interest in me. He wanted to know

Figure 4. Mountan Jewish merchants at the market, 1996. (Photo by author)

about life in America, and he was the first Mountain Jew to introduce me to his family and friends.

The fair surrounded a large and round stadium at the top of a hill. To get to it, we walked along a muddy pathway and up a flight of steps. After we circled the large stadium, we walked into a narrow alleyway where Caucasian men were selling a variety of items. We were quickly swallowed up by a river of moving people. Sergei looked back at me and told me to hold on to him, so that I would not get lost. Jokingly, I grabbed onto his sleeve but soon let go. The alleyways between the kiosks seemed to open up spontaneously, giving the whole market a maze-like quality. When we reached what seemed to be the center of the area, Sergei headed for a large tube that was lying on the ground to our left. It looked to be about twenty feet high. As we got closer, I saw that inside, along the walls, were rows of stalls. He said that his cousin worked on the other side of the tube. We walked into the blackness.

Later, I told Aleksandr Elizarovich, a forty-five-year-old Mountain Jewish entrepreneur from Baku and a main sponsor of the Mountain Jewish community at the Central Synagogue, that I had visited the *Is-mailovskaia iarmarka*. He commented that I was certainly "very brave" to have gone there. "It is wild. It goes on forever, " he said.

This "wildness" of the market marked it as a man's domain. While Sergei and I sat on large bags of clothes in his cousin's kiosk, I noticed that all of the Mountain Jews who worked at the market were men, although I did see several Russian women selling items there. I asked Sergei if Mountain Jewish women also worked in the market-place. "Women?" he asked, taking a drag from his cigarette, "No. They stay home with the family. That is their job. If they go to work, who will look after the young children and the old parents and grand-parents? No. We have a more Eastern culture. The Russian Jews are more European than we are. We Mountain Jews are poor Jews. The Russian Jews were surrounded by educated Europeans, so they themselves got educations and are smart. We Mountain Jews were surrounded by animals and so we stayed like animals. We don't have higher educations."

Sergei's statement mirrors what Irina said about Jews picking up the culture of their surroundings. Sergei blamed the "Eastern" men-tality of the Muslim population in Azerbaijan and Dagestan for the "animal"-like ways of Mountain Jews. He believed that Mountain Jews treated their women poorly because of this "savage mentality."

Making adequate money has been the mark of a Mountain Jewish man's strength and capacity, as well as his sexuality. When Mountain Jewish men traveled to sell items, many had affairs on the road. I once asked Anna, a widowed Mountain Jewish woman in her thirties, if Mountain Jewish men cheated on their wives. She said, "It is a 100 per-cent probability that they will have affairs. This is so because Mountain Jewish men travel a lot for their work. They live in hotels." She told me that her husband had had an affair and that she found out about it only after his death.

While it is a man's job to earn enough money to attract a wife and to support her after the marriage, a woman, on the other hand, has to be highly guarded by her family until marriage. In the past, the parents would find a bride for their son (Murzakhanov 1994:28). This practice still continues, although now young men and women have the option of declining the offer (Murzakhanov 1994:38). The overprotection of young women has been one of the reasons for the practice of *brak ukhoda* (wife stealing), in which a young man kidnaps a woman so they can marry despite her parents' disapproval. Once he has sex with her, her parents have to recognize the marriage. I met several Mountain Jewish women who had been kidnapped with their consent. Tales of wife stealing and on-the-road affairs paint a picture of Mountain Jewish men as savage and dangerous. Accordingly, both Mountain Jewish men and women alike stressed how young marriageable girls had to be protected and guarded at home.

Shalom used these Mountain Jewish discourses and practices about the separation of the sexes in the market, home, and Orthodox synagogue to construct his community in Moscow. He founded it so that Mountain Jewish men who migrated to work in the city's kiosks and markets would not lose touch with their heritage. Kostia told me:

> Half of the families of the Mountain Jews who work here [in Moscow] are in Israel, Baku, Kuba, and Derbent. They are dispersed. And therefore, they [the men] live a sort of bachelor life here. They are torn away from their families. And [because of] that, we need a place for religious life, so even if the people are torn away from their families, they will not be torn away from their roots. And that can only be done here [at the Central Synagogue], so that they remember and feel that they are not alone, that they are not dispersed, that they are not lost. So they have somewhere to come if it is hard for them, even [if it is] morally hard. They can come here to remember their fathers who died. They have nowhere else to go [for that].

By building the Mountain Jewish community at the Central Synagogue, Shalom tried to move Mountain Jewish culture from the family into the synagogue. This was a great challenge for two reasons. First, the majority of Mountain Jewish men do not know much about the format of Jewish prayer, nor can they read Hebrew, although this is changing rapidly due to the increase in Jewish education of young boys in Moscow.[6] Second, although it incorporates some elements of Jewish tradition, Mountain Jewish culture has been, as Aleksandr Elizarovich once said, "family oriented. The family keeps Mountain Jewish culture alive." Boris Semyonovich, a Mountain Jew from Baku visiting Moscow, commented, "Religion is in the family. We study Torah and praise God under one roof. The most valuable treasure is children. The Mountain Jews are against abortion. As many children as God gives. You ask Shalom. He will tell you that in Kuba there are families with ten to fifteen children. The health of the mother and children is the most important thing in the family."

In his effort to bring Mountain Jewish culture to the synagogue, Shalom drew less on the knowledge of the sacred texts and more on spatial and symbolic means to attract Mountain Jewish men. Synagogues in Azerbaijan and Dagestan had one large room illuminated with windows, a floor covered with rugs, and an ark on the western wall, as opposed to the eastern wall of the Ashkenazic and European synagogues (Anisimov 1888:68–69). One of the most important aspects of the traditional Mountain Jewish synagogue was that it did not have a women's section. In 1888, the ethnographer Ilya Anisimov wrote on his trip to Dagestan: "Women are not allowed into the synagogue, and not even one of them can read the prayers. Several of the God-fearing old women come up to the front part of the synagogue during Shabbat and the major holidays to stand at the window or at the door of the synagogue, in order to see the sermon and hear the service" (Anisimov 1888:69). Some Mountain Jewish men continued to believe in this concept, and they told me to stand on the street outside the synagogue even after religious services were finished.

I visited Aleksandr Elizarovich, a sworn bachelor, at his apartment for dinner during the Passover holiday. Like at his place of business, Aleksandr was dressed in a suit and tie. His girlfriend, a Russian woman named Lena whom he had been dating for several weeks, had prepared the meal. While she was getting the food ready to be served, Aleksandr gave me a tour of his one-room apartment. He was especially proud of the bowls he had brought back from Azerbaijan. They were made out of iron and quite heavy. On the same shelf was a stone mortar and pestle that his grandmother had used to grind spices.

A small table stood in the corner set with plates of chicken, cabbage salad, marinated and fried mushrooms, whole tomatoes and cucumbers, and matzah. Most of his walls held bookshelves, and two ram horns hung behind his bed. In the hallway to the bathroom and kitchen, there was a picture of a scantily dressed woman, which I could see from my seat at the table.

After eating some of the first course, Lena went into the kitchen to bring out the turkey. She returned several seconds later, telling us that we would not be having a second course because she burned it. Aleksandr said to her, "I told you that I thought something smelled like it was burning when we came in." She responded, "No, it was still cooking then. Your oven does not have one of those timer things." "See?" he turned to me, "See how modern-day women cannot live without such devices?" He turned to Lena. "Imagine. My grandmother cooked all day in those pots [he pointed to the pots on the shelf] and the food tasted great. Civilization is not always progress." He laughed slightly, but he had a serious and depressed look on his face.

Aleksandr liked to reminisce about his childhood in Baku, and as he cut up the cucumbers and tomatoes, he told us stories about his family. "On Passover, my grandfather used to drink wine out of a ram's horn. Do you know why? Because you cannot put down the horn until you have finished the wine or the wine will spill out on the table." He went on to say:

> I remember Passover at my house. We would all sit around the table, and we could not eat until my grandfather sat down. Then, my grandmother would come around with one of those big pots and put meat on everyone's plate. She served my grandfather last. Then, she would take pieces of meat off his plate and put it on mine or someone else's. At first, I felt sorry for my grandparents that they did not have enough meat to feed everyone. But then, I realized that they believed that it was harmful for an old man to eat meat since he would get too tired to work. But young men need meat. It gives them energy.

I asked Aleksandr if only men sat at the table, and he said that was so. "Where were the women?" I wanted to know. "They waited until the men ate, reset the table, and then ate," he said. Lena mumbled sarcastically, "That's a woman's right." From reading ethnographies of Mountain Jews, I knew that the separation of women and men during the meal was a sign of a woman's modesty and respect for her male in-laws. The same could apply to prayer. I said, "I really want to see a service in the Mountain Jewish community, but I cannot because there is no place for women." "Correct, men and women do not pray to-gether." Lena shook her head in disbelief.

Middle-aged men like Aleksandr waxed nostalgic over home and synagogue etiquette, and the older men attempted to keep these tra-ditional practices going. Thus, although Kostia and Sergei tended not to follow these customs, Shalom always sided with the more estab-lished and respected men in his community. It was not surprising then, that my presence in the Mountain Jewish prayer hall caused much controversy from both Mountain and Russian Jewish men. Most Mountain Jewish men saw my socializing with them as a sign of my immorality, while Russian Jewish men worried about my safety. In this context, Mountain Jews demarcated their space as separate from the rest of the synagogue by demanding overtly modest behavior from all the women who entered their sanctuary.

By the summer of 1996, Sergei's hospitality toward me in the Mountain Jewish prayer hall had convinced Shalom and Kostia that it was acceptable to talk with me. Every morning after I attended a prayer service, Kostia invited me to sit with him and drink tea. In fact, Kostia and Sergei were so used to my presence in the Mountain Jewish prayer hall that they no longer saw me as a guest but as a regular part of the daily routine. However, not all of the Mountain Jews had the same point of view. This difference of opinion turned into an argument.

One morning in July, Sergei invited me into the Mountain Jewish community to have tea after services. When I walked in, an older Mountain Jewish man named Gavriel sat at the table. After I poured myself some tea, Gavriel looked at me and said, "Put a scarf on your head." I said, "Well, services are over." "I know the law. Put something on your head." I answered, "I am not married, and therefore, according to Jewish law, I do not have to do so."[7] He got extremely angry and said, "All women have to. I know the law." I was not sure what to do. Kostia kept silent, but Sergei said that Gavriel was wrong. Gavriel exclaimed, "I know the law, and she has to wear something on her head. Who are you to say she does not?" "I am a member of the community!" Sergei yelled, standing up. Gavriel yelled back, "There is no leadership here!" Sergei walked over to Tzvi, a Georgian Jew who had just entered the room, and explained the situation to him. Tzvi agreed with Sergei. Gavriel voiced his dissent again, and someone suggested asking Khakham Eliahu, a Georgian rabbi who was leading the prayer services for the Mountain Jews until they could hire their own rabbi. He came in and agreed with Tzvi. Sergei yelled at Gavriel triumphantly, "How dare you think that you have some kind of higher authority here!"

On one level, the argument between Sergei and Gavriel was a generational and regional dispute. Gavriel was in his sixties and lived most of his life in Derbent, a city in Dagestan. His view that a woman should cover her hair was probably extrapolated from Mountain Jewish custom that a woman, when engaged, must be extremely formal in front of her potential in-laws. She "must not walk around without her head covered, without stockings, and with her arms and legs uncovered" (Murzakhanov 1996:30). Sergei, on the other hand, was raised in Baku, spoke fluent Russian, and spent much time traveling around the Soviet Union. In addition, he was more interested in what Jewish law (the Torah and talmud) had to say than in what Mountain Jewish tradition might be. According to Jewish law, a married woman should cover her hair for at least three reasons: because a married woman should not make herself attractive to anyone else besides her husband, as a sign of dignity, and because of the belief that exposed hair is a sign of licentiousness (Greenberg 1983:187).[8] Sergei's attitude toward the issue of a woman's head covering corresponded to the growing influence of religious dogma on Jews in Moscow. The majority of Western and Israeli-sponsored Jewish schools in Moscow stressed learning talmudic law as the way to become a "real" Jew (as opposed to an assimilated Jew under the Soviet regime). The tension between Gavriel and Sergei was whether to base proper behavior on Mountain Jewish traditions or on Jewish law as interpreted by Ashkenazic Orthodox Jews. On another level, by stating that I had to wear something on my head, Gavriel turned what Russian Jews labeled an oppressive and Asian attitude toward women into a proclamation of how Mountain Jews maintained a higher degree of religious practice than Russian Jews.

By August, every time he saw me in the synagogue, Shalom said, "Bring a scarf [to put on your head] when you come [to the Mountain Jewish community]." He said that Gavriel complained to him, stating that he (Shalom) had set up a "hotel" in the synagogue, because I was always present in the Mountain Jewish prayer hall. Gavriel was thus questioning my integrity, since it was common knowledge in Moscow that single women who hung around hotels were prostitutes. He said that Shalom was "holding meetings, eating food, and socializing with women," and that he had thus corrupted what Gavriel saw as the high moral standards of Mountain Jews, namely their separation of the sexes. I decided to bring a hat with me to the synagogue and to wear it whenever I spent time in the Mountain Jewish prayer hall.

Unfortunately, one day in late August, Shalom caught me bareheaded as I crossed the threshold into the Mountain Jewish community. He yelled out to me, "I beg you, please put something on your head!" I said, "I have it with me. I am putting it on now. See?" I reached into my bag, grabbed my hat, and quickly placed it on my head. Sergei repeated his opinion to Shalom that I was not married, and therefore I did not have to wear a hat. For that whole day, I felt restless. I kept putting my hat on and taking it off, depending on where I was in the synagogue. When Shalom left, Sergei and Kostia insisted that I did not have to wear a hat, but I kept it on anyway, and, from that point until the end of my fieldwork in November 1996, I wore it every time I came to the synagogue.

Despite their disagreement with Gavriel, Sergei and Kostia repeatedly said that their strict customs about female modesty and the separation of the sexes made them more Jewish than Russian Jews. When Kostia said that the Ashkenazim think of themselves as white, Sergei agreed, commenting, "The Ashkenazim think they have a better way of life than Mountain Jews here. . . . [But] Mountain Jews are more traditional than the Ashkenazim." "Right," Kostia said, "We [Mountain Jews] preserved. . . . We are more conservative . . . in relation to women [and] in relation to Jews."

Kostia and Sergei challenged the sites of discourse that marked them as low by reversing the symbolic hierarchy of Russian Jew over Mountain Jew. According to many Mountain Jews, their "conservative" nature in relation to women and other Jews made them more Jewish than Russian Jews; it made them the true People of the Body. Mountain Jews viewed what Russian Jews called the "oppression of women"— the separation of the sexes and rules about extreme modesty—as comprising legitimate Jewish bodily practices. Kostia said that, because they lived in the mountains, Mountain Jews were able to maintain the real Jewish relations among men and women. He said, "the community of Mountain Jews in the Caucasus is the most ancient community of all the communities of the world." Mountain Jews frequently stated that they had forgotten some Jewish traditions due to their isolation, but they insisted that "we are still Jews" and cited their "traditional" attitudes as proof.

Genetics also plays an integral part in this story about Mountain Jewish heritage. As Aleksandr Elizarovich told me during our Passover dinner:

Mountain Jews are very reserved people. But, I think that they are the most interesting out of all the Jews. Mountain Jews are very colorful. They have absorbed some of the culture and traits of the Azeris. We even look sort of like them. You know, there were some local peoples who converted to Judaism, and therefore there was intermarriage. But, there is still a Jewish feature in every Mountain Jew. We have kept that, and some Mountain Jews look like they have stepped out of the Bible. Russian Jews were not told about their heritage when they were growing up. It was kept from them. Mountain Jews were taught to be proud of being Jewish. Every young man wore a large, gold Star of David on a chain around his neck.

He pulled out his gold-star necklace from under his shirt and placed it over his tie. "We showed everyone that we are proud."

The many Mountain Jews who left their homes for Moscow faced the threat of becoming assimilated into Russian culture. As Aleksandr Elizarovich said, they had come "down from the mountains into civilization." With their prayer hall, the Mountain Jewish community at the Central Synagogue was able to reach out to other Mountain Jews in the city who might not otherwise have kept up, or even been aware of, their religious traditions. Kostia and Aleksandr Elizarovich felt that they had a mission to educate all Jews about the unique culture of Mountain Jews.[9] Kostia specifically told me that, since being the treasurer of the Mountain Jewish community, "I have more understanding . . . that the history of our people, of our community, of our Mountain Jews . . . has much value. There will come a time when the world will find out and hear a lot of important things about the Mountain Jews. . . . Mountain Jews are one of the most important elements in the history of the Jewish people."

Not only did Mountain Jews redefine their "uncivilized nature" to assert their membership in the Jewish nation, but they also stated that their "savageness" made them good Russian citizens. Mountain Jews were proud of their so-called innate ability to be shrewd businessmen, and they said that this characteristic gave them superiority over Russian Jews. As Aleksandr Elizarovich told me, "Russian Jews are intellectuals. They don't know how to do business. The Georgian Jews were also intellectuals. The Georgians let the Jews occupy high positions in society. But in Azerbaijan and Dagestan, the Jews could only make their living by trade. That is why we are so skilled at it today." In a symbolic reversal of hierarchies, Mountain Jews said that, because of their "animal"-like upbringing, they were more equipped than the Russian Jews to take advantage of Russia's new market economy.

And yet, there were times when the Mountain Jewish community provided a space for Mountain, Russian, and even Georgian Jews to come together equally as Jews. With a constant supply of hot tea for visitors and a refrigerator tucked away in the back of the room, this prayer hall attracted other Jews who wanted to sit and chat for a while after prayer. Particularly in conversations over vodka and snacks, Russian, Georgian, and Mountain Jews told stories about their sexual liaisons with women (see Limón 1989:478). These narratives broke down the boundaries between the "intellectual" Russian Jewish man and the "savage" Mountain Jewish man, allowing both to traverse race and class lines that otherwise seemed unbridgeable. These times also provided the space for Georgian Jews to discuss their sexual desires within the synagogue context without a sense of shame. The men naturalized their male gender and sexuality as the impetus for their shared "Jewish" behavior. Instances like these built the Jewish nation on top of and through women's bodies (Biale 1997).

A Vodka-Drinking Episode

The Mountain Jewish prayer hall was divided into four spaces: (1) the front of the room where Shalom made business calls and drank tea with visitors; (2) the long corridor that functioned as a seating area during prayer services and festivals, remaining empty during the weekdays; (3) the bimah and ark that were used during religious rituals;

and (4) the small nook in the back of the room to the left of the bimah that served a place to have private drinking parties.

On the days when he did not have to race off to a business deal, Beniamin, the large Georgian Jewish businessman in his early forties, relaxed in the Mountain Jewish prayer hall. One morning in June 1996, I walked into the Mountain Jewish community after services to find him, Kostia, Sergei, and Evgenii Moiseivich sitting around the front desk talking and sipping tea. I sat down next to them. Beniamin told us that it was his son's twelfth birthday, and he invited us to drink some vodka with him in celebration. He asked Evgenii to come with him to buy vodka and snacks down the street.

They returned twenty minutes later with two bottles of Absolut vodka and some fresh cucumbers and tomatoes. We moved to the back of the room to watch Evgenii prepare the food. He cut the vegetables into thick slices and then took some leftover radishes out of the refrigerator and placed them in a bowl with some raw and salted salmon he had brought from home. He placed these items, a half a loaf of black bread, a bottle of tomato juice, and several glasses onto a small wobbly table. Kostia sprinkled salt onto the cucumbers and tomatoes with his fingers, and Evgenii handed him a large kosher *kolbasa* to cut up and distribute.

Beniamin stood up to give the first toast. He wished us all health, happiness, and luck. We drank. Still standing, Beniamin began to reminisce about his youth: "I remember at the institute [in Moscow], I would spend the day in classes, and at night, we would hang out with some girls. I did not want to sleep. I would lay down to nap for a while and then get up and do it all over again. Now, if I don't get a good night's sleep, I feel sick all day long. . . ." Kostia sympathized, "It is age. . . . You are just getting older."

Lyonia walked up to us to ask where Shalom was. Beniamin invited him to join us. "Do you want to drink one hundred grams of vodka?" Lyonia smiled and said, "Why not?" Beniamin poured him a drink and then continued, "I remember when I would pull up in my car to pick up some girls [at the synagogue]. There were so many of them. Of course, I would never tell my father that I was doing that . . ." Lyonia said, "I also did that. I would come here. I remember this one time, I picked up a girl and was taking her home. When we got into the light of a street lamp, I saw that she was really young. I asked, 'How old are you?' 'Sixteen.' 'What class are you in?' 'The tenth.' 'You cannot be sixteen and be in the tenth class. Forget it.' 'But why?' 'I just said so.' My young daughter asked me the other day, 'Dad, why can't I do that [sex]?' 'Because, you won't use protection and that is the way babies are made and you can't support a baby right now,' I told her.

She said, 'But that is what parents are for.' " Kostia nodded and commented, "She is just at that age."

Lyonia sighed, "I want to get remarried. Right now, I am married to a *goika* [non-Jewish woman]. I was married two times before that." Sergei piped up, "That means that your daughter is not a Jew." "No, I was married before to a Jew. She is from that marriage. Of course, my current wife does not want me to get remarried. . . ."

They all had another toast, finishing the bottle. Kostia put it under the table. Beniamin said, "Kostichka, let's have another round." Kostia hesitated. "We all have to get back to work, and one of us is a *dama* [lady]." Beniamin retorted, "She is not a *dama*, she is a sister. There is a difference." Suddenly, I was now the topic of conversation. Kostia asked me if I were engaged. Someone said, "She is engaged to a *goi* [non-Jew]." Kostia looked shocked. "Why are you studying this topic then?" he said, giving me a disapproving look. Beniamin stood up and walked around behind me. He put his hands on my shoulders. "She is not married yet, is she? She is our sister."

This conversation undermined the racializing narratives I heard about the black Mountain Jews and the civilized Russian Jews. Over shots of vodka, Lyonia, who had once commented to me that Mountain Jews were a "wild people," now talked about his own sexual desires. By discussing intermarriages, he and the others explored their common concern about the fate of their people—the Jews. On one level, these Russian, Georgian and Mountain Jews came together as equals because drinking vodka and tea in Russia works to establish community (Pesmen 2000). Tales of sexual conquest are a popular Russian male genre that emerges at casual drinking parties (Ries 1997:65–66). By performing a typical Russian male discourse, they all bonded as men with similar interests, namely having intercourse with women.

There was another element besides the Russian ethics of drinking that forged a connection among them. Through eating and discussing procreation, Russian Jews lowered themselves to the level of the body and the material, the central image in Russian Jewish and Mountain Jewish categorizations of Mountain Jews. All the men at the table became part of a common grotesque Jewish body—a body that eats, defecates, and copulates (Bakhtin 1984:19–20).

The conversation revealed that, just as it is important in Russia for a man to have sex to be a man, it is doubly important for a Jewish man to have sex with a Jewish woman, so as to continue the Jewish people. Under Orthodox law, a Jew is anyone born of a Jewish mother, and thus a big part of Jewish identity is maintaining proper sexual relations. At that moment, the body—with its acts of procreation, pregnancy, and birth—became the most important factor in defining a common Jewish identity. Being Jewish in this context meant being People of the Body.

Throughout my fieldwork, the topic of procreation was the main way that Jews of all backgrounds discussed their common Jewishness. In individual conversations, Mountain, Georgian, Russian, and Bukharan Jews repeatedly told me that it was important for me, a Jewish woman, to marry a Jew, no matter what his geographical origin. They said that this union would "continue the Jewish people," as well as cause me less emotional anguish. They predicted that if I married a non-Jew, he would call me a *zhidka* in a heated argument some day, and then I would be sorry he was my husband. Many Jews said that Russians were anti-Semites "in their hearts," and Adom once lectured me, "The most important thing is the Jewish family. Jews belong with Jews. Russians are very hospitable people. When they have bread and vodka, they will invite you to join them. But, as soon as the money runs out, they will call you a dirty Jew."

The tales of picking up women that I heard in the Mountain Jewish community placed me in an uncomfortable situation. Beniamin must have wanted to show me that I was safe, that I was not going to be the object of their desire. Perhaps as a Georgian Jew, he felt embarrassed about mentioning sex in the synagogue, albeit this kind of sex talk teetered on the edge of respectable conduct. In a gesture of protection, Beniamin stood behind me with his hands on my shoulders. He told everyone that I was their "sister," demonstrating how at that moment Russian, Georgian, and Mountain Jews were "brothers," and how I was off limits to all of them.

The Gendered Nation

Incidents like the one above occurred very rarely, and, for the most part, Russian and Mountain Jews consistently engaged in a racializing discourse that conflated race with class. This kind of talk endured because both groups had much invested in articulating their differences. On the most basic level, Russian Jews believed that their claim to "natural" superiority gave them the means to recapture the synagogue from Western and migrant Jews. Russian Jews constantly asserted that the immorality of Mountain Jews made them unsuitable for synagogue life. Russian Jews thus re-created the old Soviet order; they naturalized the "uncivilized" market practices of Mountain Jews as the expression of their "blackness." But more was at stake than just synagogue resources. Any claim to the superiority of one group over another had to rest on the falsity of the other's assertion of Russian citizenship and membership in the Jewish nation. That is why Russian Jews portrayed themselves as intellectuals, and Mountain Jews used their "wild" nature to counter Russian Jewish claims. Mountain Jews said their innate savageness made them better Jews and better citizens of the new capitalist Russia. They demonstrated that they had every right to be in the synagogue.

And yet, all the talk about race, class, and the nation (both Jewish and Russian) rests on images of female morality. Russian Jews conceptualized the "blackness" of Mountain Jews in terms of their poor treatment of women. Russian Jews believed that I had an innately higher intellect and sense of propriety than Mountain Jews because I am an Ashkenazic woman, and, by spending time with them, I was not acting normally (or morally). They commented that I was in grave danger of being abducted, raped, and/or killed. In turn, Mountain Jews redefined their savageness as true Jewish bodily practices that were manifested in keeping their women safe at home, and my presence among them highlighted the importance of female modesty. Assertions of Russianness and Jewishness thus rely on perceptions of Jewish women as moral or immoral.

The gendered nature of the racialized categories provided Mountain and Russian Jewish men with a way to become Jewish brothers, but again, only in reference to women. They became Jews through their need and desire to have sex with Jewish women and by their protection of a Jewish woman (me) from their lustful gazes. At that latter moment, I was made into kin, but this was done not out of a recognition of my equal status but out of a concern for my welfare. In the context of the synagogue, the men had full membership in the Jewish and Russian nations because they defined the terms of belonging. The women served mainly as vehicles for entry (literally and metaphorically) into it.

Chapter 5
The Madman and His Mission to Unite the Sephardim

> Shalom went from one political figure to the next to get them to recognize the Mountain Jews. He even worked hard enough to get a space for us in the Central Synagogue. He is doing a big deed for us. He spends all of his time trying to build the Mountain Jewish community. We will thank him when it is finished. He is an amazing person. He gave up his family to do this work.
> —Aleksandr Elizarovich

In order to create a place for Mountain Jews in the synagogue, Shalom not only attempted to reproduce family values and structure within the prayer setting, but he also tried to provide Mountain Jews with a political base of power. As chairman of the Mountain Jewish community, Shalom created an organization called MEROS (*Moskovskaia evreiskaia religioznaia obshchina sefardov* [Moscow Religious Community of Sephardic Jews]), of which he was president. According to him, two Bukharan Jews, two Georgian Jews, and three Mountain Jews signed the constitution. It was ratified in December 1992 and registered with the Moscow Justice Department in March 1993. Citing the Russian law "about the freedom of religion," MEROS's constitution established the organization as "an autonomous, legal entity" that could secure and give out religious items, set up study groups for children and youth, provide charity for the needy, spread information about Judaism, participate in conferences, own property, organize the production of cultural items and consumer goods, and hold bank accounts.

It was probably not a coincidence that *MEROS* sounded almost identical to *MERO*, the Moscow Jewish Religious Community, which was historically Ashkenazic. Shalom wanted to create an organization

146   Chapter 5

that would rival MERO in power and stature. He tried to build up momentum for change by declaring that the synagogue had reached a *kriticheskoe polozhenie* (crisis situation), in which the *ashkenazkoe rukovodstvo* (Ashkenazic administration) discriminated against Bukharan, Mountain, and Georgian Jews. He said the present administration excluded them from the governing process, making it difficult to practice their own unique rituals. He sent the following letter to the World Sephardi Federation and the American Sephardi Federation on September 12, 1996:

The Moscow Religious Community of Sephardic Jews (MEROS) greatly needs your help and participation to solve two very pressing problems. First, we do not have our own rabbi. We urgently need a specialist in Sephardic culture to be the spiritual leader of our community. Second, we do not have our own synagogue. At the present time, approximately fifty thousand Sephardic Jews (Mountain, Georgian, and Bukharan Jews) live in Moscow. The space given to us in the Central Synagogue is very small and not suitable for the full realization of our religious rituals (Mountain Jews especially suffer from this situation).
It has come to our attention that "Joint" (Joint Distribution Committee) will subsidize the construction of a Jewish cultural center on an empty lot across from the Central Synagogue. We believe that it would be expedient to build a Sephardic synagogue and cultural center on a small piece of this land.
Please help us!
We wish you and your families a very happy and healthy new year.
May the year 5757 bring all the Sephardic Jews closer together.
Respectfully yours,
The President of MEROS
Shalom Simanduev

Sephardic Jews have ties to Spain, having been expelled from there in 1492. Mountain and Georgian Jews are *Mizrahim*, because their ancestors arrived in the Caucasus from Jerusalem through Persia. Bukharan Jews are Sephardim; even though they have origins similar to Georgian and Mountain Jews, they adopted a Sephardic liturgy in the late 1800s.[1] At the Central Synagogue, Georgian, Mountain, and Bukharan Jews shared a Sephardic ethnicity that drew on a shared "set of relations" which excluded Western and Russian Jews (Comaroff and Comaroff 1992:54). This identity manifested itself through the dual processes of "material motivation"—conflicts over the procurement and distribution of ritual items and funding—and "cultural formulation"— the development of traditions based on remembering and "intercultural conversations" (Williams 1989:428; Gilroy 1993:276; Fischer 1986). As Rabbi Silverstein told me, "We cannot ignore the Sephardim. There are thirty thousand of them in Moscow. Eighty percent of the student population of the religious schools is Sephardim." According to him, Georgian, Bukharan, and Mountain Jews "could be a strong force," if they came together politically and financially. Kostia agreed: "Eighty percent of the *tzedoka* given to the synagogue comes from Sephardim." Shalom wanted to develop the ties among the non-Ashkenazic Jews to institute a new power regime in the synagogue.

Portrait of a Madman

Shalom was born in the mid-1940s to a poor Mountain Jewish family in Kuba. He dropped out of school early to make a living. At age eighteen, he moved to Piatagorsk, in the Dagestan Republic, to sell pastries on the street. He later worked in a factory there and then found jobs in various cities across Dagestan and Azerbaijan. Shalom told me that he became interested in building a Mountain Jewish community in 1972, when he was residing in Baku; that was when his "national consciousness" began. When I asked him why he was concerned with Mountain Jews in particular, he said, "Everyone is for their own. Can't you see that here [at the Central Synagogue]?" Shalom has dedicated his life to ensuring that Mountain Jews, as a people, do not "disappear" when they leave their homeland. He also helped establish Mountain Jewish communities in Germany and Canada.

In 1993, Shalom tried to find an official meeting place for MEROS. He wrote to many government officials, hoping to obtain a space in one of the two apartment buildings near the Central Synagogue, which had been owned by the synagogue's congregation before 1917. His requests were repeatedly denied. In 1994, Shalom succeeded in renting the storage space in the Central Synagogue for somewhere between forty million roubles (eight thousand dollars) to fifty million roubles (ten thousand dollars) a year.[2] When I asked Kostia to explain the relationship between MERO and MEROS, he said:

In general, Rabbi Silverstein does not bother us, but when Shalom wanted to set something up two to three years ago, he was not allowed to do so. The synagogue administration saw him as starting financial competition here because our Jews give out so much *tzedoka*. The administration thinks that more of us will come here [to the Mountain Jewish community] and less will go there [to the main hall]. It said that we could set up a *minyan* here, but our respected Shalom began to yell so that all could hear that a *minyan* would not suit us. We needed an organization [MEROS], registered on an equal level with them. That worried them even more.

Shalom's plans put the synagogue administration on the defensive. According to Kostia, Shalom was allowed to establish the Mountain Jewish community in the Central Synagogue only after he agreed to pay rent to alleviate the synagogue's financial problems. "We offered them forty million roubles. The next day, the executive director, Mr. Sharogradskii, asked us, 'Where is the money? Where is the money?' He announced to Shalom and then to me, 'You must give us fifty million every year.' I asked why. He said, 'Why do you ask why? Don't you use the light? Don't you use the heat? Don't you use the water? Don't you come here?' Why don't the Ashkenazim, who pray in the big hall and use more services than we do, have to pay? The situation is very complex and even sort of comical."

Kostia implied that MEROS's difficulties with the administration signaled a larger conflict between Ashkenazim and Sephardim. Although Kostia was prominently involved in the struggle for Sephardic sovereignty, Shalom led this movement with his loud and confrontational style.

When I arrived in Moscow, people at the synagogue said that they were fed up with Shalom. He and Kostia constantly got into shouting matches that reverberated down the corridor, and Evgenii Moiseivich complained jokingly to me that "working with crazy people in a psychiatrist's office is quieter than working with Shalom." Lyonia explained to me how Russian Jews viewed Shalom: "He wastes his time on trifles. People here relate to him with a little bit of irony, you know that of course. He takes everything very personally and close to his heart. He shouts when it might be better not to shout. He fusses when there is absolutely nothing wrong. He undertakes things that he thinks are very important."

Aleksandr Elizarovich had his doubts about Shalom's sanity. He said that I needed to understand Shalom: "He is not a normal and healthy man. A normal man would think about making money, raising a family. Shalom does not think about those things. Instead, he concentrates on making a synagogue for the Mountain Jews." When I mentioned that I had hoped Shalom would take me to a Mountain Jewish wedding, Aleksandr said that Shalom, as a religious person, could not explain to everyone why he was escorting a woman. He was divorced, and he lived alone in a hotel near the synagogue. He thus had to keep his distance from me.

Shalom's demeanor so unnerved the administration that it gave in to his demands, just to get rid of him. As Anton Rizovskii, the former executive director of MERO, commented, "Every community needs a madman. I told Simcha to give Shalom a phone and an office so that he would shut up." Many Jews talked about how Shalom's displays of emotion proved that he was "crazy," and some even stated that he was "clinically insane." Shalom, when asked, attributed what he called his "carbonated" personality to his Mountain Jewish mentality. "We [Mountain Jews] are an emotional people," he stated matter-of-factly. His lack of emotional control, however, proved to many that the image of Mountain Jews as "uncivilized" was valid.

Russian Jews often told me how Shalom did not know how to read Hebrew and that he had trouble reading Russian. Yehuda commented, "That Shalom, he does not know even one Hebrew letter! He pretends to pray." Yurii said, "Shalom is illiterate. During morning prayer, he sits at the table and reads the newspaper. He can read [Russian] okay, but he does not really know how to write." These comments slipped into the larger historical discourses about how Mountain Jews are a people who lost their Jewish knowledge. As Yehuda and Yurii would argue, how could Shalom lead the Sephardim in ritual and prayer if he could not even read Hebrew? By talking about Shalom's inability to read, Russian Jews attempted to undermine Shalom—and to ensure the future of their own Ashkenazic *minyan* and the synagogue itself.

Anton Rizovskii once claimed that Shalom was "dividing the synagogue," and at times Russian Jews interpreted Shalom's actions as "nationalistic"—an attempt to establish Sephardic autonomy at the expense of others at the synagogue. These statements reverberated with Soviet, and even Russian nationalist, rhetoric about maintaining national unity.[3] Yurii Isaakovich blocked Shalom's and Kostia's applications for membership in the *dvadtsatka* on the grounds that, Shalom "got himself written up as the president of the Sephardic community. He wants to set up a separate synagogue, like [what is happening] in Chechnya." Yurii equated Russia's war with Chechnya over the ownership of gas lines in that republic to Russian Jews' need to keep the Sephardim in the synagogue in order to hold on to their *tzedoka* and *minyan* members. Yurii implied that all resources should be directed toward the center—Moscow, in the case of Chechnya, and MERO, in the case of the Sephardim. Russian Jews identified with the administration because it was Ashkenazic, and as such, they wanted the Ashkenazim to continue to have authority. Shalom's goal to break away from the Central Synagogue rejected this nationalist discourse. In a discussion with fellow Mountain Jews, he said, "They [the Ashkenazim] did not want us to have a place [in the Central Synagogue]. They said it would cause nationalistic divisions. The pope of Russia came to my side. He explained that in America, Sephardim and Ashkenazim are separate. Rizovskii helped. We [finally] got registered."[4]

Shalom played up his lack of formal education and religious knowledge to persuade others to work for him. At first, he was wary of my questions, but by mid-summer, he realized that, in return for information about the Mountain Jewish community and MEROS, I would aid him in his cause. He demanded my full allegiance, stating that I must help him since he was only "*malogramotnyi*" (slightly literate). Although I never committed myself fully to the Sephardic project (in keeping with my attempt to remain as partial as I could), I sympathized with the situation of Georgian, Bukharan, and Mountain Jews in the synagogue and wanted to see them obtain more space.

While Shalom played his role as an illiterate with such skill that it seemed to be his true nature, he also sometimes struggled with this image of himself, trying to prove to others that, despite his inability to read Hebrew, he did have the qualities needed to lead a religious community. He presented himself as a religious leader by performing what he saw as his Jewish morality as manifested in his Mountain Jewish heritage.

He liked to tell people "I am a religious man" and "My work belongs here in the synagogue"; he constantly berated other Jews for what he saw as their lack of religious practice. For example, after morning services in the small hall on March 7, 1996, Berl shook my hand and said, "I want to congratulate you on the upcoming holiday [International Women's Day on May 8]. May you have luck." Shalom came up on my left, having just entered the room. He yelled at Berl. "Don't you know that religious men do not shake women's hands?! You should act religiously!"[5] Berl said, "She took my hand first." Shalom continued, "Sascha, I respect you. You are like a sister to me. This is not allowed." "He is old. I don't mind," I said. Shalom calmed down and walked away. Berl leaned over to me and whispered in my ear, "We may be old, but we still like *devushki* [girls]."

Shalom made himself into a religious authority by citing talmudic law, admonishing Berl like a child, and worrying about me as a younger sister. Berl, seemingly scared of Shalom, only voiced his dissenting opinion to me in a whisper. Perhaps Shalom was right. A seemingly innocent handshake might have been Berl's excuse to touch a *devushka*.

In June, Shalom started a lengthy moral campaign against the synagogue kiosk that allegedly sold kosher food at high prices. Shalom declared that this food was humanitarian aid for poor Jews, and he demanded that the synagogue administration make amends by giving discounts or a percent of the profit to the needy. He was also outraged that the kiosk was only infrequently open for business. He persuaded Rabbis Silverstein and Dubinovich to sign a note declaring that the kiosk should open at 9:15 A.M. He posted copies of it around the synagogue and on the kiosk door. When the woman who worked at the kiosk crossed out his note, Shalom accused the administration of actively thwarting his efforts. He said to me, "They are scared of me.

They know that I know that the kiosk sells charity products for 30 percent more than the normal price." By the time I was ready to leave Moscow in November 1996, the administration was so annoyed with Shalom's constant complaining and nagging about the kiosk issue that Rabbi Dubinovich joked with me, "Do a favor to the community. Take Shalom away with you to America."

Despite what some Russian Jews claimed, Shalom did have a method to his madness. It was possible to unite the Sephardim because Mountain, Georgian, and Bukharan Jews experienced structural inequality, both materially and ideologically, within synagogue life. This subordination led these Jewish groups to see themselves as belonging to one larger entity—the Sephardim—and to differentiate between themselves and Russian Jews. Sometimes, these opposing relationships emerged due to conflicts within the prayer service, and at other times, they came about through the informal creation of a Sephardic tradition.

Creating Sephardic Tradition through Conversation

Ethnicity in the post-Soviet context is quite flexible, as evidenced in the relations between Russian and Georgian Jews. But I did not understand the extreme creativity of this phenomenon until a conflict erupted about my presence at morning services. Because I had to sit so far in the corner of the small hall, I wanted to tape the service from the bimah in order to catch the words and activities in more detail. On May 6, Yurii allowed me to walk up to the bimah, just before the Torah reading, to flip over the tape to record the rest of the service. However, Yurii turned off the tape recorder because Zviad and Yose got into the fistfight that morning. A week later, I tried to record the service again. When I went up to the bimah to turn over the tape, Semyon demanded that I leave the prayer hall. He screamed, *"Nel'zia byt' muzhchinami i zhenshchinami!"* which I loosely translated to mean "Men and women should not be together in the same room during prayer!" My moving to the center of the room had broken the law about the separation of the sexes. While none of the Ashkenazic Jews came to my aid, Shalom insisted quietly that I come to "our service," the Georgian reading simultaneously going on in the main hall. I decided instead to go outside into the hallway to clear my head. Several minutes later, Aleksei came out to find me. He said, "Please, don't be upset. I will look into the situation."

After services, Sergei invited me into the Mountain Jewish prayer hall for some tea. Aleksei soon joined us. He said to me, "Don't listen to Semyon. It is okay. I talked with the rabbi [Silverstein]. He said that Semyon is crazy." Aleksei reassured me that I would still be welcome at prayer. Then he added, "Come to our Torah reading. They [Russian Jews] do not respect you because we see you as a Mountain Jew or a Georgian Jew." I asked, "The Ashkenazim do not respect the Georgian or Mountain Jews?" "It is not that, but the fact that they are Russian," Aleksei said. Sergei added, "They look down upon us. They think that they are better."

Aleksei and Sergei understood my being expelled from prayer in terms of ethnicity, and they showed me once again how ethnic affiliation was a key way worshipers understood prayer activities. This situation was not a case of "Georgians" versus "Russians." Instead, it indicated how Mountain and Georgian Jews saw themselves as belonging at times to a separate ethnic group. Aleksei said that because "we," the Mountain and Georgian Jews, saw me as a Mountain or Georgian Jew, the Russian Jews did not "respect" me. Sergei added that Russian Jews looked down on "us," referring to Georgian and Mountain Jews. In this context, the Georgian Jewish Torah reading, which was usually attended by one or two Mountain Jews, became a vehicle for the expression of the differences between "us," Mountain and Georgian Jews, and "them," Russian Jews.

Membership in the Sephardic ethnic group at the synagogue was based on alliances. Some Georgian and Mountain Jews saw me as one of their own because I had been spending much more time with them in the Mountain Jewish prayer hall for several months leading up to the incident. Accordingly, Georgian and Mountain Jews understood my expulsion from the small hall as signaling the rupture of my relationship with the Russian Jews.

When I first arrived in Moscow, I had talked primarily with Ashkenazic Jews, especially Yurii. These contacts provided me with a specific history of synagogue life that centered on the "heroics" of Russian Jews and denied the long-term presence of Georgian, Mountain, and Bukharan Jews at the synagogue. Although the elderly Russian Jews were in a subordinate position to the Western administration, their rendition of synagogue history gave them authority in ritual matters. Western publications about Soviet Jews (Gitelman 1988; Levin 1990) and archival materials about the Central Synagogue focus almost solely on Russian Jewish activities. Georgian, Mountain, and Bukharan Jews understood these stories as indicative of how Russian Jews refused to "respect" them. By excluding the Sephardim from the Central Synagogue's history, Russian Jews denied them an active part in its present—and future.

When I became one of "us," Georgian, Mountain, and Bukharan Jews began to tell me about their important role in synagogue history. After I had tea with Sergei and Aleksei, Tzvi told me a tale of how

Georgian Jews conducted business in the synagogue. Tzvi, a Georgian Jew in his seventies, sat drinking tea with Dmitri, a Georgian Jew in his fifties. They conversed with one another in Georgian in the corner of the Mountain Jewish prayer hall. In the middle of their conversation, Dmitri told Tzvi (in Russian) to tell me his story. Tzvi, who had hardly said two words to me until now, crossed the room and sat down next to me. He said to me in Russian:

I have been coming here [to the synagogue] for forty-six years. I moved here in 1949. There was a man who came here—a businessman. He had old tsarist money for sale—gold money. I introduced him to our Georgian Jews. That kind of money was a rare thing to see. At that time, it was really hard to buy shoes and clothes. But he had everything. He gave our Jews the products, and they made money [from selling them]. . . . It was dangerous, but such stuff! When he died in 1955, I said to our people who had made a profit, "Let's bury him the Jewish way." But no one wanted to come. Only Beniamin's father and I went to his [the businessman's] wife, and said to her, "Look here, this is our law. We bury every person by Jewish law." She sent his body to the crematorium. That is not allowed! I went [to his funeral] anyway because he was my good acquaintance. They burned him! He left a lot of everything—money, gold, diamonds. . . . He gave his daughter a huge diamond brooch and earrings. She came to me recently and said, "I want to sell [these]." She gave them to our Jews so that they could sell them for her. [6]

Through an informal network at the synagogue, Georgian Jews in Moscow sold goods on the black market, and there was an understanding that once those connections were established, they would continue to exist, even if submerged for many years. So, while Russian Jews at the synagogue declared commerce "immoral," Georgian Jews used the synagogue to make good business deals, as well as to keep up religious practice. And, as Tzvi demonstrated by his choice to attend the funeral, friendship and business sometimes outweighed religious belief and conviction. By making business a "tradition," Tzvi opened up a space for Georgian Jewish communion with Mountain Jews, a process that had the potential to legitimate Mountain Jewish claims to Jewish identity. Georgian and Mountain Jews built up a shared tradition that functioned, as Paul Gilroy suggests (1993:276), as "a process rather than an end . . . a way of conceptualizing the fragile communicative relationships across time and space that are the basis not of diaspora identities but of diaspora identifications, [making] intercultural, transnational diaspora conversations between them possible."

These conversations fostered a sense of closeness and shared identification among Mountain, Georgian, and even Bukharan Jews; and because these conversations sometimes centered around the practice of business itself, they extended this "tradition" into the future. On one occasion, Isaak, the elderly cantor of the Bukharan Jewish community, met with Beniamin to have him sell several pieces of diamond jewelry. Beniamin told Isaak that he would have the pieces appraised and then make a sale for him.

At other times, these chats were exploratory, since Bukharan, Georgian, and Mountain Jews did not know much about one another's histories. Tzvi once asked Shalom if all the Mountain Jews had the same language. On another occasion, Rakhmin Efraimovich Abramov, the chairman of the Bukharan Jewish community, started a discussion with several Mountain Jewish women who had come to buy matzah. He was shocked to find out that they were from Tbilisi, because he thought Mountain Jews were restricted to the Azerbaijan and Dagestan regions.

Georgian and Mountain Jews enjoyed exchanging stories about their homelands, and these tales usually centered on business practices. Kostia, Sergei, and Tzvi sat in the Mountain Jewish prayer hall one day after services discussing kosher food. Tzvi convinced Kostia and Sergei that "Jews cannot eat vultures."[7] Tzvi then commented, "Speaking of fowl, I have an anecdote, a Georgian anecdote. A [Jewish] man goes out to buy four geese. He buys them and on the way back, a Georgian sees him. He says to the [Jewish] man, 'I have to tax you because you bought these geese, but I will give you one goose back.' "

Everyone laughed and agreed that this anecdote was funny. Sergei said, "I have another story. In Baku, Jews would go to the mountains to sell produce to the Azeris. In this case, they sold them flour. They would go up the mountain with the flour, and the Azeris would order one kilo, or two kilos, or four kilos." As Sergei said this, he gestured that he was putting his hand down on one end of a scale, so as to make the flour seem heavier than it really was, to show us how Jews cheated Azeris into paying more money than the flour was worth. Everyone laughed, but Tzvi shook his finger at Sergei, saying, "You know, Jews are never supposed to lie. It is a sin to lie." Sergei retorted, "But how about if you lie to a non-Jew?" Tzvi answered sternly, "You should not lie to other people,[8] even to the Muslims, since they are the older brothers of the Jews. If you know the [biblical] history, Avraham had two sons, Isaak and Ishmael. Ishmael was the older son whom Avraham kicked out of the house. Ishmael became the founder of the Muslims."[9]

In Tzvi's story, the Gentile took advantage of the Jew, but in Sergei's story, the Jew cheated the Gentile. This transformation of the Jew from victim into oppressor spurred Tzvi to give a lesson about the ethics of Judaism. Tzvi acted like a father or older brother, admonishing Sergei for not believing that Jews have a moral responsibility to their people and their neighbors. Tzvi also told Sergei about the relationship between the Jews and Muslims. Tzvi's stories worked to transcend the differences that existed between the "Georgian" or "Mountain" Jewish experiences in order to unite Georgian and Mountain Jews together through shared history. In this way, the traditions of Georgian Jews, the Jewish group considered to be the most religious out of all the Soviet Jewish groups, became part of the traditions of Mountain Jews, the Jewish group considered to have the weakest connection to Judaism.

While the telling of these tales created bonds among Mountain, Bukharan, and Georgian Jews, they also created resistance to Shalom's attempts to unite them as Sephardim. Although Mountain, Georgian, and Bukharan Jews felt discriminated against, they also experienced a connection with Russian Jews as Jews. The discussion between Sergei and Tzvi about the morals of Judaism indicated how Georgian, Mountain, and Bukharan Jews sometimes talked about themselves as members of the Jewish people at large. At such moments, Jews from the republics felt that being Jewish in general was more important than being a Sephardic Jew. Beniamin expressed this sentiment in a speech he gave at a Mountain Jewish bar mitzvah. Holding up a plastic cup of vodka, he said, "May we increase so that no one can destroy us and so that every year there are more and more of us in this country. I try not to fall into that [kind of talk] about 'Mountain Jews, Georgian Jews, Bukharan Jews.' God does not have Georgians or Azeris. He has only one nation. The Jews are his children. We are all Jews. Let God hear what we ask him, and may he bless our business. Glory to the Jewish people."

There were times as well when Mountain Jews specifically questioned the validity of the term *Sephardic*. One afternoon in the Mountain Jewish prayer hall, Sergei asked Valeri why Mountain Jews are Sephardim. Valeri said that they are considered Sephardim because they are not Ashkenazim; he also noted that the Sephardim lived in Spain, and Mountain Jews do not have any Spanish Jewish heritage. Several days later, Sergei told Vitia, another Mountain Jew, "You know that we are not Sephardim." Vitia was visibly confused. Sergei tried to explain to him that "the Sephardim came from Spain, and we are not from Spain."

At the bar mitzvah attended by Beniamin, Sergei's friend Misha asked Sergei, "Was Avraham [the first Jew] a Georgian or a Mountain Jew? What kind of Jew was he?" Sergei responded, "He was not a Jew at all. . . . He lived in Iraq at the time." "Iraqi Jews speak our language [Farsi], right?" "Right." "That means that they made him a Sephardic

Jew." They laughed. Misha's humorous comment indicates how Mountain and Georgian Jews were aware of the politics behind this ethnic identification.

Creating Sephardic Ethnicity through Ritual

Through his tactical use of morning ritual, Shalom institutionalized the relations among Georgian, Bukharan, and Mountain Jews into a statement of Sephardic ethnicity. From July until November 1996, weekday services took place in the main hall to accommodate the construction in the small hall. Although Semyon rejected my presence at morning services, this change of location allowed me to observe the men from the vantage point of the women's section. No one could object to my presence now.

Monday, July 22 was the first day that morning services took place in the big hall. I observed the *minyan* sit or stand close to the bimah at the front of the room until the Torah reading. Then, the Georgian Jews (and Shalom, Sergei, and Kostia) began to separate from the Russian Jews, just like they did in the small hall. However, the spatial logistics were different. The Russian Jews gathered at the bimah at the front of the room while the Georgian and Mountain Jews surrounded the large table in the back of the room, which Khakham David had arranged into a bimah. When they finished reading the Torah, the Georgian and Mountain Jews returned to their original seats.

Having two Torah readings going on in the same room at the same time left some worshipers with the impression that prayer was not going "correctly." Talking about the new situation, Sergei told Kostia that the service was like "a bazaar," loud and disorderly, and that the "Georgians" should find another place to read. Kostia said that he already asked the Georgians to move, but they refused to do so. When Sergei asked why, Kostia said flatly, "They just don't want to." Perhaps Khakham David did not want to move the Georgian Jews upstairs to their own prayer hall, since it might have divided the two groups for the entire service. This would have endangered both *minyans* since it was unclear at the beginning of services if each group would have ten men.

Two weeks later, the situation grew even more complicated. Kostia and Sergei did not join Khakham David, Shalom, and the Georgian Jews. Instead, they stood talking to one another in the center of the room. Finally, Rabbi Silverstein called them to the bimah to hear the Ashkenazic Torah reading. Shalom, Aleksei, and Beniamin watched this development with keen interest from the back of the room. Kostia and Sergei hardly ever took part in the reading among the Georgian

Jews, but this time, among the Ashkenazim, Kostia received the second *aliyah*, and after Rabbi Silverstein received the third *aliyah*, Sergei lifted the Torah scroll, with Yurii's help. Rabbi Silverstein recited his passage in a booming voice to compete with Khakham David's recitation. Prayer practice in the main hall had thus begun to weaken the usual ethnic division between the Georgian Jews (with Shalom, Kostia, and Sergei) and the Ashkenazic Jews.

In late August, Shalom rearranged the entire spatial logistics of prayer. During the service, Yurii went to obtain the Torah scroll from the small hall. When he returned to the bimah, all the worshipers stayed in their places. I assumed this meant that they had decided to read the Torah together. But then Shalom and Sergei quickly headed for the door to the hallway, and as Shalom reached it, he said, "Let's go!" Kostia and Khakham Eliahu (the second Georgian rabbi) followed them into the Mountain Jewish prayer hall. Tzvi, Beniamin, and some of the other Georgian Jews slowly walked out after them, but Aleksei and Dmitri stayed behind to sit in the back of the big hall.

From that point until the reopening of the small hall in November, the "Georgian Jewish" Torah reading took place in the Mountain Jewish prayer hall. This relocation actually changed the meaning of the ritual. By insisting that it take place in the Mountain Jewish prayer hall, Shalom enacted the sentiment he had expressed to me the day I was expelled from the small hall, namely that the Georgian Jewish Torah reading was "our service," meaning a service for all Sephardim. Officially, the Mountain Jewish prayer hall was the location of MEROS, and as such, those Jews who prayed within MEROS were considered to be "Sephardim." Shalom made this Torah reading into a statement of Sephardic ethnicity and sovereignty. Once the Torah reading in the Mountain Jewish prayer hall began, it was Khakham Eliahu who led the Sephardim. This choice made the reading less "Georgian," since Khakham David, the official rabbi for the Georgian Jews, continued to remain behind in the big hall. For a few months prior, Khakham Eliahu had been reading the Torah for the Mountain Jews on Shabbat. In this way, the Georgian Jewish Torah reading became an expression of both Mountain Jewish and Sephardic ethnicities.

After services one morning in October 1996, I went into the Mountain Jewish community to ask Gavriel, the elderly Mountain Jew who had insisted that I wear a hat in the prayer hall, why the Mountain Jews gather together on Shabbat.

Gavriel: [*Sredi*] *Svoikh* [To be among our own kind].
Sascha: But Khakham Eliahu is Georgian.
Gavriel: He reads the Torah in his language, and I do it in mine . . .

Kostia: He [Khakham Eliahu] reads the Torah in Hebrew.
Gavriel: But sometimes it sounds like Georgian.
Shalom: We are all Sephardim.
Gavriel: We [the Mountain Jews] pray *na svoyom iazike* [in our own language].

Gavriel stated that Judeo-Tat, the language of the Mountain Jews, expressed the essence of Mountain Jewishness. He indicated that this expression lies not in the language's grammar and vocabulary but in its pronunciation. Accordingly, because Khakham Eliahu was "Georgian," he "spoke" Georgian when he read the Torah, meaning that he pronounced Hebrew as he pronounced Georgian. Kostia had a similar point of view. He said, "Each person reads Hebrew differently. For example, the Mountain Jews read Hebrew approximately as they speak Farsi." These semantics of language created the impression that there were mutually exclusive Mountain Jewish and Georgian Jewish ethnicities. In Russian, the word *iazik* means both language and nation. Shalom, realizing that such a view threatened the creation of a religious community of Sephardic Jews within the Mountain Jewish synagogue, attempted to correct Gavriel. Shalom insisted that these ethnic differences did not matter because "We are all Sephardim." For him, the notion that Georgian and Mountain Jews were Sephardim eclipsed any differences there may be between these two groups. Gavriel, however, refused to budge from his original position. This conversation brought up the ambiguities involved in a having a "Sephardic" ritual in a Mountain Jewish space.

By relocating the Georgian Jewish Torah reading to the Mountain Jewish prayer hall, Shalom finally made himself into the religious Sephardic leader he imagined himself to be. I had the chance to observe this ritual firsthand during Shabbat. I had wanted to see a service in the Mountain Jewish prayer hall from the inside instead of sneaking peeks at it from the hallway during Monday and Thursday mornings, so I asked Shalom if I could sit on the steps in the Mountain Jewish community. This staircase goes up to the bookkeeper's office; there is a folding door at the bottom, and the steps are draped in lace material, so there is material to hide behind. Shalom retorted that there would be no place to sit, but Sergei cut in, saying that I did not really need to pray because I was there to do research. Shalom relented, but not before reminding me to wear something on my head.

I arrived the next morning on Shabbat. Services had just started, and Shalom met me at the door. He walked me through the room to the staircase. I tried not to look at anyone so as not to cause too much trouble, but as soon as I walked up the steps and Shalom closed the door, I heard someone ask, "Who is she?" I heard Shalom say, "She is an American. She is doing research." Through the lace curtains, I could observe the bimah and the congregation.

When the Georgian Jews read the Torah in the main hall, Shalom stood on the parameter of the bimah, speaking only when he wanted Khakham David to say prayers for deceased or sick Mountain Jews. In the Mountain Jewish prayer hall, however, Shalom was in charge of the whole service. He was very adamant about directing every aspect of the reading. He chose who would get *aliyah* and told Khakham Eliahu when to say specific prayers. It seemed that not all the Georgian and Bukharan Jews liked his dictatorial ways, since many of them did not volunteer to come into the Mountain Jewish prayer hall for the Torah reading on Mondays and Thursdays. This situation forced Shalom to actively seek out Georgian and Bukharan Jews to make a *minyan* in his prayer hall.

Shalom also used the controversies over the distribution of prayer shawls and phylacteries during morning prayer to prove his point that the Sephardim were at a material disadvantage within an Ashkenazic synagogue—and to convince Georgian and Bukharan Jews to participate in the Sephardic reading. These items were always scarce, and by mid-January 1996, I came to realize that the worshipers understood the distribution of phylacteries and prayer shawls in terms of ethnic preferences. Yurii Isaakovich complained to me:

For five years, we have not gotten any new phylacteries and prayer shawls. I only have old ones that we received from men who died. The other day, the brothers [Aleksei and Zviad] asked for a pair of phylacteries for a Georgian. They asked me why I give out old ones. I said because I do not have any others. Then, this new guy came in. Simcha automatically liked him and told me to give him the new phylacteries. I said that we do not have any, and he said that we do. We actually do have one pair, with nice long head straps, but this one is only for bar mitzvahs, only for boys. I keep them on the top [of the cabinet]. I had to give them to him [Simcha], because he knew about them. The brothers were offended. They said, "Ah ha. You give the nice ones to Simcha but not to us." I explained to them that they are only for the bar mitzvahs and that Simcha knows that they are here.

A conflict regarding three new prayer shawls and phylacteries that Mr. Hirsch, a Swiss (Ashkenazic) Jewish businessman who prayed at the synagogue, donated to the morning *minyan* further highlighted the issues surrounding the dispensation of ritual objects. Right away there were disputes over who could use them. Kostia wanted to claim one pair as his own, but Mr. Hirsch did not want anyone to use them exclusively, and he told Kostia, "When you need them, you can use them. And when he [pointing to Sergei] needs them, he can use them." This conflict over Mr. Hirsch's gifts came to a head in October.

On the morning of Thursday, October 17, Mountain Jews and Georgian Jews attended a bar mitzvah in the Mountain Jewish prayer hall. Beniamin paced back and forth from the Mountain Jewish prayer hall to the big hall. He was worried about a mix-up over the prayer items needed for the Mountain Jewish bar mitzvah boy. He said that Shalom walked into the main hall during the *Amidah* to ask Yurii Isaakovich for them. Yurii refused, because he was praying, and Shalom started yelling. Finally, Shalom decided to give his own prayer shawl and phylacteries to the boy.

I heard Zviad in the main hall. He was yelling at Rabbi Dubinovich. From the hallway, the only words I could catch were Dubinovich's "you should have ordered them earlier." Zviad was obviously complaining about how Yurii did not give Shalom the ritual items.

Later that day, Sergei and I asked Yurii about the controversy. Yurii said Shalom came up to him during the *Amidah* and that Shalom did not know that one cannot talk during that prayer. Yurii explained how Shalom had disregarded Yurii's suggestion the day before to ask him for the items before prayer this morning. Yurii then added that he thought Shalom had taken two of the three new phylacteries to "sell" them. Yurii often said that Shalom established his community only to make money. In one of his more critical moods, Yurii commented vehemently, "Shalom is a predictable person. He wants to make money, so he sets up this community. It is okay if a person takes a little for himself. But when a person takes a lot and leaves a little, that is bad. Shalom went to Germany. He convinced stupid people there that he had to make a Mountain Jewish community, but all he wanted to do was make money. He lies to people. He says that he is building a community."

While Shalom, Zviad, and Aleksei complained that the Ashkenazim deliberately kept religious items away from the Sephardim, Yurii claimed that Georgian Jews, Shalom, and the administration hoarded religious items for business purposes. It was clear that whoever had the most access to ritual items had more authority in the synagogue. Once again, Yurii drew on the image of the "uncivilized" and "cunning" Mountain Jewish businessman to challenge Shalom's growing power in the synagogue. Shalom, in turn, knew that Yurii wanted to expel him from the community. After the *dvadtsatka* meetings, I asked Shalom why Yurii did not want him to be on the synagogue board. He said, "He is a *khitryi chelovek* [cunning person]. He came in here yesterday to tell us about the meeting, but he did not say the same things he said today." Kostia, sitting near by, agreed: "Yes, he is cunning, but he is getting old." In a twist of discourse, Kostia and Shalom turned the stereotype of Mountain Jews back onto Yurii. In their eyes, Yurii and Russian Jews, not Mountain Jews, were the sneaky and greedy ones.

Crisis of Ethnicity: The Performance of Body and Blood

Despite his success using ritual to institutionalize Sephardic solidarity and to politicize what he saw as Sephardic subordination, Shalom ultimately obstructed his ability to gather official support from Georgian and Bukharan Jews. In September 1996, Shalom admitted to me that the Georgian Jews as a group did not favor a separate Sephardic synagogue because Rabbi Silverstein had guaranteed them the exclusive use of their prayer hall that was large enough to meet their ritual needs. Shalom then looked for more help from the Bukharan Jews, since they, like the Mountain Jews, had inadequate space for their congregation. Bukharan Jews no longer used the synagogue library; they now gathered in a tiny room near the back of the main hall. Not only was this room small, but it also smelled like sewage due to the constantly overflowing toilet next door. In October 1996, Rakhmin Efraimovich, the chairman of the Bukharan community, walked into the Mountain Jewish prayer hall to tell Shalom that the Bukharan Jews did not want to take part in his project. He warned Shalom, "Don't get involved in Bukharan business. The only new synagogue will be the one on *Poklonnaia gora*."[10] After Rakhmin left, Shalom said that he had a secret to tell me: "The Central Synagogue offered to redo the Bukharan hall, so that the Bukharans would not take an interest in building a separate synagogue."

Shalom was right. Construction began in the Bukharan prayer hall in November. The synagogue administration promised to expand the room, making a separate entrance into it from the street and fixing the toilet area. In a telephone conversation with me, Rakhmin commented that Shalom was just "dreaming" about building a Sephardic synagogue:

We [Bukharan Jews] do not want to be included in his personal bazaar. We do not want papers, a president. It is enough to pray calmly. I asked Dubinovich last night and he said that there would not be a Sephardic synagogue. Our community will get even bigger. The young come. Thirty-five young men were there on Simchat Torah. We do not do it for money, like Shalom. He gets paid for his hotel room and his laundry. I work for free. Write that in your book, that Rakhmin Efraimovich Abramov works for free. I do not mess with Shalom. *On ne v etom mire* [He is not in touch with reality].

Shalom's emotional character and visions of leadership distanced him from others. Georgian and Bukharan Jews indicated that his Mountain Jewish mentality (his so-called need to make money off of others) was stronger than his ability to represent the needs of Sephardic Jews. Rakhmin's statement echoed what Lyonia had said about Shalom, namely that he made much to-do about nothing in order to create nationalistic and political problems within the synagogue. Georgian and Bukharan Jews thus agreed with Russian Jews that Mountain Jews were members of an "uncivilized" race. In this case, Shalom's inherent "blackness" undercut the creativity of Sephardic ethnicity. Ironically, Georgian and Bukharan Jews viewed Mountain Jews as unable to work for the benefit of the larger group, even though they had made their own separate deals with Rabbi Silverstein.

After he lost the support of the Bukharan and Georgian Jews, Shalom insisted on my allegiance to his synagogue project, making me promise that I would not tell Rabbi Silverstein about it until MEROS had the support of the American Sephardi Federation (ASF) and the World Sephardi Federation. He tried to reinforce my loyalty by pointing out how I was really a *gorskaia evreika* ("Mountain Jewess"). He frequently tried to convince me of my genetic heritage in front of everyone, saying things like "You look like me, don't you? How could you not be a Mountain Jew? Your eyes are as dark as mine." He played on a question Russian Jews often asked me when they tried to ascertain my Jewish heritage: *Ty chistokrovnaia evreika?* ("Are you a full-blooded Jew?"). He claimed that all of Russia knew that I was a Mountain Jew by saying vague statements like "You are a Mountain Jew, they showed it on TV" and "You are a Mountain Jew, they told me on the phone." At one Mountain Jewish bar mitzvah attended by Russian, Georgian, Bukharan, and Mountain Jews, he instructed a Mountain Jew to take a picture of me. Shalom yelled at him, "She is a Mountain Jew. Go photograph her!" "Show your eyes!" he commanded me, while the man took my picture. Shalom's behavior and statements that blood was proof of loyalty to a group caused many Bukharan and Georgian Jews to doubt his commitment to a Sephardic, rather than a Mountain Jewish, cause. In a serious tone, Rakhmin Efraimovich Abramov constantly asked me if I were a Bukharan Jew or a Mountain Jew.

Shalom also frequently slipped between talking about "us Mountain Jews" and "us Sephardim," making it unclear whether he was using his status as the president of MEROS to help his "own kind." When Nikolai Dzhinashvili, a Georgian Jew, came to the Central Synagogue as a representative of the ASF to ascertain the extent of the "crisis situation" there, Shalom arranged a meeting between him and MEROS.

However, Shalom invited only Mountain Jews. During a conversation about the ASF's interest in establishing a Sephardic yeshiva in Moscow, Shalom yelled, "We don't have our own rabbi!" Dzhinashvili tried to explain to Shalom that a Sephardic yeshiva would supply rabbis to the community in ten years or so, Shalom said he wanted an immediate solution. He complained, "There is a very big problem with rabbis. The Mountain Jews need our own rabbi, immediately. Do not build a school, but help us with our community in this extremely small room. A woman [the bookkeeper] walks up over the ark. It is forbidden to ascend over the Torah scroll!"

His focus on the needs of Mountain Jews within a discussion about Sephardic sovereignty indicated not only how Shalom sometimes placed the concerns of Mountain Jews first, thus proving the suspicions of Bukharan and Georgian Jews, but also how Mountain Jews were more mentally and emotionally involved in the Sephardic project. It was evident that they had the most to lose in the plan's failure, since they were the only Sephardim without what they saw as a special arrangement with the administration. The friendly inter-cultural conversations among Sephardic Jews began to devolve into smoldering antagonism.

One afternoon soon after the Bukharan declaration of sovereignty, Sergei had tea with Rakhmin Efraimovich in the Mountain Jewish community. Sergei asked Rakhmin why he did not support the building of the Sephardic synagogue.

Rakhmin: I do not need the headache, the papers. For me, the most important thing is that people come.
Sergei: More people will come [if it is built].
Rakhmin: Sure they will. [That will be] the next generation.
Sergei: Look into the future. You will need a bigger space.
Rakhmin: They are doing renovations. [We will get] one hundred square meters.
Sergei: Maybe you don't want a Sephardic synagogue because you don't respect Shalom.

The room fell silent. Rakhmin sat legs apart, leaning over his large, protruding stomach. His face was stony. Sergei sat sideways in his chair, neck slightly strained, expressing his anger at the situation, but trying to keep himself under control. The atmosphere was tense, but Rakhmin kept a distanced attitude.

Rakhmin: I respect him. I come here.
Sergei: No you don't.

Rakhmin:	What does respect have to do with anything? You can build a Sephardic synagogue without me. We will come as your guests.
Sergei:	Sure we can build it without you. But you said yourself that without you, the synagogue will not be built.
Rakhmin:	Yes, I said that.

By the time I was ready to leave the field in November, Kostia, Sergei, and Shalom were the only ones still invested in the project, for it ultimately meant improving the size of the Mountain Jewish prayer hall. Shalom and the board of the Mountain Jewish community even voted to make me their official representative to the American Sephardi Federation. I was to prove to the federation how inadequately the Sephardim were treated at the Central Synagogue.

The day before I concluded my fieldwork and returned to America, Shalom hired a local photographer to shoot a video, documenting how the "Ashkenazic administration" mistreated the Sephardim by comparing the size of the main prayer hall with the Mountain Jewish prayer hall. I narrated in English. As the camera panned the Mountain Jewish prayer hall, Kostia, Sergei, and Shalom invited Rabbi Silverstein to come sit down with them at the desk to wish me good luck in the future. After the rabbi said some kind words about me, Kostia decided to finally tell the rabbi about how I would represent MEROS in America. He said, "[I want to talk to you] about the issue of the Sephardic community. Now, a person is going to America to talk to the Sephardic community [there], to talk to the world, and to represent us. We are not hiding this issue. We want everyone to know about it. Concretely, can you say that you wish the Sephardic community good luck, so that the Sephardic community finally has its own spacious synagogue that enjoys full rights, so that there is a head Ashkenazic rabbi and a head Sephardic rabbi, so that we associate according to our rights?"

Shalom looked at Rabbi Silverstein and said, "Say a blessing for that, [and] say a *Mi Shebayrakh* for Sascha and for these golden words. We really want [you to do that]." The room was silent, and then Rabbi Silverstein said that the plan to strengthen the Sephardic culture and religion was "a wonderful deed, and it will have the assistance of the head rabbi of Russia and the head rabbi of Moscow. But the question of a synagogue is a question of money, and the question of money is related to the question of people, and all of that is related to how many people this community can attract. And in that, I wish you very much success."

Rabbi Silverstein thanked me on the video for giving him a deeper understanding of synagogue life. He reminded us that yesterday he recited a blessing for my safe return. The camera followed him out the door and then focused back on Shalom, Sergei, Kostia, and me standing inside the Mountain Jewish prayer hall. Shalom said to me, "God give you health. That's it. We did not get the blessing, Sascha. That's it. Give mama and papa a big *shalom* ["hello" in Hebrew] from us."

The Finale

Despite his efforts to create a Sephardic movement at the synagogue, Shalom was unsuccessful. The contingent alliances that existed among Mountain, Georgian, and Bukharan Jews were not strong enough to withstand the pervasive bodily discourse about racial essences. While Shalom played up his perceived wild Mountain Jewish nature to get what he wanted, his performances of passion ultimately did not help his cause. They not only reinforced the image of the savage Mountain Jew, but they also alienated Georgian, Bukharan, and even Russian Jews from Shalom's cause. In addition, Rabbi Silverstein used this situation to increase his hold on the synagogue's *minyans*. He made deals with Georgian and Bukharan Jews to control their optimal ritual space at the synagogue. Because Shalom, Kostia, and Sergei became isolated, they turned to me to save the struggle for Sephardic sovereignty. Sympathetic to their needs for a bigger prayer space and grateful for their help with my ethnographic project, I talked with the American Sephardi Federation and showed them the video, but, after several meetings, I was unable to gather international support for the building of a separate Sephardic synagogue.

Several months later, Sergei called me to tell me that Shalom had emigrated to Germany and that Rabbi Silverstein had appointed him (Sergei) to look after the Mountain Jewish prayer hall at the synagogue. And so, when that video camera focused on Sergei, Kostia, Shalom, and me standing in the Mountain Jewish prayer hall, it captured the end of Shalom's attempt to build both a Mountain Jewish community and a Sephardic synagogue in Moscow.

Conclusion

About twenty years ago, there was an article by a Jew from Latvia who moved to Israel. It was translated into Russian. It was about a daisy—you know, "Loves me, loves me not"—and how Jews count on the daisy, "To emigrate, not to emigrate." This is very poignant. The article was copied many times and passed around. He wrote another piece called "The Last Jewish Grave in the Graveyard." He said that no one wanted to be the last Jew to die in Russia.

—Yehuda Levi

The End of an Era

In September 1996, Yurii Isaakovich took me to the Vostriakova cemetery to visit his parents' graves. Vostriakova has Jewish and non-Jewish sections, but they had overlapped recently due to lack of space. As we entered the Jewish area and walked along the narrow dirt path overgrown with tall weeds and bushes, Yurii read the names on the headstones. It gave him great joy to see Jewish surnames; he had a friend named Fishbane, he knew a Cohen who was a good doctor, and he once had a Rabinowitz for a neighbor.

Yurii pointed out the graves near us that had gone to ruin. One headstone was crooked and covered with vines, while another was a pile of rubble. He said there was no one left to care for these plots, since the relatives of the dead had emigrated. "Now, people are ordering stronger headstones, so when they leave the country, they know nothing will happen to the graves."

The choice of emigrating from Russia informed events chronicled in this book. While Georgian, Bukharan, and Mountain Jews migrated to Moscow to make better lives for themselves, they maintained family connections in other countries, so they could go there if Russia experienced drastic economic, social, or political destabilization. Russian Jews also contemplated leaving their homes for Israel or the West, if life in Moscow was not beneficial for them. All these individuals weighed the positive and negative affects of staying or leaving. Elderly Russian Jews at the synagogue faced different circumstances. Declaring that they were too old to uproot themselves or that their families refused to leave, they watched fellow *minyan* members leave or become ill and die.

In October 1996, Moshe, the eighty-year-old Russian Jew who read the Torah in the small hall, went into the hospital to be treated for pneumonia. He returned to the synagogue several weeks later to attend a *Yahrzeit* meal in honor of Rabbi Dubinovich's mother. Usually stately in appearance, Moshe arrived hunched over and haggard-looking. Lyonia and Yurii joked that Moshe had "crawled" into the prayer hall. They did not address him directly or show any sympathy for him. Other *minyan* members shook his hand, but they kept their distance. I gave my seat at the table to Moshe and handed him a plastic cup of soda. He looked around hungrily for recognition from his peers, especially Berl, Shloimie, and Shmuel Berl. But it was as if he were already lost to them. They hardly noticed him.

When I returned to the Central Synagogue for a short visit in June 2000, I sat with Yurii in the refurbished small hall, bright and marble-floored. Elderly Russian Jews no longer gathered there on Shabbat, but there was no youth *minyan* either, since the religious younger generation preferred to pray in their own yeshivas.

I asked Yurii to tell me what had happened to the Russian Jewish *minyan*. He said that Moshe, Shloimie, and Berl had died; Shmuel Berl had emigrated to the West to join the rest of his family, and Yehuda Levi no longer attended services. Lyonia, having continued his Jewish education, was now the cantor and Torah reader for weekday services in the small hall, but the remaining Russian Jews could no longer gather a morning *minyan* without the help of Georgian Jews, who were now in the majority and sometimes led the service. Yurii lamented that he paid the four elderly Russian Jews to come to morning and evening *minyans*; otherwise, they refused to attend. Yurii then complained about the small hall renovations. He was still upset that the solid old pews had been replaced with new ones. Some had already broken. "See the paint chipping in the corner of the room?" he said, pointing to the blotched wall near the ark, his voice straining. He had held fast to his sense of duty, representing himself as one of the last Russian Jews heavily invested in small hall religiosity and Soviet morality.

Down the hallway in the Mountain Jewish prayer hall, Evgenii Moiseivich said to me with a sigh, "There are too many synagogues and not enough Jews." The Mountain Jewish religious community had split up: one group remained at the Central Synagogue, still calling itself the *gorskaia evreiskaia obshchina* (Mountain Jewish community), while another group had obtained funding from wealthy Mountain Jewish businessmen to build a separate small synagogue, informally called the *gorskaia sinagoga* (Mountain [Jewish] Synagogue), in the courtyard of the Central Synagogue. They had taken over space allocated to the Bukharan Jews, who, as a result, returned to praying in the library. Due to the split in the Mountain Jewish community, Kostia left his job as treasurer, and Sergei became the head of the new synagogue. During my visit, Bukharan and Georgian Jews were looking for sponsors to help them build their own independent places of worship. All the while, Jews continued to leave Russia—and to move to Moscow. Some left, only to return again, admitting they did not feel at home anywhere, as the following joke articulates: "A man goes to Israel, then back to Russia. He is not happy in Israel. He is not happy in Russia. Where is he happy? On the road."

The Beginning of a New Age

While this joke is an exaggeration, it points to a key aspect of post-Soviet Jewish identity: it is inherently transnational. The movement back and forth to Moscow, especially from the former Soviet republics, confounds the classical notion of the nation-state building project in which a homogeneous ethnic group pledges allegiance to its own state. Jews at the synagogue searched for national belonging on two levels: they wanted to be influential Russian citizens and valuable members of the Jewish people. Two critical issues arise from such a situation. What happens to Jewish identity when membership in the Jewish nation hinges on being a Russian citizen in a market economy? And, what are the implications for the new Russian nation when Jews define their Jewishness in terms of Russianness?

Russian Jews have experienced Moscow change dramatically in a short amount of time. No longer confined by Soviet rule, they are free to worship as they please, and they can purchase ritual goods on the open market. But the high price for this freedom has been the devaluation of their worldview and way of life. While the Soviet system restricted Russian Jews at the synagogue, it also created a system of meaning—a way of living in the world—that they incorporated into their religious practices. Surveillance and restriction of synagogue activities encouraged silent inner belief; scarcity emphasized the use value of sacred items and the creation of personal networks to obtain them; paternalistic redistribution compelled an appeal to bureaucracy for assistance; and the ethical power of the intelligentsia made intellect an essential component of Jewish identity. This cultural framework produced the notion that morality is communal and that immorality is individualistic. In the Soviet context, money moved a person away from the former and toward the latter.

The dissolution of the Soviet Union, the influx of Jews from the republics and the West, and the implementation of a market economy shook the very foundations of Russian Jewish identity at the Central Synagogue. A new focus on being "religious" supported outwardly visible activities of Orthodox Judaism, namely religious education and keeping kosher. The widespread availability of ritual items shifted emphasis away from the inherent value of an object to its market price. The elimination of Soviet bureaucracy had a twofold effect: the reproduction of administrative power on the synagogue level and the removal of any governmental organization able to hear complaints. Finally, the loss of power among the educated placed a new importance on success in business as the actualization of personal self-worth. Money had become the key to success, and the market symbolized the power of the individual in spite of the community.

Being a Jew is no longer self-evident in Moscow. Russian Jews are one of many Jewish groups; they have to share space with Georgian, Mountain, Bukharan, and Western Jews in the synagogue and the city. Trying to find a place for themselves, each group must address why it belongs there—and to do that, it must assert why it is an integral part of Russian society. As a result, Jewish identity revolves around claims to Russian citizenship and evaluations of how Jews can contribute to the new Russian state.

By placing themselves in the national narrative, Jews at the synagogue used the racial and ethnic categorizations involved in the creation of the Russian nation-state to their advantage. Their manipulation of these elements reveal an ongoing tension between a post-Soviet past and a market-oriented future, as well as conflicts between center and periphery. Post-Soviet Jews often conflated race and ethnicity with emerging class differences. Evaluations of the morality of the new business culture were central to each Jewish group's self-identification and ability to add to Russia's potential.

Due to their perception of their own poverty, Russian Jews were heavily invested in maintaining the value of intellectual endeavors and religious belief within the heart. Georgian and Mountain Jews reveled in the new market economy, applying their own history of commerce to achieve personal success, which they invested in their families and communities. And yet, these distinctions among Jewish groups made sense only in reference to one another. Post-Soviet Jewish identity is thus contextual; one cannot simply be "Jewish" in Russia today. Jewishness has meaning only when one claims to be a Georgian Jew, Russian Jew, or Mountain Jew. Even the pronunciation of Hebrew is an act of differentiation. Jews at the synagogue consciously created and demonstrated their identities in front of one another.

This very Soviet and Russian formula of us versus them provided Shalom with the means to gather support for the creation of a Sephardic synagogue, since Georgian, Mountain, and Bukharan Jews shared common alienating experiences in a primarily Ashkenazic religious community. While Jews at the synagogue were able to play creatively with ethnicity—be it Sephardic, Georgian, or Russian—they expounded the Russian nationalist discourse about race; Mountain Jews were placed outside the Jewish people. Unlike Georgian and Russian Jews who were able to shift the boundaries of belonging between their groups, Mountain Jews had to work hard to prove the benefits of their "blackness." In contrast to a perception of ethnicity that can shift and expand, skin color represents a mark of difference that is extremely difficult to overcome.

Bodily differences can be transcended, however, but only through a descent into a discourse placing all participants on the level of sexuality. The "savage" space of the Mountain Jewish prayer hall provided the parameters in which Georgian, Russian, and Mountain Jews could assert their brotherhood by talking about having sex with Jewish women. The vodka-drinking episode illustrates how male desire can create a shared Jewish identity. This community is a male one; women are the means for inclusion into it, but not the recipients of it. Images of gender simultaneously unify and divide the Jewish nation.

Storytelling in the Field:
The Ethnographer's Responsibilities

Soon after I arrived in Moscow in 1995, Rabbi Silverstein and a visiting American rabbi teased me, saying if I wanted to see morning services, I would have to dress up like a man. We laughed at the preposterous nature of this suggestion, but as I walked away from them, I frowned with indignation. The joke highlighted my biggest problem in the field: how could I, a young woman, study a religious community of Orthodox Jewish men? As I gained access to morning services and experienced my troubles with Aleksei and Yehuda Levi, I realized that I could not change who I was at that time, nor could I significantly alter who people thought I should be. I decided to make the best use of the situation, understanding it as a process whereby I was able to obtain important relational information about synagogue life. If I were a man, this ethnography would have turned out differently, but this story is just as inherently incomplete as any other (Clifford 1986).

Shifting perspectives among Mountain, Georgian, Russian, and Bukharan Jews, I honored some silences, while I broke others. Ethnographers have to choose which stories to tell and which tales to let lie undisturbed. We also have to look out for ourselves, weighing our research successes and physical safety against how these concerns might affect the people we study. At the same time, we must forfeit some control over our fieldwork—events can drag us in, without our being conscious of it at the time. We can easily become part of the tale.

In the growing transnational realities of Russian society, ethnographers have a responsibility to investigate how Westerners, even the ethnographer, influence the trajectory of Russian culture, economics, and politics. Although Rabbi Silverstein represented himself as a proponent of business-like competition, he used Soviet strategies of paternalistic redistribution and surveillance to obtain his goals. And, as people informed on each other in front of me, a possible American Jewish redeemer, I myself became a spy for the administration. Postsocialist reality is thus not so much "post" as it is "in between" an uncertain, but market-oriented, future and a socialist past. Those invested in preserving the Soviet past or reaching for a capitalistic future use similar techniques of domination and resistance. Those who are successful, like Rabbi Silverstein or the Mountain Jews (with their new synagogue), have access to personal and financial resources. Those who fail, like Yehuda Levi, do not have the ties and accounts they need to succeed.

Russianness and Jewishness

Jews in Russia have defined their Jewishness in terms of Russianness, applying their own values to the new economy. This process signals a turning point for Russia. Russians are faced with a myriad of "others" in their territory, as the Russian and Soviet anti-Semitic image of the Jewish trader/traitor fractures due to the large numbers of Caucasian market men in Moscow. Although Russian Jews have internalized the negative stereotypes of themselves as greedy and individualistic (and thus outside the Russian community), Georgian, Mountain, and Bukharan Jews provide new models for Jewish identity that exemplify the contributions "outsiders" can make to Russian society. Just like Russian Jews at the Central Synagogue, Russians cannot prosper without their "ethnics" (Ukrainians, for example) and "blacks" (like Gypsies and Caucasians), because Georgian and Mountain Jews, with their market experiences and customs, are able to profit in the new economy and help Russia develop its resources.

The dissolution of the Soviet Union made Russia conscious of its need to have relations with the new republics in order to survive. It is not clear whether the majority of this awareness will take the form of territorial expansion or peaceful negotiations. Russians could learn from Jews at the synagogue about the creativity of ethnicity and how to survive with others despite perceived cultural and racial differences. The recognition of a common humanity (the Jewish *mensch* and the Russian *chelovek*) can undercut prejudices and open cultural borders. It is my hope that Jews and Russians find their place together in this fast-changing, post-Soviet world.

Notes

Introduction

1. The following discussion of the history of the Moscow Jewish population draws on information from Dubnow (1918:162–70 and 1920:127); "Moskva," in *Kratkaia evreiskaia entsiklopediia* (1991:471–83); and Lobovskaya (1996).

2. Even though official accounts state that the synagogue has been open continuously since 1906, several elderly Russian Jews mentioned that police barred them from entering the synagogue. They would not tell me the exact dates of these encounters.

3. The synagogue in Cherkizovo was erected in 1927, and the Mar'ina Roshche synagogue was built in 1929. After the government liquidated the Cherkizovo synagogue in the early 1970s, its congregation moved to the Central Synagogue. In 1993, the Mar'ina Roshche synagogue burned down, and, in 1996, Rabbi Berl Lazar, the head Lubavitcher rabbi of the former Soviet Union, oversaw its reconstruction and consecration in preparation for its becoming a Jewish center. Many local Jews told me about their visits to the old Mar'ina Roshche synagogue and how they felt a sense of warmth, community, and belonging there. In 1992, the Lubavitcher Hasidim acquired and refurbished a former small synagogue building near Bolshaia Bronnaia Street. People say that Lazar Poliakov built it either for his own use or for the local Hasidim. The Soviet government made it into a Soviet House of Culture in the 1930s. During the time of my research, Bolshaia Bronnaia functioned as a synagogue and place to buy kosher meat and bread. By the year 2000, the Lubavitchers had obtained a new synagogue near the metro station Otradnoe.

4. *Khakham* is the Sephardic term for a rabbi. It means "the wise."

5. A mullah is a Muslim teacher or interpreter of religious law. By calling Isaak Khaimov their mullah, the Bukharan Jews acknowledged their long history of living among Muslims in Central Asia.

6. For more information on the use of many synagogues in Eastern Europe, see Bohlman (2000).

7. Men wear phylacteries during weekday morning prayer. Phylacteries are a set of small boxes with accompanying leather straps. One box is placed on the forehead and the other on the inner muscle of the left forearm. The boxes contain four passages from the Bible (Exodus 13:1–10, Exodus 13:11–16, Deuteronomy 6:4–9, and Deuteronomy 11:13–21) that command the wearing of the phylacteries during prayer.

8. In 1996, the Central Synagogue was still "nationalized" property. After the collapse of the Soviet Union, the city of Moscow retained ownership of

much former state property, and the Moscow Jewish Religious Community (located at the Central Synagogue) did not utilize its opportunity to repurchase the synagogue. As a result, the Community leased the synagogue from the Moscow city government.

9. For example, see GARF (the State Archive of the Russian Federation), *fond* (f.) 6991s, *opis* (op.) 4, *delo* (d.) 54. Page numbers *(listi)* are indicated by l. or ll. This and all subsequent translations of archival documents are my own.

10. For example, in 1956, the Council authorized the publication of three thousand copies of the prayer book *Siddur Hashalom* to be distributed to the Moscow Jewish Religious Community and other synagogues in the Soviet Union (GARF, f. 6991s, op. 4, d. 37, l. 58). In addition, in 1957, the Council for the Affairs of Religious Cults had a chart listing (1) the cities in the Soviet Union that had synagogues that received Jewish calendars and prayer books from the Central Synagogue, (2) the number of calendars received, and (3) the number of prayer books received (GARF, f. 6991s, op. 4, d. 76, ll. 51–54).

11. GARF, f. 6991s, op.4, d. 23, ll. 26–27.

12. GARF, f. 6991s, op. 4, d. 71, l. 104.

13. GARF, f. 6991s, op. 4, d. 23, ll. 32–35.

14. On January 13, 1953, Stalin accused nine doctors (six of whom were Jewish) of poisoning prominent Soviet leaders and planning to murder current party leaders. He charged them with being Zionist spies. It was rumored that if Stalin had not died, he would have authorized the trial of the doctors, which would have led to a nationwide pogrom (Korey 1973:16).

15. The number of Jews allowed to emigrate rose from 299 persons in 1968 to 1,027 persons in 1970 (Levin 1990:667).

16. By 1973, Soviet Jewish emigration slowed down and continued at a slow pace until 1976. In addition, the pattern of *Noshrim* (a Hebrew word for "dropouts") emerged when Soviet Jews began to immigrate to other countries instead of Israel. In 1974, 18.7 percent of the emigrants chose not to go to Israel. By 1976, this number had increased to 48.6 percent. This shift in the pattern of Jewish emigration from the USSR reflected the practical problems of life in Israel: a bureaucratic insensitivity and impatience with or lack of understanding of the varied cultural and psychological background of the newcomers, the day-to-day hardships of getting adjusted to a new life, and the onset of the Yom Kippur War in 1973 (Levin 1990:710). By 1978, the number of Jews allowed to emigrate had risen and then peaked at over 51,000 in 1979 (Gitelman 1988:280). The Soviet invasion of Afghanistan in December 1979 broke the already tenuous international relations with the West and greatly curtailed Jewish emigration. In 1980, the government cut back emigration by 60 percent, and from 1983 to 1986, only about 1,000 Jews left the country, as compared to 25,000 in the 1970s (Gitelman 1988:286).

17. The word *prikhozhanin* means parishioner, and it comes from the verb *prikhodit'* which means "to come." While the Central Synagogue has no official membership policy, Americans are used to the idea of membership in a religious organization, so I use the term "members of the congregation" or "congregants" to refer to these self-described frequent visitors.

18. I use the term *tactic* here to refer to practices that are resistant and counter-hegemonic (see de Certeau 1984:xix).

19. Five thousand roubles roughly equaled one dollar in 1995.

Chapter 1

1. The *Shema* is the following prayer: "Hear, O Israel: the Lord is our God, the Lord is One."

2. The term *Amidah* means "standing" in Hebrew, and the prayer is so named because the worshiper recites it while standing. This prayer is included in the morning *(Shacharit)*, afternoon *(Mincha)*, and evening *(Ma'ariv)* services. Even though the Ashkenazim refer to this prayer as the *Shemoneh Esrei* (the "eighteen benedictions"), the *Amidah* actually contains nineteen benedictions: (1) the blessing for the patriarchs; (2) the praise of God's might; (3) the *Kedushah*, which praises God's holy name; (4) petitionary prayers for insight; and prayers for (5) repentance, (6) forgiveness, (7) redemption, (8) health and healing, (9) a year of prosperity, (10) the ingathering of the exiles, (11) the restoration of justice, (12) the punishment of heretics, (13) the reward of the righteous, (14) the rebuilding of Jerusalem, (15) the return of the Davidic reign, (16) the acceptance of prayers, (17) the rebuilding of the holy temple, (18) thanks to God, and (19) the establishment of peace.

3. GARF, f. 6991s, op. 4, d. 54, l. 8.

4. GARF, f. 6991s, op. 4, d. 54, l. 9.

5. GARF, f. 6991s, op. 4, d. 54, l. 12.

6. GARF, f. 6991s, op. 4, d. 37, 1. 58.

7. GARF, f. 6991s, op. 6, d. 1621, l. 39.

8. GARF, f. 6991s, op. 4, d. 79, ll. 186–8.

9. GARF, f. 6991s, op. 4, d. 71, ll. 103–9; d. 73, ll. 88–96; op. 6, d. 1192, ll. 74–76, l. 124, and ll. 154–55.

10. The prayer for peace corresponded to the government's international propaganda of being concerned with stopping the use and spread of atomic weapons. As for the prayer for the Soviet Union, Jews always pray for the health of the country in which they live. This prayer took on even more significance in the 1970s, when the Soviet government portrayed Jews who wanted to emigrate as traitors to their country. See Gitelman (1988) and Levin (1990).

11. It is a prayer that "does not speak about death, or mourning, or the soul of the deceased," and many who say it "see it as a simple affirmation of faith that is spoken in the midst of community—that even in my grief and sorrow, I can still rise amongst my fellow Jews and praise God" (Dosick 1995:232).

12. For details, see Rothenberg (1971:54).

13. There has never been an official membership policy at the Central Synagogue due to the Soviet government's antagonistic policy toward organized religion. During the Soviet years, frequent worshipers at the synagogue would unofficially "buy" a seat in the main hall in order to raise money to bake matzah on Passover. Recently, Rabbi Silverstein has continued this practice, but the prices for seats are extremely high. Those who buy them are rich businessmen, influential lawyers, and Jewish members of the government. However, hardly any of these people come to the synagogue on a daily basis.

14. The Hasidim (Hasids) began as a mystical and popular movement in southern Poland and Ukraine in the eighteenth century. The founder of the movement, the Baal Shem Tov, provided a new way of being a religious Jew. He revolted against the rabbinic standards of learning and piousness as a sign of religious devotion to give the poor Jewish masses a way they could get in

touch with God. He practiced mystical healing and believed in serving God with joy and song.

15. This conversation is based on notes that I took immediately after meeting with Rabbi Silverstein.

16. This conflict between the *Mitnaggedim* and the Lubavitcher Hasidim came to a head in June 2000, when the Hasidim of Russia elected a Hasidic rabbi to be the chief rabbi of Russia. At that time, the Putin administration recognized both the Hasidic rabbi and Rabbi Dubinovich, who was elected chief rabbi of Russia in 1990 by a different Jewish council.

17. Because of the shortage of ritual objects, each member of the *minyan* used his own prayer book. Shloimie led the service with the 1979 version of the *Siddur Hashalom*. Even though his prayer book incorporates several Sephardic customs (since it was intended for distribution across the Soviet Union), Shloimie led the service according to the Ashkenazic liturgical style. Some of the members of the congregation used the *Siddur Tehillat Hashem*, distributed by the Lubavitcher Hasidim. It follows the *nusach Ha-Ari Z"l*. The Georgian Jews prayed with either their own prayer book, called the *Siddur Shirat Avner* (*Siddur* Songs of Avner), which they brought with them from Georgia, or any prayer book they could find.

18. Perhaps the absence of this custom among Russian Jews in Moscow relates to how the Soviet press at times labeled the selling of seats and Torah portions as financial transactions prohibited under Soviet law (Rothenberg 1971:57).

19. For more information on this prayer, see Nulman (1996:244).

20. Beniamin translated this Georgian Jewish prayer service that I audiotaped on Monday, May 20, 1996.

21. Based on my one tape recording of the service on May 20, 1996, Khakham David recited only the *Menuhah* portion of the prayer. This section names the deceased and says, "May the repose that is prepared in the celestial abode."

Chapter 2

1. Russian Jews sometimes called the *Yahrzeit* a *pominka*, due to the similar nature of the two rituals. The *pominka* is a traditional Russian meal of remembrance that takes place after the deceased is buried and on the forty-day anniversary of his/her death. The word *pominka* comes from the Russian verb *pomnit'*, which means "to remember." The main point of a *pominka* is to maintain the memory of the deceased (Kuz'menko 1996:88).

2. Western accounts of Jewish life in Georgia also share this opinion (Rothenberg 1967; Cale 1970).

3. This brief discussion of Georgian Jewish history comes from Dzhindzhikhashvili (1994:126–28); Kandel' (1990:269–72); "Gruzinskie evrei" in *Kratkaia evreiskaia entsiklopediia* (1982:235–45); Rothenberg (1967:16–19); Gitelman (1988:297–304); and Zand (1991:378–444).

4. GARF, f. 6991s, op. 4, d. 23, ll. 32–35.

5. GARF, f. 6991s, op. 4, d. 56, l. 9.

6. GARF, f. 6991s, op. 4, d. 56, l. 78; d. 57, l. 22.

7. GARF, f. 6991s, op. 4, d. 54, l. 41.

8. Cheese without the kosher label could contain rennet, a product taken

from the stomach of a calf. The calf might not have been slaughtered correctly, and the rennet's inclusion in the cheese could break the kosher law of not mixing milk and meat (Klein 1979:306).

9. One of the three *mitzvot* (Jewish laws) that a woman must fulfill relates to the making of bread *(challah)*. She must take of a piece of dough from the yeast batter, throw it into the oven so that it burns, and say the proper blessing. This law reenacts the days of the Temple when the Jews brought offerings to God from the harvest. Bread is kosher when it is made by religious Jewish women or under rabbinic supervision. It must not contain any animal products, so that it can be eaten with both milk and meat dishes (Greenberg 1983:111).

10. A bar mitzvah is a ceremony marking a boy's transition to manhood at age thirteen. *Bar mitzvah* means "son of the law" and indicates that he is now able to fully participate in a *minyan*.

11. GARF, f. 6991s, op. 4, d. 54, l. 178.

12. GARF, f. 6991s, op. 4, d. 23, l. 34.

Chapter 3

1. There is a minor stipulation to this statement. In 1996, amendments were made to the law about religious freedom in the Russian Federation. The Duma indicated that the new constitution of the Russian Federation passed in 1993 did not adequately control the myriad of new religious organizations that flourished under the 1990 freedom of religion law. The 1996 amendments (sent out first in the law project entitled, "About the Explanation of the Changes and Additions to the Law 'About the Freedom of Religion,' " approved in 1996) were aimed at the growing number of foreign "cults," like Mormons, in Russia. Some of the amendments stated that religious organizations could only be created by persons who have continuously lived in the Russian Federation, that these organizations had to be registered (and have a membership of at least ten), and that the public prosecutor would monitor these organizations for any violation of the freedom of conscience of any of its members. So far, Judaism has been considered to be a "local" religion. While this law might restrict the parameters of the practice of Judaism within Russia, the mayor of Moscow, Yurii Luzhkov, made it clear that he openly supported the maintenance and growth of Jewish religious institutions in his city. Not only did he wear a yarmulke to the opening of the new Lubavitcher synagogue in 1996, but he also stated at the Russian Jewish Congress, "There are 140 nations in Moscow. One of the biggest, brightest, and most respected is the Jewish diaspora. It has become smaller, a fact which I very much regret. Our most important task is to stop the exodus of Jews from Moscow. . . . We want the Jewish diaspora in Russia and Moscow to take an interest in our government, and we want to preserve all the traditions of the Jewish people and its religion" (translated from my recording of the Congress).

2. There was a movement among Russian Jews to lessen their reliance on Western agencies and to fund their own projects. In January 1996, the Russian Jewish Congress met for the first time to bring together rich Russian businessmen with local Jewish communities in need of financial support. In 1996, Rabbi Silverstein sat on the board of the Congress and helped decide the funding parameters. For example, he told me that at the first budget

meeting, 20 percent of the money gathered went to religion, 44 percent went to education, and the rest to charity for the sick, poor, and elderly. In reality, however, the categories of education and religion were mainly the same, since most Jewish schools (at least in Moscow) were sponsored by religious organizations. In this way, the majority of the money collected from local businessmen went to religious leaders.

3. Maria Abramovna, the head of the charity center located on the second floor of the synagogue (in the women's section of the big prayer hall) solicited money from foreigners and distributed it to the poor and elderly as she saw fit. The amount of cash that she raised and handled was small in comparison to the synagogue accounts supervised by Rabbi Silverstein.

4. I was never given a straight answer to my questions as to who provided Rabbi Silverstein with his salary. His wife and aunt refused to tell me his sponsors, stating that it would not be polite to talk about such things. But they hinted that he received funds from many Western organizations and individuals. He would have needed to do so in order to make enough money to support his family.

5. "Smert' rybotorgovtsa," *Moskovskii komsomolets*, March 8, 1996, p. 8.

6. "Killery vypustili v zhertvu bol'se 20 pul'," *Moskovskii komsomolets*, March 31, 1996, p. 1.

7. Dale Pesmen writes that the term *bespridel* also means without limits, and it was "originally prison slang for the end-of-the-world chaos of a prison rebellion" (Pesmen 2000:283).

8. This opinion is very strong among the Russian right. They see capitalism as an invasion from the West, arguing that, "since Russian psychology and moral values differ radically from those of the West and East, capitalism is bound to fail in Russia in any case. It would merely turn Russia into a Third World country" (Lacquer 1993:133).

9. For more information on the development of the communist ruling class, see Zemtsov (1985) and Matthews (1972 and 1978).

10. In the 1990s, the synagogue administration continued to function officially along the parameters of the *dvadtsatka* as established by the Soviet government. In 1996, the Duma reinstated these guidelines when it amended the law about religious freedom in the Russian Federation. For example, article 9/4 in the draft copy states, "In order to be registered, a religious organization must have no less than ten persons, and the organization must send to the organs of justice the following: a statement of registration, signed by the leaders of the religious organization; a list of persons who created the organization and proof of their citizenship, place of residence, and dates of birth; the confirmed constitution of the religious organization; [and] the protocol of a foundation meeting. In the case of the official registration of a religious organization, it must give information about its dogma and corresponding practice and provide documents that certify the location of the administrative organ of the religious organization."

11. I found many statistical reports on synagogue employment and finances at GARF, f. 6991s, op. 4 and op. 6.

12. GARF, f. 6991s, op. 4, d. 23, l. 32.

13. GARF, f. 6991s, op. 4, d. 23, l. 35.

14. I found many notes of the meetings between Rabbi Shliefer and Council members during which the rabbi asked for certain religious items, only to be told to put those requests in writing. In April 1956, Rabbi Shliefer asked about

resuming the production of prayer shawls and the officials told him to formally submit the request (GARF, f. 6991s, op. 4, d. 56, l. 109). The government had stopped producing them with the reasoning that "the believers themselves can sew the prayer shawls" (GARF, f. 6991s, op. 4, d. 171, l. 4). Also during that year, Shliefer asked if it could be arranged for the synagogue to buy *etrogim* (citrons) from Israel for the holiday of Sukkot. He was told that it was unlikely that he would receive this item, since it was too late to submit a request to the external trade office, as it had already set up a plan for "issues related to foreign money" (GARF, f. 6991s, op. 4, d. 56, ll. 138–39).

15. One elderly Russian Jewish woman told me that during the Soviet regime, when matzah cost two roubles a kilogram, she went to the synagogue to buy some for her mother, herself, and a friend. She stood in line at the synagogue to get a *talon* (coupon) that allowed her to buy a certain amount of matzah. Then, she took the next day off from work to stand in line at the synagogue to receive the matzah when her number was called. She said that certain old ladies sold their *talony* to people who did not want to wait in line for a coupon. Or, they sold the matzah itself for a high price. Those who had money and did not want to stand in line paid the price.

16. I found many reports written by Rabbi Shliefer and Rabbi Levin to the Council about the visits they received from foreign Jews. In these reports, the rabbis recited the party line. They said that anti-Semitism did not exist in the Soviet Union and negated the rumors heard abroad about the Soviet government's close control of religious activity. For numerous examples of these letters, see GARF, f. 6991s, op. 4, d. 54.

17. In my brief archival work at GARF, I did not find any earlier letters that the *dvadtsatka* might have written to complain about the activities of synagogue officials.

18. This period ended in 1964, however, when Khrushchev was removed from the leadership. The party viewed his reforms as too rash, since they endangered the positions of many party members who had been involved with Stalin. Brezhnev took over and implemented his plan for the "stability of the cadres," which solidified the bureaucratic system of the Soviet Union. Intellectuals began to speak freely again only in the late 1980s, during Gorbachev's reforms of *perestroika* and *glasnost'*.

19. GARF, f. 6991s, op. 4, d. 108, ll. 3–5.

20. GARF, f. 6991s, op. 4, d. 108, l. 4.

21. GARF, f. 6991s, op. 4, d. 108, l. 4.

22. GARF, f. 6991s, op. 4, d. 108, ll. 39–43.

23. GARF, f. 6991s, op. 4, d. 108, l. 41.

24. GARF, f. 6991s, op. 6, d. 784, ll. 31–44, ll. 56–57; d. 988, ll. 111–112.

25. I had access only to the Council's files up to 1985, since secret documents were inaccessible to the public for ten years. From 1977 to 1978, L. P. Kogan, an eighty-two-year-old veteran of World War II who frequented the synagogue, wrote reports about how the new chairman, S. Kleiman, misused funds (GARF, f. 6991s, op. 6, d. 1192, ll. 189–204; d. 1394, ll. 68–71, 73–76ob., 77–78, 81–82ob., 155–57a; and d. 1621, ll. 45–47, 53, 54). At the same time, there was an investigation of L. P. Kogan by the Council (GARF, f. 6991s, op. 6, d. 1192, ll. 187–88; d. 1394, l. 63; and d. 1621, l. 43). In 1980, the Council investigated a report by Ch. Ya. Lerner, a "frequent visitor" to the synagogue, about how chairman Kleiman and his replacement Minkenberg misappropriated synagogue funds (GARF, f. 6991s, op. 6, d. 1853, ll. 71–81).

Later that year, "members of the synagogue board" and "frequent visitors" to the synagogue wrote more complaints against Minkenberg and his associates (GARF, f. 6991s, op. 6, d. 1853, ll. 83–89). In 1981, G. M. Manevich (who wrote a letter against Tandetnik in 1975) complained about the administration's taking charity money from the community and congregation (GARF, f. 6991s, op. 6, d. 2101, ll. 112–14). In 1985, several "frequent visitors" to the synagogue wrote letters against B. M. Gramm, the new chairman of MERO (GARF, f. 6991s, op. 6, d. 3033, l. 20, ll. 21–24, 32).

26. This situation became clear to me during the following conversation with Rabbi Silverstein in August 1996:

Sascha: If someone has a problem with the synagogue, what do they do?
Rabbi: They call Feldman.
Sascha: If they have a problem with Feldman?
Rabbi: They call the *dvadtsatka*.
Sascha: If they have a problem with the *dvadtsatka*?
Rabbi: Tough luck.
Sascha: Before, members of the congregation called the government. . . .
Rabbi: Those days are over.
Sascha: Who is a higher authority than Feldman?
Rabbi: God.

Rabbi Silverstein's tone was jocular, but I took his statement to be a serious commentary on administrative politics.

27. Shalin (1996:72) writes, "The Soviet government had no intention of making the intellectuals' capitulation easy. It spared no effort in showing them who was boss, in drumming into their heads the conditions of surrender, for which they would be rewarded according to the sincerity of their remorse and willingness to inform on their brethren still persisting in their obstinate ways."

28. The Haftorah (which means the "termination") is the prophetic reading following the recitation of the day's Torah portion on Shabbat.

29. The *get* is the bill of divorce that a husband gives his wife in the presence of a rabbinical court. Only the husband has a right to divorce his wife, but there are specific grounds in Jewish law entitling one of the parties to seek a divorce. In such a case, the person seeking a divorce can apply to the rabbinical court that will then decide what kind of pressure to put on the recalcitrant spouse (Werblowsky and Wigoder 1965:118). By not giving his wife a *get*, Yehuda made it impossible for her to marry again.

30. The adjective *prodazhnyi* means "corrupt," and it comes from the word *prodazha*, "sale" or "selling." In other words, a person who is corrupt is "for sale."

Chapter 4

1. It was difficult to make an accurate estimate of the number of Mountain Jews in Moscow or what professions they practiced. Informal reports about the population of Mountain Jews in Moscow varied, ranging from 10,000 to 20,000 persons, depending on whether illegal and legal immigrants were counted. Not all Mountain Jews in Moscow were migrant businessmen. There were several families of Mountain Jews who lived in Moscow for over fifty years, and some Mountain Jews worked as lawyers and doctors. However,

most of the Mountain Jews who attended the Mountain Jewish prayer hall were involved in business in some way.

2. The status of German Jews as modern citizens of an enlightened and humanistic German nation was threatened by the presence of traditional Russian Jews. Steven E. Aschheim argues that the modern German Jew was created in opposition to its antithesis—the *Ostjuden* (eastern Jew) who embodied the negative traits German Jews were trying to overcome (Aschheim 1982:5). German Jews described the *Ostjuden* as dirty, loud, coarse, immoral, and culturally backward.

3. Information on the Mountain Jews comes from Zand (1985, 1986, and 1991:408–26); Gitelman (1988:315–18); and "Gorskie evrei" in the *Kratkaia evreiskaia entsiklopediia* (1982:182–91).

4. According to unofficial estimates, there were 41,000 Mountain Jews in Dagestan and 21,000 Mountain Jews in Azerbaijan in 1995.

5. According to my friend, the majority of the policemen (*menti*) are on the take and thus in competition with one another.

6. Mikhail Y. Agarunov, a Mountain Jewish scholar, writes, "For many centuries and until the 1920s, the vast majority of Mountain Jews were illiterate; the only exceptions were the rabbis and several of their students who could read the Torah. According to one historian, at the beginning of the 20th century, there was only one Mountain Jew with higher education. In the 1920s, the Mountain Jews acquired a written language based on the Latin alphabet. At about the same time, they gained various privileges from the Soviet government that made it easier for them to receive higher education. Since then, this small group of people has shown immense creative potential and has brought forth many scientists, doctors, composers, musicians, poets and writers. The first generation of Mountain Jewish intelligentsia was born" (Agarunov 1996:29).

7. "The Talmud forbids the loose exposure of the hair in the street by married women (citing this even as grounds for divorce) but the rigid development of this regulation—whereby a woman shaves off her hair at marriage and thereafter never appears in public without a wig—dates only from the fifteenth century. In some Orthodox circles, married women cover their hair with wigs although among Oriental and Hasidic Jews, a kerchief is used as the covering" (Werblowsky and Wigoder 1965:402).

8. Blu Greenberg writes that these disparate reasons stem from "the difference in rabbinic understanding of the Biblical law of the unfaithful wife. A married woman, charged with infidelity, was required to undergo an ordeal of bitter waters, during which the priest uncovered the woman's head. From this law, and from other sources, it was commonly understood that proper Jewish women of the past went about with their hair covered, mostly likely with shawls or head veils" (Greenberg 1983:187).

9. Mountain Jewish intellectuals also stated this idea. The writer Amaldan Kukullu has spent most of his life translating and publishing the oral history of Mountain Jews. The Mountain Jewish scholar Mikhail Agarunov organized a conference on Mountain Jews in Moscow in 1996 and established the Jewish Genealogical Society of Baku. He writes, "The mass emigration of Mountain Jews and their consequent assimilation with the nationals of the countries to which they are emigrating necessitates that systematic research be carried out promptly [by Mountain Jews] to preserve all information concerning this group" (Agarunov 1996:30).

Chapter 5

1. Information on the Bukharan Jews comes from "Bukharskie evrei" in the *Kratkaia evreiskaia entisklopediia* (1967:565–72).

2. Both Evgenii Moiseivich and Shalom told me on different occasions that the Mountain Jews paid eight thousand dollars in rent. Kostia, however, told me that the rent was later increased to ten thousand dollars.

3. Claims that Shalom's decision to set up MEROS was "nationalistic" reverberated with the tenets of the nationality policy of the Soviet Union. According to Khazanov, its basic principles were "(1) the maintenance of an over-centralized and unitary Soviet state despite official declaration of its federative structure; (2) political domination by the Russians in the Soviet Empire; (3) suppression of all manifestations of nationalism among the non-Russian peoples including their attempts at real autonomy; (4) creation of a new social structure of all the Soviet peoples including loyal ethnic elites dependent on the Soviet state and therefore interested in its preservation; (5) enforced simplification of the ethnic composition of the USSR" (Khazanov 1995:11).

4. By "pope of Russia," Shalom was referring to the leader of the Russian Orthodox Church, Patriarch Alexy II of Moscow and All Russia.

5. There are two Jewish customs behind Shalom's statement that religious men do not touch women's hands. First, according to Jewish law, menstrual blood is impure, and thus a woman is impure when she has her period. She can then pass on her impurity to objects and other people through physical contact with them. Thus, if a religious man touches an impure woman, he himself becomes impure and passes that contamination on to other people and objects, maybe even to the Torah itself (Eilberg-Schwartz 1990, on the ancient Israelites' views on the transmission of impurity; Biale 1984, for a good discussion of the Halakhic tractate of *Niddah*—the Laws of the Menstruant). Second, according to Jewish custom, men must not touch women who are not close relatives, since that touch might lead to improper behavior or thoughts. This kind of "gatekeeping" concept is common in Judaism. In this case, a Jewish man is supposed to feel confident that he will not break the law against adultery or coveting his neighbor's wife (Exodus 20:13–14), because he will never touch a woman who is not his relative.

6. Traditional Judaism prohibits cremation on at least three grounds. First, "Jews have invariably buried their dead in the earth, for it is written 'dust thou art and to dust thou shalt return' (Genesis 3:19)" (Rabinowicz 1964:25). Second, the sages teach that "cremation is an indignity, an affront to man as the highest form of creation. The body, the temple, and the servant of the soul must be guarded against sacrilegious desecration" (Rabinowicz 1964:26). Third, religious Jews believe, in the tradition of Maimonides, that the dead will be physically and spiritually resurrected when the Messiah reappears. "Ezekiel's vision of the dry bones is taken by our Sages to imply that the 'righteous are destined to arise (from the dead) clothed in all their garments' [Sanhedrin 90b]. This physical resurrection, our Sages tell us [Leviticus Rabbah XVIII; Genesis Rabbah XXVIII.3], will begin from a bone called *Luz*, the nut spinal column (*Os Coccyx*)" (Rabinowicz 1964:28).

7. Deuternonomy 14:3–21 and Leviticus 11:1–47 name the animals that the Jews are not allowed to eat, and Leviticus 13:11 specifically places vultures on the list of forbidden birds. Because the exact identities of most of the birds

mentioned on this list are uncertain, religious Jews only eat birds that are known by tradition to be kosher, such as chickens, turkeys, ducks, geese, and pigeons (Jacobs 1995:124).

8. Tzvi referred to a basic tenet in Judaism, "Thou shalt not hate thy brother in thy heart. . . . thou shalt love thy neighbor as thyself" (Leviticus 19:17–19).

9. Genesis 16:1–21:21.

10. The Moscow city government planned to build a synagogue, alongside a mosque and a Russian Orthodox church, on *Poklonnaia gora* as a way to acknowledge and deal with the suffering experienced by Muscovites during World War II.

Personae

The following is an index of people discussed in the book. Everyone alive during the time of the research for this book is referred to by a pseudonym. Some have first names, while others have an additional patronymic (-vna for women or -vich for men), which indicates their status in the community and/or their adherence to a more traditional Soviet and Russian way of address. Alphabetization is by first name.

Russian Jews

Anastasia Davidovna. Seventy-eight-year-old retired doctor and professor, who told me a story about how the synagogue was corrupt.

Anton Rizovskii. Businessman and former chairman of the Moscow Jewish Religious Community (MERO), in his late fifties, who spoke at the *dvadtsatka* meetings.

Avraham. Former member of the *minyan* at the Cherkizovo synagogue, in his mid-seventies, who frequently came to Shabbat services in the main hall of the Central Synagogue; he invited me to join the small Russian Jewish *Yahrzeit* meal in the corner of the main hall.

Berl. Regular at morning services and concentration camp survivor who came to Moscow from Poland in 1946; in his late seventies, he got into a fight with Yaakov at the Georgian Jewish *Yahrzeit*.

David. Ninety-eight-year-old member of the morning *minyan* who reminisced about how he had prayed in the small and main prayer halls.

Evgenii Moiseivich. Sixty-year-old retired navy doctor and administrator of the Mountain Jewish community.

Froim. Seventy-year-old member of the morning *minyan* who showed me where he had prayed in the main hall.

Grigorii Sharogradskii. Executive director of the Central Synagogue, in his late thirties.

Igor. Eighty-year-old administrator of the main hall.

Irina Maksovna. Fifty-four-year-old retired electrical engineer and administrator of the women's section in the main prayer hall.

Izzi. Frequent attendee of Shabbat services in the main hall; in his mid-sixties, he offered me some homemade wine at a Russian Jewish *Yahrzeit*.

Lyonia. Forty-three-year-old administrator of the small hall in the afternoons and formerly a chemist.

Maiia. Frequent attendee of Shabbat services in the main hall; in her early forties, she told me that money is dirt.

Maria Abramovna. Head of the charity center at the Central Synagogue, in her late eighties.

Rabbi Mark Samuelovich Dubinovich. Fifty-four-year-old chief rabbi of Russia who was the rabbi of the Central Synagogue from 1983 until 1990.

Moshe. Eighty-year-old Torah reader in the small hall.

Musia. Young woman in her mid-twenties who occasionally came to Shabbat services in the main hall; she talked about how hard it was for Russian Jews to return to their Judaism.

Natan. Assistant executive director of the Central Synagogue, in his late fifties.

Natasha. Twenty-three-year-old daughter of Evgenii Moiseivich, who told me a story about her father's waiting in line for matzah.

Semyon. Eighty-year-old recalcitrant member of the small hall *minyan*.

Shloimie. Eighty-three-year-old cantor in the small hall.

Shmuel Berl. Long-time member of the small hall *minyan* from a Hasidic family; at age sixty-seven, he told me about the hardships of keeping kosher and observing Shabbat during the Soviet regime.

Rabbi Solomon Shliefer. Served as chief rabbi of the Central Synagogue from 1943 to 1957 (deceased).

Valeri. Fifty-year-old editor at a local Jewish press who talked with me about visiting the synagogue as a youth and then later to say Kaddish for his father.

Viatcheslav Yurov. Sixty-year-old entrepreneur who spoke at the *dvadtsatka* meetings.

Yaakov. Seventy-eight-year-old beggar who frequented the synagogue.

Rabbi Yaakov Fishman. Chief rabbi of the Central Synagogue from 1971 to 1983 (deceased).

Rabbi Yegudah-Leib Levin. Chief rabbi of the Central Synagogue from 1957 to 1971 (deceased).

Yehuda Levi. Fifty-six-year-old engineer and part-time professor of Jewish history who contested the ability of Rabbi Silverstein to run the synagogue.

Yurii Isaakovich. Fifty-nine-year-old retired engineer and administrator of the small hall.

Bukharan Jews

Isaak Khaimov. Cantor for the Bukharan Jewish community, in his late seventies.

Rakhmin Efraimovich Abramov. Chairman of the Bukharan Jewish community; in his mid-sixties, he opposed building a Sephardic synagogue.

Mountain Jews

Aleksandr Elizarovich. Entrepreneur and main sponsor of the Mountain Jewish community; in his mid-forties, he invited me to his home for Passover dinner.

Anna. Widow who visited the Mountain Jewish prayer hall at the synagogue; in her mid-thirties, she said it was common for Mountain Jewish men to cheat on their wives.

Boris Semyonovich. Head of the Mountain Jewish synagogue in Baku; in his early sixties, he came to Moscow to raise money for his congregation.

Gavriel. Member of the Mountain Jewish community at the Central Synagogue who, in his mid-sixties, demanded that I cover my hair in the Mountain Jewish prayer hall.

Kostia. Treasurer of the Mountain Jewish community, in his early forties.

Misha. Thirty-five-year-old friend of Sergei who joked about Avraham being a Sephardic Jew.

Sergei. Thirty-five-year-old frequent visitor to the Mountain Jewish prayer hall who took me to visit the Ismailovskaia fair.

Shalom Simanduev. Chairman of the Mountain Jewish community and president of the Moscow Religious Community of Sephardic Jews (MEROS), in his mid-fifties.

Vitia. Visitor to the Mountain Jewish community; in his mid-fifties, he and Sergei discussed how Mountain Jews are Sephardim.

Western Jews

Mr. Feldman. President of the Moscow Jewish Religious Community (MERO), Belgian citizen, and diamond dealer, in his mid-fifties.

Mr. Hirsch. Swiss businessman, in his mid-fifties, who donated ritual items to the Central Synagogue.

Rabbi Simcha Silverstein. Thirty-three-year-old French citizen who became chief rabbi of Moscow and head of the Rabbinical Court of Russia in 1990.

Yose. Thirty-year-old Israeli businessman and morning *minyan* member who started a fight with Zviad.

Georgian Jews

Adom. Businessman and long-time member of the morning *minyan*; in his early fifties, he invited me to his house for dinner.

Albert. Congregant in his mid-fifties who went to the morning *minyan* to say Kaddish.

Aleksei. Thirty-five-year-old businessman and Zviad's brother, who took me to his store.

Beniamin. Forty-one-year-old businessman who was raised in Moscow and regularly attended morning *minyan*; he hosted a drinking party in the Mountain Jewish community to celebrate his son's twelfth birthday.

Dmitri. Congregant in his mid-fifties; he talked with Tzvi in the Mountain Jewish prayer hall.

Joseph. Newly arrived immigrant to Moscow; in his early forties, he told me that Georgian Jews keep kosher.

Khakham David. Official rabbi of the Georgian Jews, in his mid-sixties.

Khakham Eliahu. Rabbi, in his mid-sixties, who led services for the Sephardim in the Mountain Jewish prayer hall.

Leah. Adom's wife, in her mid-forties.

Mordechai. Businessman, in his mid-thirties, who hosted a *Yahrzeit* meal in honor of his deceased mother.

Niko Aleksandrovich. Restaurant owner, in his mid-fifties, who hosted a party to celebrate his son's bar mitzvah.

Nikolai Dzhinashvili. Delegate from the American Sephardi Federation, in his mid-thirties, who met with the Mountain Jews.

Tzvi. Seventy-eight-year-old regular attendee of morning services in the small hall; he told me a story about a Georgian Jewish businessman and lectured the Mountain Jews about kosher food.

Zviad. Thirty-three-year-old businessman and Aleksei's brother, who fought Yose during morning prayer.

Glossary

All terms are defined in the text when they first appear. Select terms that appear often in the book are listed here for reference.

Russian Words

beznravstvennost'. Immorality; *beznravstvennye* (pl. adj.), immoral.

chelovek. Man or human; *chelovecheskii'*, human (adj.) or humane; ***chelovecheskoe chuvstvo,*** humane feeling; *byt' chelovekom,* to be human.

chernyi. Black (adj.), black (n.).; *chernye* (pl.).

devushka. Girl; *devushki* (pl.).

dikii. Wild; *dikie* (pl.); *dikii narod*, wild people.

dusha. Soul.

dvadtsatka. Synagogue board.

etnos. Ethnicity.

evrei. Jew; *evreika,* Jewess; *evreiskii,* Jewish (m.); *evreiskaia,* Jewish (f.); *evreistvo,* Jewishness.

glasnost'. Openness.

gorskii. Mountain (adj); *gorskie* (pl.).

gruzinskie. Georgian (pl. adj.) or Georgians (pl. n.).

guliat'. To stroll, to have a good time.

karman. Pocket.

kolbasa. Sausage.

kolkhoz. Collective farm; *kolkhozi* (pl.).

kommunisty. Communists.

kul'tura. Culture; *nekul'turnye,* uncultured (pl. adj.).

mentalitet. Mentality.

Moskovskaia evreiskaia religioznaia obshchina. Moscow Jewish Religious Community.

na khaliavu. For free.

narod. People.

natsional'nost'. Nationality.

perestroika. Reconstruction.

prikhozhanin. Frequent visitor, parishioner.

prodazhnyi. Corrupt; *prodazhnyi chelovek,* corrupt person.

rasa. Race.

religioznye. Religious (pl. adj.).

russkie. Russian (pl. adj.) or Russians (pl. n.).

samizdat. Self-published illegal literature.
solianka. Beef stewed with vegetables, pickles, and spices.
sredi svoikh. Among your own kind.
styd. Shame; *mne stydno,* I am ashamed.
veruiushchie. Religious believers; *byt' veruiushchim,* to be a believer.
zhid. Kike (m.); *zhidka,* kike (f.); *zhidit'sia* (v.), to be stingy, to show stinginess.

Jewish Words

All words are Hebrew, unless otherwise noted.

aliyah. Privilege of being called up to the Torah when portions are read during prayer;
aliyot (pl.); the reading is usually divided into three portions, which gives
three people the chance to be called up to the Torah.
Amidah. Main prayer; consists of nineteen blessings and is said standing.
Ashkenazim. Jews whose ancestors came from Germany (Russian and Western Jews).
bar mitzvah. Ceremony marking a boy's transition to manhood at age thirteen; bar mitzvah means "son of the law" and indicates that the young man
is now able to fully participate in a *minyan*.
bimah. Raised portion of a prayer hall at the front of the room.
get. Certificate of divorce.
Kaddish. Mourner's prayer said every morning in a *minyan* for eleven months
following the death of a parent or loved one.
Kedushah. Third blessing in the *Amidah* that praises God's holy name; according to Ashkenazic tradition, the *minyan* recites the *Kedushah* responsively in a
standing position during the repetition of the *Amidah*.
khakham. Sephardic word for rabbi and "the wise."
matzah. Unleavened bread.
mensch. Yiddish word for a decent person.
mikvah. Ritual bath.
minyan. A prayer quorum of ten that, according to Orthodox Jewish law, cannot include women.
Mi Shebayrakh. Prayer that invokes God's blessing on a community or an
individual.
Mitzvah. Good deed, Jewish law.
Mizrahim. Oriental Jews from lands either once ruled by Persia or located "in
the East."
Sephardim. Jews having ties to Spain.
Shacharit. Morning prayer.
Simchat Torah. Holiday celebrating the end of the yearly cycle of Torah
readings.
tzedoka. Charity, social justice.
Yahrzeit. The anniversary of the death of a congregant's close relative.
yeshiva. Religious school for boys.

Works Cited

Abramsky, Chimen. 1970. "Biro-Bidzhan Project, 1927–1959." In *The Jews in Soviet Russia since 1917*, ed. Lionel Kochan, 62–75. London: Oxford University Press.

Abu-Lughod, Lila. 1990. "The Romance of Resistance: Tracing Transformations of Power through Bedouin Women." *American Ethnologist* 17 (1): 41–55.

———. 1993. *Writing Women's Worlds: Bedouin Stories*. Berkeley: University of California Press.

Agarunov, Mikhail Y. 1996. "The Mountain Jews of the Caucasus." *Avotaynu* 12 (2): 29–30.

Alexeev, Michael, and Ali Sayer. 1987. "The Second Economy Market for Foreign Made Goods in the USSR." *Berkeley-Duke Occasional Papers on the Second Economy in the USSR*, no. 11.

Alexeyeva, Ludmilla. 1985. *Soviet Dissent: Contemporary Movements for National, Religious, and Human Rights*. Trans. Carol Pearce and John Glad. Middletown, Conn.: Wesleyan University Press.

Alexeyeva, Ludmilla, and Paul Goldberg. 1990. *The Thaw Generation: Coming of Age in the Post-Soviet Era*. Boston: Little, Brown, and Company.

Anderson, John. 1994. *Religion, State, and Politics in the Soviet Union and Successor States*. Cambridge: Cambridge University Press.

Anisimov, I. Sh. 1888. *Kavkazskie evrei-gortzi*. Moscow: Dashkovskoe Etnograficheskoe Muzei.

Appadurai, Arjun. 1996. *Modernity at Large: Cultural Dimensions of Globalization*. Minneapolis: University of Minnesota Press.

Appiah, Kwame Anthony. 1990. "Racisms." In *Anatomy of Racism*, ed. David Theo Goldberg, 3–17. Minneapolis: University of Minnesota Press.

Arkangelsky, Vitaly D. 1998. "Modern Russian Social Security." *Social Service Review* (June): 251–68.

Aschheim, Steven E. 1982. *Brothers and Strangers: The East European Jew in German and German Jewish Consciousness, 1800–1923*. Madison: University of Wisconsin Press.

Bakhtin, Mikhail. 1984. *Rabelais and His World*. Trans. Helene Iswolsky. Bloomington: Indiana University Press.

Balzer, Marjorie Mandelstam. 1999. *The Tenacity of Ethnicity: A Siberian Saga in Global Perspective*. Princeton, N.J.: Princeton University Press.

Banting, Mark, Catriona Kelly, and James Riordan. 1998. "Sexuality." In *Russian Cultural Studies: An Introduction*, ed. Catriona Kelly and David Shepherd, 311–51. Oxford: Oxford University Press.

Baron, Salo W. 1976. *The Russian Jew under the Tsars and the Soviets*. 2nd ed. New York: Macmillan.

Bauman, Richard. 1986. *Story, Performance, and Event: Contextual Studies of Oral Narrative*. Bloomington: Indiana University Press.

Berdahl, Daphne. 1999. *Where the World Ended: Re-Unification and Identity in the German Borderland*. Berkeley: University of California Press.

Berdahl, Daphne, Matti Bunzl, and Martha Lampland, eds. 2000. *Altering States: Ethnographies of the Transition in Eastern Europe and Russia*. Ann Arbor: University of Michigan Press.

Biale, David. 1997. *Eros and the Jews: From Biblical Israel to Contemporary America*. Berkeley: University of California Press.

Biale, Rachel. 1984. *Women and Jewish Law: An Exploration of Women's Issues in Halakhic Sources*. New York: Schocken Books.

Bohlman, Philip V. 2000. "To Hear the Voices Still Heard: On Synagogue Restoration in Eastern Europe." In *Altering States: Ethnographies of the Transition in Eastern Europe and Russia*, ed. Daphne Berdahl, Matti Bunzl, and Martha Lampland. Ann Arbor: University of Michigan Press.

Bourdieu, Pierre. 1984. *Distinction: A Social Critique of the Judgement of Taste*. Trans. Richard Nice. Cambridge, Mass.: Harvard University Press.

Boyarin, Jonathan. 1991. *Polish Jews in Paris: The Ethnography of Memory*. Bloomington: Indiana University Press.

———. 1992. *Storm from Paradise: The Politics of Jewish Memory*. Minneapolis: University of Minnesota Press.

Boym, Svetlana. 1994. *Common Places: Mythologies of Everyday Life in Russia*. Cambridge, Mass.: Harvard University Press.

Brodkin, Karen. 1998. *How Jews Became White Folks and What That Says about Race in America*. New Brunswick, N.J.: Rutgers University Press.

"Bukharskie evrei." 1976. In *Kratkaia evreiskaia entsiklopediia*, vol. 1, ed. Y. Oren and M. Zand, 565–72. Jerusalem: Keter.

Burawoy, Michael. 1995. "From Sovietology to Comparative Political Economy." In *Beyond Soviet Studies*, ed. Daniel Orlovsky, 72–102. Washington, D.C.: Woodrow Wilson Center Press.

Burawoy, Michael, and Katherine Verdery, eds. 1999. *Uncertain Transition: Ethnographies of Change in the Postsocialist World*. Lanham, Md.: Rowman and Littlefield Publishers.

Cale, Ruth. 1970. "The Jews in Soviet Georgia." *Hadassa Magazine* 51: 6–7, 22–23.

Chervyakov, Valeriy, Zvi Gitelman, and Vladimir Shapiro. 1997. "Religion and Ethnicity: Judaism in the Ethnic Consciousness of Contemporary Russian Jews." *Ethnic and Racial Studies* 20 (2): 280–305.

Clifford, James. 1986. "Introduction: Partial Truths." In *Writing Culture: The Poetics and Politics of Ethnography*, ed. James Clifford and George E. Marcus, 1–26. Berkeley: University of California Press.

Cohen, Stephen, ed. 1982. *An End to Silence: Uncensored Opinion in the Soviet Union from Roy Medevedev's* Underground Magazine. New York: Norton.

Comaroff, Jean, and John Comaroff. 1992. "Of Totemism and Ethnicity." In *Ethnography and the Historical Imagination*, 49–67. Boulder, Colo.: Westview Press.

The Complete Artscroll Siddur. 1990. Translated with anthologized commentary by Nosson Scherman. Brooklyn: Mesorah Publications.

de Certeau, Michel. 1984. *The Practice of Everyday Life*. Trans. Steven F. Rendall. Berkeley: University of California Press.

d'Encausse, Helene Carrere. 1992. *The Great Challenge: Nationalities and the Bolshevik State, 1917–1930*. New York: Holmes and Meir.

Deshen, Shlomo. 1972. "Ethnicity and Citizenship in the Ritual of an Israeli Synagogue." *Southwest Journal of Anthropology* 28: 69–82.

De Soto, Hermine G., and Nora Dudwick, eds. 2000. *Fieldwork Dilemmas: Anthropologists in Postsocialist States*. Madison: University of Wisconsin Press.

Dominguez, Virginia R. 1989. *People as Subject, People as Object: Selfhood and Peoplehood in Contemporary Israel*. Madison: University of Wisconsin Press.

Dosick, Wayne. 1995. *Living Judaism: The Complete Guide to Jewish Belief, Tradition, and Practice*. New York: HarperCollins Publishers.

Douglas, Mary. 1970. *Purity and Danger: An Analysis of Concepts of Pollution and Taboo*. Baltimore: Penguin Books.

———, ed. 1984. *Food in the Social Order: Studies of Food and Festivities in Three American Communities*. New York: Russell Sage Foundation.

Dragadze, Tamara. 1988. *Rural Families in Soviet Georgia*. London: Routledge.

Dreizin, Felix. 1990. *The Russian Soul and the Jew: Essays in Literary Ethnocriticism*. Lanham, Md.: University Press of America.

Dubnow, S. M. 1918. *History of the Jews in Russia and Poland from the Earliest Times until the Present Day*, vol. 2: *From the Death of Alexander I until the Death of Alexander III*. Philadelphia: Jewish Publication Society of America.

———. 1920. *History of the Jews in Russia and Poland from the Earliest Times until the Present Day*, vol. 3: *From the Accession of Nicholas II until the Present Day*. Philadelphia: Jewish Publication Society of America.

Dumont, Jean-Paul. 1978. *The Headman and I*. Austin: University of Texas Press.

Dunlop, John B. 1998. *Russia Confronts Chechnya: Roots of Separatist Conflict*. Cambridge: Cambridge University Press.

Dzhindzhikhashvili, Zoia. 1994. "Georgian Jews." Trans. Dale Pesmen. In *Encyclopedia of World Cultures*, vol. 4: *Russia and Eurasia/China*, ed. Paul Friedrich and Norma Diamond, 126–28. New York: G. K. Hall and Company.

Eilberg-Schwartz, Howard. 1990. *The Savage in Judaism: An Anthropology of Israelite Religion and Ancient Judaism*. Bloomington: Indiana University Press.

———. 1992. "Introduction: People of the Body." In *People of the Body: Jews and Judaism from an Embodied Perspective*, ed. Howard Eilberg-Schwartz, 1–15. Albany: State University of New York Press.

Fischer, Michael M. J. 1986. "Ethnicity and the Post-Modern Arts of Memory." In *Writing Culture: The Poetics and Politics of Ethnography*, ed. James Clifford and George E. Marcus, 194–233. Berkeley: University of California Press.

Fitzpatrick, Shelia. 1996. "Signals from Below: Soviet Letters of Denunciation of the 1930s." *Journal of Modern History* 68: 831–66.

Foster, George M. 1967. "Peasant Society and the Image of Limited Good." *American Anthropologist* 65 (2): 293–315.

Frankel, Jonathan. 1991. "The Soviet Regime and Anti-Zionism: An Analysis." In *Jewish Culture and Identity in the Soviet Union*, ed. Yaacov Ro'i and Avi Beker, 310–54. New York: New York University Press.

Gellner, Ernest. 1990. "Ethnicity and Faith in Eastern Europe." *Daedalus* 119 (1): 279–94.

Gilman, Sander. 1986. *Jewish Self-Hatred: Anti-Semitism and the Hidden Language of the Jews*. Baltimore: Johns Hopkins University Press.

———. 1991. *The Jew's Body*. New York: Routledge.

Gilroy, Paul. 1987. *"There Ain't No Black in the Union Jack": The Cultural Politics of Race and Nation*. Chicago: University of Chicago Press.

———. 1993. *The Black Atlantic: Modernity and Double Consciousness*. Cambridge, Mass.: Harvard University Press.

Gitelman, Zvi. 1988. *A Century of Ambivalence: The Jews of Russia and the Soviet Union*. New York: Schocken Books.

Goldberg, B. Z. 1961. *The Jewish Problem in the Soviet Union: Analysis and Solution*. New York: Crown Publishers.

Golovnev, Andrei V., and Gail Osherenko. 1999. *Siberian Survival: The Nenets and Their Story*. Ithaca, N.Y.: Cornell University Press.

Goluboff, Sascha L. 2000. "Re-Enabling the Disabled: The Struggle of Blind Russian Jews for Citizenship in the New Russia." *Anthropology of East Europe Review* 18 (1): 27–31.

Gorlizki, Yoram. 1990. "Jews." In *The Nationalities Question in the Soviet Union*, ed. Graham Smith, 339–59. New York: Longman.

"Gorskie evrei." 1982. In *Kratkaia evreiskaia entsiklopediia*, vol. 2, ed. Y. Oren and M. Zand, 182–191. Jerusalem: Society for Research on Jewish Communities.

Graeber, David. 1996. "Beads and Money: Notes toward a Theory of Wealth and Power." *American Ethnologist* 23 (1): 4–24.

Greenberg, Blu. 1983. *How to Run a Jewish Household*. New York: Simon and Schuster.

Gregory, C. A. 1982. *Gifts and Commodities*. London: Academic Press.

"Gruzinskie evrei." 1982. In *Kratkaia evreiskaia entsiklopediia*, vol. 2., ed. Y. Oren and M. Zand, 235–45. Jerusalem: Society for Research on Jewish Communities.

Hall, Stuart. 1992. "New Ethnicities." In *"Race," Culture, and Difference*, ed. James Donald and Ali Rattansi, 252–59. London: Sage Publications.

Handler, Richard. 1985. "On Dialogue and Destructive Analysis: Problems in Narrating Nationalism and Ethnicity." *Journal of Anthropological Research* 41 (2): 171–82.

Hann, C. M., ed. 1993. *Socialism: Ideals, Ideologies, and Local Practice*. London: Routledge.

Hayden, Robert M. 1996. "Imagined Communities and Real Victims: Self-Determination and Ethnic Cleansing in Yugoslavia." *American Anthropologist* 23 (4): 783–801.

Heilman, Samuel C. 1976. *Synagogue Life: A Study in Symbolic Interaction*. Chicago: University of Chicago Press.

Holquist, Peter. 1997. " 'Information Is the Alpha and Omega of Our Work': Bolshevik Surveillance in Its Pan-European Context." *Journal of Modern History* 69: 415–50.

Humphrey, Caroline. 1995. "Creating a Culture of Disillusionment: Consumption in Moscow, Chronicle of Changing Times." In *Worlds Apart: Modernity through the Prism of the Local*, ed. Daniel Miller, 43–68. London: Routledge.

Institute of the World Jewish Congress. 1996. *Annual Report on Post-Soviet Jews*. Jerusalem: Institute of the World Jewish Congress.

Jacobs, Louis. 1995. *The Jewish Religion: A Companion*. New York: Oxford University Press.

Kandel', Felix. 1990. *Ocherki vremen i sobytii iz istorii rossiiskikh evreev*. Jerusalem: Association "Tarbut."

Katz, Lev. 1970. "After the Six-Day War." In *The Jews in Soviet Russia since 1917*, ed. Lionel Kochan, 321–36. London: Oxford University Press.

Keller, Mark. 1979. "The Great Jewish Drink Mystery." In *Beliefs, Behaviors, and Alcoholic Beverages: A Cross-Cultural Survey*, ed. Mac Marshall, 404–14. Ann Arbor: University of Michigan Press.

Kertzer, David I. 1988. *Ritual, Politics, and Power*. New Haven, Conn.: Yale University Press.

Khazanov, Anatoly M. 1995. *After the USSR: Ethnicity, Nationalism, and Politics in the Commonwealth of Independent States*. Madison: University of Wisconsin Press.

Kideckel, David A., ed. 1995. *East European Communities: The Struggle for Balance in Turbulent Times*. Boulder, Colo.: Westview Press.

"Killery vypustili v zhertvu bol'se 20 pul'." 1996. *Moskovskii komsomolets*, March 31, p.1.

Klebnikov, Paul. 2000. *Godfather of the Kremlin: Boris Berezovsky and the Looting of Russia*. New York: Harcourt.

Klein, Isaac. 1979. *A Guide to Jewish Religious Practice*. New York: Jewish Theological Seminary of America.

Kon, Igor S. 1996. "Moral Culture." In *Russian Culture at the Crossroads: Paradoxes of Post-Communist Consciousness*, ed. Dmitri N. Shalin, 185–207. Boulder, Colo.: Westview Press.

Kopytoff, Igor. 1986. "The Cultural Biography of Things: Commoditization as Process." In *The Social Life of Things: Commodities in Cultural Perspective*, ed. Arjun Appadurai, 64–91. Cambridge: Cambridge University Press.

Korey, William. 1973. *The Soviet Cage: Anti-Semitism in Russia*. New York: Viking Press.

Kuehnast, Kathleen. 2000. "Ethnographic Encounters in Post-Soviet Kyrgyzstan." In *Fieldwork Dilemmas: Anthropologists in Postsocialist States*, ed. Hermine G. De Soto and Nora Dudwick, 100–118. Madison: University of Wisconsin Press.

Kugelmass, Jack. 1986. *The Miracle of Intervale Avenue: The Story of a Jewish Congregation in the South Bronx*. New York: Columbia University Press.

Kukullu, Amaldan. 1995. *Zhardakhai Ovsholum: Pesni, stikhi, khvali, epitafii*. Moscow: Amaldanik.

Kulick, Don. 1995. "Introduction: The Sexual Life of Anthropologists: Erotic Subjectivity and Ethnographic Work." In *Taboo: Sex, Identity, and Erotic Subjectivity in Anthropological Fieldwork*, ed. Don Kulick and Margaret Willson, 1–28. London: Routledge.

Kuz'menko, Pavel. 1996. *Russkii pravoslavnyi obriad pogrebeniia*. Moscow: Bukmen.

Lacquer, Walter. 1993. *Black Hundred: The Rise of the Extreme Right in Russia*. New York: HarperCollins Publishers.

Ledeneva, Alena V. 1998. *Russia's Economy of Favours: Blat, Networking and Informal Exchange*. Cambridge: Cambridge University Press.

Lemon, Alaina. 1998. " 'Your Eyes Are Green like Dollars': Counterfeit Cash, National Substance, and Currency Apartheid in 1990s Russia." *Cultural Anthropology* 13 (1): 22–55.

Levin, Nora. 1990. *The Paradox of Survival: The Jews in the Soviet Union since 1917*, vols. 1 and 2. New York: New York University Press.

Lewin, Moshe. 1995. "Society, Past and Present in Interpreting Russia." In

Beyond Soviet Studies, ed. Daniel Orlovsky, 56–71. Washington, D.C.: Woodrow Wilson Center Press.

Limon, Jose E. 1989. "Carne, Carnales, and the Carnivalesque: Bakhtinian *Batos,* Disorder, and Narrative Discourses." *American Ethnologist* 16 (3): 471–486.

Lobovskaya, Margarita. 1996. *Moskovskaia Khoral'naia Sinagoga.* Moscow: Moscow Government and Moskovskie uchebniki.

Magomedov, R. M. 1994. "K voprosu o tatakh." In *U nas Rodina odna—Sovetskii Soiuz.* Makhachkala (1981). Reprinted in *Taty fol'klor,* ed. Io. B. Simchenko and B. A. Tishkov, 157–59. Moscow: Rossiiskaia akademiia nauk, Institut etnologii i antropologii im. N. N. Miklukho-Maklaia.

Markowitz, Fran. 1988. "Jewish in the USSR, Russian in the USA." In *Persistence and Flexibility: Anthropological Perspectives on the American Jewish Experience,* ed. Walter P. Zenner, 79–95. Albany: State University of New York Press.

Mars, Gerald, and Yochanan Altman. 1987. "Alternative Mechanisms of Distribution in a Soviet Economy." In *Constructive Drinking: Perspectives on Drink from Anthropology,* ed. Mary Douglas, 270–29. Cambridge: Cambridge University Press.

Matthews, Mervyn. 1972. *Class and Society in Soviet Russia.* New York: Walker and Company.

———. 1978. *Privilege in the Soviet Union: A Study of Elite Life Styles under Communism.* London: George Allen and Unwin.

———. 1986. "Poverty and Patterns of Deprivation in the Soviet Union." *Berkeley-Duke Occasional Papers on the Second Economy in the USSR,* no. 6.

Miles, Robert. 1987. *Capitalism and Unfree Labour: Anomaly or Necessity?* London: Tavistock Publications.

Millar, James R., and Elizabeth Clayton. 1987. "Quality of Life: Subjective Measures of Relative Satisfaction." In *Politics, Work, and Daily Life in the USSR: A Survey of Former Soviet Citizens,* ed. James R. Millar, 31–57. Cambridge: Cambridge University Press.

Moore, Sally Falk. 1987. "Explaining the Present: Theoretical Dilemmas in Processual Ethnography." *American Ethnologist* 14 (4): 724–36.

"Moskva." 1991. In *Kratkaia evreiskaia entsiklopediia,* vol. 10, ed. Y. Oren and N. Pratt, 471–83. Jerusalem: Society for Research on Jewish Communities.

Murzakhanov, Yu. I. 1994. *Gorskie evrei: Annotirovannyi bibliographicheskii ykazatel', Chast' I. XVIII—nachalo XX v.* Moscow: Choro.

———. 1996. *Sovremennia sem'ia u gorskikh evreev Kabardino-Balkarii.* Moscow: Choro.

Myerhoff, Barbara. 1979. *Number Our Days.* New York: E. P. Dutton.

———. 1992. *Remembered Lives: The Work of Ritual, Storytelling, and Growing Older.* Ann Arbor: University of Michigan Press.

Nulman, Macy. 1996. *The Encyclopedia of Jewish Prayer: Ashkenazic and Sephardic Rites.* Northvale, N.J.: Jason Aronson.

Ortner, Sherry B. 1973. "On Key Symbols." *American Anthropologist* 75 (5): 1338–46.

———. 1995. "Resistance and the Problem of Ethnographic Refusal." *Comparative Studies in Society and History* 2: 173–93.

Pesmen, Dale. 2000. *Russia and Soul: An Exploration.* Ithaca, N.Y.: Cornell University Press.

Pilkington, Hillary. 1998. *Migration, Displacement, and Identity in Post-Soviet Russia.* London: Routledge.

Pinkus, Benjamin. 1991. "Soviet Government Policy toward the Extraterritorial National Minorities: Comparison between the Jews and the Germans." In *Jewish Culture and Identity in the Soviet Union*, ed. Yaacov Ro'i and Avi Beker, 290–309. New York: New York University Press.

Polyani, Karl. 1997. "The Semantics of Money-Uses." In *Primitive, Archaic, and Modern Economies: Essays of Karl Polyani*, ed. George Dalton, 175–203. Garden City, N.Y.: Doubleday.

Prell, Riv-Ellen. 1989. *Prayer and Community: The Havurah in American Judaism*. Detroit: Wayne State University Press.

Rabinowicz, Rabbi H. 1964. *A Guide to Life: Jewish Laws and Customs of Mourning*. London: Jewish Chronicle Publications.

Ramet, Sabrina Petra. 1993. "Religious Policy in the Era of Gorbachev." In *Religious Policy in the Soviet Union*, ed. Sabrina Petra Ramet, 31–52. Cambridge: Cambridge University Press.

Redlich, Shimon. 1982. *Propaganda and Nationalism in Wartime Russia: The Jewish Antifascist Committee in the USSR, 1941–1948*. Boulder, Colo.: East European Quarterly: United States of America.

Rethmann, Petra. 2000. "Land, Democracy, and Indigenous Rights in Russia." *Anthropology of East Europe Review* 17 (8): 21–26.

Ries, Nancy. 1997. *Russian Talk: Culture and Conversation during Perestroika*. Ithaca, N.Y.: Cornell University Press.

———. N.d. " 'Honest' Bandits and 'Warped' People: Russian Narratives about Money, Corruption, and Moral Decay." Unpublished paper.

Roediger, David R. 1991. *The Wages of Whiteness: Race and the Making of American Workers*. London: Verso.

Rosaldo, Renato. 1989. *Culture and Truth: The Remaking of Social Analysis*. Boston: Beacon Press.

Rosten, Leo. 1968. *The Joys of Yiddish*. New York: Pocket Books.

Rothenberg, Joshua. 1967. "The Special Case of the Georgian Jews." *Jewish Frontier* 34 (6): 16–19.

———. 1970. "Jewish Religion in the Soviet Union." In *Jews in Soviet Russia since 1917*, ed. Lionel Kochan, 159–87. London: Oxford University Press.

———. 1971. *The Jewish Religion in the Soviet Union*. New York: KTAV Publishing House.

Schapiro, Leonard B. 1974. "The Jewish Anti-Fascist Committee and the Phases of Soviet Anti-Semitic Policy during and after World War II." In *Jews and Non-Jews in Eastern Europe: 1918–1945*, ed. Bela Vago and George L. Mosse, 283–300. New York: John Wiley and Sons.

———. 1979. "Anti-Semitism in the Communist World." *Soviet Jewish Affairs* 9 (1): 42–52.

Sewell, William H., Jr. 1992. "Introduction: Narratives and Social Identities." *Social Science History* 16: 479–88.

Shalin, Dmitri. 1996. "Intellectual Culture." In *Russian Culture at the Crossroads: Paradoxes of Post-Communist Consciousness*, ed. Dmitri Shalin, 41–97. Boulder, Colo.: Westview Press.

Shatz, Marshall S. 1980. *Soviet Dissent in Historical Perspective*. Cambridge: Cambridge University Press.

Shokeid, Moshe. 1995. *A Gay Synagogue in New York*. New York: Columbia University Press.

Sidorov, Pavel I. 1995. "Russia." In *International Handbook on Alcohol and Culture*, ed. Dwight B. Heath, 237–53. Westport, Conn.: Greenwood Press.

Simis, Konstantin M. 1982. *The Corrupt Society: The Secret World of Soviet Capitalism*. Trans. Jacqueline Edwards and Mitchell Schneider. New York: Simon and Schuster.

Sinyavsky, Andrei. 1997. *The Russian Intelligentsia*. Trans. Lynn Visson. New York: Columbia University Press.

Slezkine, Yuri. 1991. *Arctic Mirrors: Russia and the Small Peoples of the North*. Ithaca, N.Y.: Cornell University Press.

"Smert' rybotorgovtsa." 1996. *Moskovskii komsomolets*, March 8, p. 8.

Stallybrass, Peter, and Allon White. 1986. *The Politics and Poetics of Trangression*. Ithaca, N.Y.: Cornell University Press.

Stark, David. 1994. "Recombinant Property in East European Capitalism." *Working Papers on Transitions from State Socialism*, no. 94–5. Mario Einaudi Center for International Studies, Cornell University, Ithaca, N.Y.

Stoler, Ann. 1989. "Making the Empire Respectable: The Politics of Race and Sexual Morality in Twentieth-Century Colonial Cultures." *American Ethnologist* 16 (4): 634–61.

Szmeruk, Ch. 1960. "Yiddish Publications in the USSR (from the Late Thirties to 1948)." *Yad Washem Studies* 4: 99–133.

Tishkov, Valery. 1997. *Ethnicity, Nationalism, and Conflict in and after the Soviet Union*. London: Sage Publications.

Tsigelman, Ludmilla. 1991. "The Impact of Ideological Changes in the USSR on Different Generations of the Soviet Jewish Intelligentsia." In *Jewish Culture and Identity in the Soviet Union*, ed. Yaacov Ro'i and Avi Beker, 42–72. New York: New York University Press.

Verdery, Katherine. 1988. "Ethnicity as Culture: Some Soviet-American Contrasts." *Canadian Review of Studies in Nationalism* 15 (1-2): 107–10.

———. 1995. "What Was Socialism and Why Did It Fall?" In *Beyond Soviet Studies*, ed. Daniel Orlovsky, 27–46. Washington, D.C.: Woodrow Wilson Center Press.

———. 1996. *What Was Socialism and What Comes Next?* Princeton, N.J.: Princeton University Press.

———. 1999. *The Political Lives of Dead Bodies: Reburial and Postsocialist Change*. New York: Columbia University Press.

Visweswaran, Kamala. 1994. *Fictions of Feminist Ethnography*. Minneapolis: University of Minnesota Press.

Voronel, Alexander. 1975. "The Search for Jewish Identity in Russia." *Soviet Jewish Affairs* 5 (2): 69–74.

———. 1991. "Jewish *Samizdat*." In *Jewish Culture and Identity in the Soviet Union*, ed. Yaacov Ro'i and Avi Beker, 255–61. New York: New York University Press.

Walters, Philip. 1993. "A Survey of Soviet Religious Policy." In *Religious Policy in the Soviet Union*, ed. Sabrina Petra Ramet, 3–30. Cambridge: Cambridge University Press.

Wedel, Janine R. 1998. *Collision and Collusion: The Strange Case of Western Aid to Eastern Europe, 1989–1998*. New York: St. Martin's Press.

Werblowsky, R. J. Zwi, and Geoffrey Wigoder, eds. 1965. *The Encyclopedia of the Jewish Religion*. New York: Holt, Rinehart and Winston.

Williams, Brackette F. 1989. "A Class Act: Anthropology and the Race to Nation across Ethnic Terrain." *Annual Review of Anthropology* 18: 401–44.

———. 1991. *Stains on My Name, War in My Veins: Guyana and the Politics of Cultural Struggle*. Durham, N.C.: Duke University Press.

Wilmsen, Edwin N. 1996. "Introduction: Premises of Power in Ethnic Politics."
In *The Politics of Difference: Ethnic Premises in a World of Power*, ed. Edwin N.
Wilmsen and Patrick McAllister, 1–24. Chicago: University of Chicago Press.
Zand, Michael. 1985. "The Literature of the Mountain Jews of the Caucasus
(Part I)." *Soviet Jewish Affairs* 15 (2): 3–22.
———. 1986. "The Literature of the Mountain Jews of the Caucasus (Part 2)."
Soviet Jewish Affairs 16 (1): 35–51.
———. 1991. "Notes on the Culture of the Non-Ashkenazi Jewish Communi-
ties under Soviet Rule." In *Jewish Culture and Identity in the Soviet Union*, ed.
Yaacov Ro'i and Avi Beker, 378–444. New York: New York University Press.
Zborowski, Mark, and Elizabeth Herzog. 1952. *Life Is with People: The Jewish
Little-Town of Eastern Europe*. New York: International Universities Press.
Zemtsov, Ilya. 1985. *The Private Life of the Soviet Elite*. New York: Crane Russak.

Index

Igor, 109
Institute of the World Jewish Congress, 27, 126
Irina Maksovna, 81–82, 84–85, 87–89, 110, 112, 133
Izzi, 92

Jacobs, Louis, 68
Jews: belonging to the nation, 61–62, 143–44, 155, 168–70; gender, sex, and the nation, 72–79, 140–44, 170; identity, 61–62, 64, 93, 168–70, 171–72; post-Soviet situation, 1, 6, 21, 33. *See also* Bukharan Jews; Georgian Jews; Mountain Jews; Russian Jews
Joint Distribution Committee (JDC), 106–7, 146
Joseph, 68, 74

Katz, Lev, 25
Keller, Mark, 83
Kelley, Catriona, 117
Kertzer, David I., 36
Khaimov, Isaak, 12, 34, 154, 173 n.5
Kideckel, David A., 5
Klebnikov, Paul, 1
Kon, Igor, 99
Kopytoff, Igor, 119
Korey, William, 19, 24, 25
Kosher food, 176 n.8, 177 n.9; deficit of and high prices in Moscow, 23, 70–71, 82, 150, 169; Georgian Jewish, 63–68, 72–79. *See also* Council for the Affairs of Religious Cults, Inspector Tagaev
Kostia, 34, 35, 122, 128, 131, 134, 136–42, 147–48, 154, 156–61, 164–65, 168, 182 n.2
Kuehnast, Kathleen, 16
Kugelmass, Jack, 6, 30
Kukullu, Amaldan, 125, 181 n.9
Kulick, Don, 76

Lampland, Martha, 5
Leah, 73–75
Ledeneva, Alena V., 5
Lemon, Alaina, 4
Lena, 135–36
Levin, Nora, 5, 17–18, 25, 152, 174 nn. 15–16, 175 n.10
Levin, Rabbi Yegudah-Leib, 11, 99, 102–6, 179 n.16

Lewin, Moshe, 99
Limon, Jose E., 140
Lyonia, 45, 59–60, 80–82, 87, 89, 117–18, 119, 127–28, 141–42, 148, 167

Magomedov, R. M., 126
Maiia, 129
Manevich, G. M., 106
Maria Abramovna, 128, 178 n.3
Market: development of, 1–2, 46–47, 121, 168–69; as morally corrupt, 4, 97–98, 128–31; speculation at the synagogue, 23–24, 27–28; visit to, 131–33. *See also* Mountain Jews; Surveillance, denunciations of corruption in the synagogue
Markowitz, Fran, 6
Mars, Gerald, 72
Mathews, Mervyn, 70, 178 n.9
Matzah, 24, 25, 29, 101–2, 154, 179 n.15
Mikvah, 23, 101
Miles, Robert, 4–5
Millar, James R., 79
Misha, 155–56
Moore, Sally Falk, 33
Mordechai, 52, 55–56, 64–67, 76
Moscow Jewish Religious Community (MERO), 9, 94, 104, 106, 145–47, 149
Moscow Religious Community of Sephardic Jews (MEROS), 145–49, 157, 162, 164, 182 n.3
Moshe, 13, 35, 43, 50, 65–67, 83, 120–21, 167
Mountain Jews: building the Mountain Jewish community, 127, 134–40, 145; *chernye*, 4, 122–24, 127–31, 133–34, 143–44, 149, 160, 162, 170; economic status, 2; emigration, 126, 166–67; history, 125–26, 146; influence on synagogue life, 1–2; Jewish identity, 138–40, 143–44; market economy, 140, 143–44; morning prayer in small hall, 12–16, 34, 50; new synagogue, 168; prayer hall, 12, 51, 122, 140–43, 151–65, 167, 170; Simchat Torah, 11–12. *See also* Moscow Religious Community of Sephardic Jews; Sephardim
Murzakhanov, Yu. I., 125, 134, 137
Musia, 79
Myerhoff, Barbara, 6, 30, 36, 90, 92

Acknowledgments

I want to acknowledge my deep gratitude to those friends and acquaintances in Russia who let me into their lives. Their generosity and patience allowed me to undertake and finish this project. I am most grateful to Alexander Yakovlevich Kleiman, Grigorii Abramovich Aksenfeld, Roman Iusufov, the Goldschmidt family, Yom-Tov Shamailov, Giul'nara Rabaeva, Mariia Zhdanova, Yurii Azar'ianovich Abramov, Vitali Rafailovich Eliyagu, Amaldan Kukullu, Maiia Ivanovna, and Yulii Vladimirovich Baronchuk.

When I first thought of the idea to study Jews in Russia (a subject and research area almost absent in anthropological literature), William Kelleher, of the University of Illinois at Urbana-Champaign, motivated me to take on the project full force. His solid knowledge of theory, his keen interest in cultural, economic, and political transformation, and his encouragement helped me to navigate my way through research and writing. Nancy Ries, of Colgate University, also deserves special recognition. She generously gave much of her time to my project, sharing important insights into Russian and Soviet culture. I also want to thank Gary Porton, Diane Koenker, Norman Whitten, and Nancy Abelmann, all of the University of Illinois.

There were many friends who helped me along the way: Nan Volinsky, Matthew LaBo, Christopher Cosner, and Alan McRae provided emotional support through the challenges of research and writing. Matti Bunzl, Heather Coleman, "The Kopi Kollective" (Thomas Trice, Paula Rieder, and Andrew Nolan), Dale Pesmen, Dana Katz, Karen Hirsch, Robin LeBlanc, and Adam Scales read drafts and clarified my ideas. Nina Glick-Schiller was instrumental in pushing me to further develop my concepts about Jewish identity and race. Finally, I am indebted to those who made this book a reality: Peter Agree at the University of Pennsylvania Press for believing in the project; Sarah Barrash Wilson for so patiently copyediting the manuscript; John Blackburn for his help with the maps; and the two anonymous readers of the book manuscript—their comments were extremely insightful and beneficial.

For work leading up to this project, I received several Foreign Language and Area Studies Grants (FLAS) from the Russian and East European Center at the University of Illinois, and I obtained a grant from the National Science Foundation, issued through the Anthropology Department at the University of Illinois, for summer research in 1994. I studied Jewish history and culture under a Graduate Training Fellowship from the Social Science Research Council during the 1994–1995 academic year. My initial research in Moscow was sponsored by an Individual Advanced Research Grant from the International Research and Exchanges Board (IREX), with funds provided by the National Endowment for the Humanities and the U.S. Department of State, which administers the Title VIII Program. I received two fellowships from the University of Illinois and one from the Illinois Program for Research in the Humanities. Two Glenn Grants from Washington and Lee University allowed me to return to Moscow in the summer of 2000 and to do further writing in the summer of 2001.

Parts of this book were previously published. Portions of Chapter 1 appeared first in *Anthropological Quarterly* 74 (2) (April 2001): 55–71. Sections of Chapter 4 were originally published as "The Savage in the Jew: Race, Class, and Nation in Post-Soviet Moscow," in *Identities: Global Studies in Culture and Power* 8 (2) (July 2001): 283–312.

Finally, I dedicate this book to my parents, Barry Stephen Goluboff and Diane Kandle Goluboff. Their unceasing love, support, and understanding made it possible.